D1720038

THE WAY OF THE
WIZARD

MARDUKITE ACADEMY OF SYSTEMOLOGY PREMIERE EDITION

THE WAY OF THE

WIZARD

UTILITARIAN SYSTEMOLOGY

(A NEW METAHUMAN ETHIC)

BY JOSHUA FREE

THE JOSHUA FREE IMPRINT
JFI PUBLICATIONS

ISBN : 978-0-578-28391-3

The Systemology Society Beta-Defrag Booster and Stabilizer for upper-level Wizard Grades. Based on the "Freedom From" lecture series given in July 2021 at Mardukite Academy and developmental research for the remaining year.

A MARDUKITE SYSTEMOLOGY PUBLICATION
Mardukite Research Library Catalog No. 3E/"Liber-Three"
Developed for Mardukite Academy & Systemology Society
cum superiorum privilegio veniaque
FIRST EDITION
April 2022
Published from
Joshua Free Imprint – JFI Publishing
Mardukite Borsippa HQ, San Luis Valley, Colorado

Your Only Ticket Off of a Prison Planet...

We all strongly benefit from the fact that at its basic state, the *Alpha Spirit* is actually righteous and good —if not otherwise *amoral* down here on Earth when serving a higher Ethic—simply working to get along in the continuation of its own existence.

Were this not the case, we would have no chance at rehabilitating presence and *Awareness* of the actual *Self* that is behind the helm and restoring to it the full control of how we experience the *beta-existence* that we each participate in maintaining as reality.

The world manifested "out there" is an agreement of participation by what is going on "in here" and there really is no distinction between the two when we get right down to it.

Accumulated involvement in dangerous situations, states of confusion, unjust destruction and being at the effect end of faulty—or blatantly false—information, all lend to fragmented purposes that may very well be painted to appear "for our own good."

Instead they are actually non-survival (or counter-survival) oriented, leading us away from routes to achieve "greater heights"—higher more ideal states of Knowing and Beingness —including the "Magic Universe" preceding this one.

Here then is the next great frontier of the Pathway crossed by participants in the "*Freedom From*" workshops led by Joshua Free at the Mardukite Academy and Systemology Society in 2021 and 2022,

A bridge from *Grade-IV* to *Grade-V* is finally available, enhanced for Seekers, Pilots, Ministers and Wizards, in a hardcover Mardukite Academy Collector's Edition.

...A Pathway Leading to Spiritual Ascension

EXPERIMENTAL RESEARCH
REPORT
Spring 2021 – Winter 2021/22

"Are you a user or being used?
Has your memory been abused?
Take random samples from your Mind
—and analyze what you may find."

"You can clear all your memory,
And be transformed when you find the Key.
Think all the things that will bring you peace.
Confusing data soon will cease."

~PETRA "*Computer Brains*"

TABLET OF CONTENTS

EDITOR'S NOTE

"The Self does not actualize Awareness
past a point not understood."
—*Tablets of Destiny*

While preparing this book for publication,
the editors have made every effort to present this
material in a straightforward manner; using clear,
easy to read and understand language.

Wherever a word that is defined in the "glossary"
first appears within this book, it will be **bold**.

Clear understanding of this knowledge is critical to
achieve actual realizations and personal benefit
applying *Mardukite Zuism* philosophies and
NexGen Systemology spiritual technology in practice.

*This present volume is intended for Seekers completing
Grade-IV Wizard Level-0 from the Mardukite Academy.*

A new *Seeker* should be especially certain not to
simply "read through" this book without attaining
proper comprehension as "knowledge." Even when
the information continues to be "interesting"—if at
any point you find yourself feeling lost or confused
while reading: trace your steps; return to just
before the misunderstanding; go through it again.

Take nothing within this book on faith.
Apply the information directly to your life.
Decide for yourself.

∞

MAN—KNOW THYSELF

"And this above all:
To thine own self be true.
And then it must result,
as that night follows day,
that thou can not be
false to anyone."

—Shakespeare, *Hamlet*

THE WAY OF THE
WIZARD

"Actualizing WILL in *Self-Honesty* requires using *Systemology Processing* to 'Process-out,' *analyze* and disperse emotional ZU-energy wound up and entangled in 'guilt' and 'blame.' Only then is a person truly *free*."

—Joshua Free "*Crystal Clear: Handbook for Seekers*"

For *Amanda Shea* &
Dedicated to *Kyra-Light-Kaos*,
whose Hostile-Acts and unprocessed Hold-Outs
caused too much guilt for her to remain on the Pathway.

:: ETHICS, CODES, MORALS & DOGMA[‡] ::
—General Information for All Systemologists—

Semantically named from the Greek word "*ethos*"—meant to infer an **individual**'s "moral character" (and the corresponding "customs" or "principles" thereof)—formal intellectual pursuit of "*ethike philosophia*" became a fundamental subject among famous "high minds" of the *Classical World*—including Aristotle, Plato and Socrates. Of course, the **concept** itself is actually much older; extending far back to the *Ancient Near East*—"**Mesopotamia**"—and **inception** of *cuneiform* writing and other civic **systems**. Even the Ancient Druids of Western Europe had already perfected their own independent philosophy of *Ethics* by the time of their first direct encounters with the Greeks—and the *Classical World*—nearly 2,500 years ago. Unfortunately, many contemporary scholars of the past century continued to falsely favor the *Classical Period* (for example, Greece and Rome, *c. 500 BC*) as the singular source or **epicenter** of all substantial **knowledge** carried forth from the ancient world.

We tend to **treat** a much wider array of source material at the Mardukite Academy and Systemology Society than practically any other "**esoteric** fellowship" in history. But, our efforts are not entirely unlike those of the Greek and Hermetic traditions from the *Classical Period*—enigmatic and "cultish" Pythagorean Schools and secretive "underground" Socratic Societies.[*] With much of the cuneiform records

---

‡ Portions of this chapter-lesson are based on the July 2021 "*Grade-IV, Freedom From*" lectures given by *Joshua Free* to the *Mardukite Academy of Systemology* at *Mardukite Babylonia SLV Borsippa HQ*; additional "*Notes On Philosophy*" sections are specially adapted from the *Grade-I* (*Route-A*) Master Edition textbook: "*The Great Magical Arcanum.*" These were issued as supplemental lecture handouts.

* Referencing John Toland's *Pantheisticon* available from Mardukite Esoteric Research Library; reprinted in *Grade-I* (*Rte-D*) Master Ed. textbook: "*Merlyn's Complete Book of Druidism*" by Joshua Free.

already lost to the shifting sands of Sumer by this time, the *Classical Age* witnessed its own revival of "**epistemological**" philosophies regarding the "truth" of "things" and strong efforts toward preserving an "absolute" **knowledge**—such as was once retained in **Babylonia**, and which once served as the true "heartbeat" of ancient **systematization**. As time bore on, similar intellectual pursuits became diluted and reduced to a wider subjective **treatment** as "moral philosophy," eventually influencing human "**consciousness**" strongest through common practices of religious "**dogma**" and upheld (or **enforced**) by whatever element of civilization stood socially responsible for maintaining civic "justice."

With small regard for linguistic analysis and the true meaning of words, common-use English is seldom a perfect language for us to communicate Systemology to the "average" individual. It can take a considerable amount of time and training to indoctrinate one of these "**standard-issue**" lifeforms to even the most basic wide-angle **understanding** of our Systemology... Unless, of course, all specialized vocabulary and terms are uniquely and concisely defined to our complete satisfaction in relation to basic purposes of our organization. This is the only way we can share certainty that a *Seeker* (or reader) is receiving (and perfectly duplicating in their Personal Universe) the exact meaning communicated (in this book) as intended. As a systematic approach to philosophy and spirituality concerning "*Life, Universes and Everything*," our Systemology naturally recognizes separate semantics for each significant component—*ethics, morals, dogma, justice* and so on—since they are not actually **identifiable** synonymously equal to one another.

> **ethics** : an intellectual philosophy concerning *rightness* and *wrongness* based on "**logic**" and "**reason**" combined with observable consequences and tendencies of action or conduct; formal name for a "moral philosophy" (study of moral choices); in ancient times, originally treated *one-to-one* with "**Cosmic**

Law" regarding *causation, order* and *sequence*; an **objective** (Universal) philosophy of *rightness* and *wrongness*, treated separate from culture-specific (subjective/"**relative**") **considerations**, such as *morals* and *dogma*; in **NexGen Systemology** (*Grade-IV Metahuman Systemology*), a **dynamic** philosophy (applying "**logic**-and-**reason**") to understand the nature of "reality **agreements**" concerning *rightness* and *wrongness*, then treating the most "**optimum**" **conditions** of continued **existence** ("SURVIVAL" in **Beta-existence**; "CREATION" in **Alpha**) for the highest affected "Sphere of Existence" (on the **Standard Model**).

morals : widely held culturally conditioned (socially **learned**) ethical standards of conduct used to "judge" *rightness* from *wrongness* of an individual's character, **personality** or actions (which may or may not be intellectually and emotionally influenced by "local" religious customs, taboos and *dogma*; basic social reality agreements determining "proper conduct" and "right actions" (behavior) based on civic *laws*, social **codes** and religious *doctrines* of a particular society or group and its own cultural experiences of **Reality**.

dogma : religious doctrines or opinion-based beliefs (**data-set**) treated socially as fact, especially regarding "divinity" or "God" (the common "Human" interpretation of the "Realm" or "boundary" of Infinity) represented by the "Eighth Sphere" on our original Standard Model of Systemology; religiously defined values, taboos and ethical standards emphasized by cultural/religious socialization and mythographic beliefs (held superior to observable causal effects, logical sequences or verifiable proofs).

code : an outline of *ethical* standards regarding social **participation** and acceptable behavior; not generally enforced as *law* itself, but a standard that reasonable individuals are **actualized** (or civil) enough to **Self-Determine** (by choice) their own following (or adherence) if it is *right* and *good*; shared reality agreements that promote optimum conditions of continued existence ("SURVIVAL" in *Beta-existence*; "CREATION" in *Alpha*) for the highest affected "Sphere of Existence" (on the *Standard Model*).

law : a formal **codified** outline (or list) of *ethical* standards regarding social participation and acceptable behavior, like a "*code*," except that it *is* enforced by civic consequences (or even "*Cosmic Law*") when not adhered to, usually with punishment coming either by the group (exclusively) or by involvement with an "outside party" or societal (legal) **authority**; a predictable sequence of naturally occurring events that will consistently repeat under the right conditions (such as "*Cosmic Law*" or "*Natural Law*").

justice : observable social actions (or consequential reaction) and predetermined civic (legal) processes employed in a society or group to uphold or enforce their reality agreements concerning "*law*"; a civic authority and administrative body responsible for carrying out practical/physical responses and penalties; the words, "*just*," "*justice*" and "*justification*," all stem from the Latin "*jus*" (meaning "*morally right*," "*law, in accordance with*" or "*lawful*") and "*iustus*" (expressing what is "true," "proper," "up-right" and "justified").

Fortunately, in view of the fact that this course is for the Mardukite Academy of Systemology—and strongly connected to "**Mardukite Zuism**" ministries and related spiritual advisement techniques—we do not exclusively restrict our understanding to contemporary academia or even 0the *Classical World*. We have a tangible 6,000-year archive to draw from. It is familiar territory for us "Mardukite Systemologists" to reference our ancient stores of "*Arcane Tablets*" and esoteric "*Mystic Scrolls*" when necessary; or when supplementing Clear Understanding for an individual's personal vision maintained of antiquity and progressive development of building upon the same **archetypal** Systems of Civilization. Yes, we treat you with a history lesson; even now as we transition from Grade-IV, when our own "total recall" of the past is still uncertain, obscured by many thin veils solidly compacted together; meaning the Self-created barriers and "unknowns"—or more correctly, what we specifically chose (at some point on the *Backtrack*) to "Not-Know" and/or not be "responsible" for.

Imposition of critical *Ethics*—in the form of *Justice* and *Law*—only increased as civic populations (and the complexity of their systems) grew. This is easily demonstrable with a simple *Back-Scan* of the past 6,000 years on Earth. Drawing from '**common knowledge**', Babylon carries a pretty bad reputation for the severity of its *Laws*, but ironically, you don't find a lot of significant criminality during that *Age*, like you might expect. Yes, of course, nations were always pitted against each other for one territorial reason or another—which is ironic when you consider just how much energy had to go into keeping that land sustainable and viable for life; you'd think at some point they would have all just banded together and overtaken more plush regions elsewhere. But, they didn't; so, obviously there is a greater significance to the hold on Mesopotamia—one which escapes more obvious observations available to the average individual. Post-Alexandrian invaders that overtook Mesopotamia did not even maintain the aqueduct system and then newer populations just let the whole place go to pieces.

In both **Sumerian** and **Babylonian** tradition, the Sun —"*Shammash*"—represents "truth," "justice" and the "wisdom of ethics." Such is the domain of *Shammash*, both: literally, as an Anunnaki representative; then celestially, as the actual embodiment of the Sun. This is also the classification for the *Fourth* "rung" along the *Pathway* on the "Ladder of **Ascension**" or "Ladder of Lights" (or "step" on the "Stairway to Heaven") and, likewise, representative of the *Fourth Gate*. This is what immediately precedes the *Fifth* gradient— or *Grade-V*—in the original "Star-Gate" **methodology**; and it seems particularly fitting and prophetic that we should be taking up the concise Systemology of **Self-Honesty** and systematic **processing** of *Ethics* at this **level**. For those that reached the basic point of **Beta-Defragmentation** attainable at this level of our applied spiritual technology (since the release of **Liber-3D**, "**Imaginomicon**"), my intent is that [**Liber-Three**, *Ethics*] will successfully "boost" and "stabilize" all personal gain achieved from completely working through *Grade-IV*. This newly released material on *Ethics*, *Self-Honesty* and "**Responsibility**" provides an effective and necessary "bridge" between *Grade-IV* and *Grade-V* for our "Pathway" in Systemology.

Looking back at records from ancient Mesopotamia—we do not find significant emphasis on violent criminality or imprisonment. While the severity of Babylonian "**Codes**" and "Laws" are particularly famous **rhetoric**, the actual Mardukite legal system is practiced with emphasis on "equality" and "balance"—with "making things whole." During initial installation of civic systems, the Anunnaki most likely held-back restimulating "Prison **Imprints**" too deeply in order to keep the masses from prematurely "waking up" to realizing that this Earth is itself something of a "Prison-Planet." Early progression of formal "*Ethics*" in Mesopotamia is concisely taken up by E.A. Wallis Budge in his century-old treatise titled "Babylonian Life and History":—

> "In primitive times in Babylonia each community or each tribe formulated its own laws and administered them according to custom, which was probably already age-old. The laws at that time were few and simple, and were drawn up chiefly to protect the property of the god and the community. Of these we know nothing. When the Sumerians conquered Babylonia and settled down in it, they observed their own laws, and it is possible they adopted some of those of their predecessors in the country..."

> "When Khammurabi* conquered the whole of Babylo-

---

* Budge employs the archaic spelling "*Khammurabi.*"

nia, he formulated a Code of Laws, by which he intended all his subjects to regulate their lives and affairs.
The Laws were not invented by him, but were drawn
up from earlier codes which had been in existence for
many centuries. He had this Code cut upon a large
stone *stele*, which was set up in the Temple of **Marduk** (*E-Sag-Ila*), so that any and every [person] could
consult it... The **condition** of peace existing throughout the country under the firm, just and vigorous rule
of Khammurabi made application of the Laws of the
Code comparatively easy. The property of the rich
and the rights and privileges of the poor were alike
safeguarded, and during the time that the Code was
observed, a woman could travel unmolested from
Babylon to the Mediterranean Sea. The text of the
Code was also edited for use in schools and studied as
a text-book for many centuries after Khammurabi's
death..."

Therefore, in c. 1800 B.C., "The Code of Hammurabi" greatly
expounded on precepts of former Kings and the cultures
they governed;‡ though he had admittedly received the
"Code" from *outside* sources, Divine (as attributed) or otherwise. While his "Code" might seem rather "excessive" at
first glance, to members of present-day **Western Civilization** now studying Babylon, its original presence in society
was intended as a cultural deterrent (to crime) and standard
of protection (for the people), which did not require excessive **enforcement**. [Although less famously known, their As-
syrian neighbors to the north held far stricter and more
militant laws.]

Early in the development of civilization, the "Law-Giving
Kings" were highly celebrated for their wisdom. Legal
"codes" in Mardukite Babylon were stylized in a very particular style of "ought not or else consequences"–type statements, which were readily accepted by the community as a

---

‡ The oldest surviving written legal code predates Hammurabi by three
 centuries and is attributed to the Sumerian King Ur-Nammu.

standard of safety and protection. These were not written out as a list of demands, such as you find with the Judeo-Christian "Law of Moses" or "Ten Commandments"—instead, they describe scenarios like: "if this man harms this other fella, he must pay him such and such or be his servant for three years."

Aside from critical matters of state or crimes against the Temple, the highest "order" or "governmental system" was seldom employed. Citizens were encouraged to handle their own affairs at a local **level**; public display copies of the "Code of Hammurabi" were simply reminders that the "World Order of Marduk, son of Enki, son of Anu" was present among the population—and that the "Sun-god of Justice" was ever watchful. Stephen Bertman notes, in his *"Handbook to Life in Ancient Mesopotamia"*:—

"If the law codes of Mesopotamia signify an ideal of justice that should govern society, how was the ideal made an everyday **reality**? To begin with, there were no lawyers. Nor was there a regular court system, as we understand it. Nor were there prisons, or even a police force. How then was justice achieved, or even approximated? The key was an innate compliance to a higher authority, a behavioral characteristic that permeated Mesopotamian culture. Society's prime personal virtue was humble and unquestioning obedience—to the gods and their earthly surrogates."

"Most controversies were resolved on the local level —the village or neighborhood—by a Council of Elders whose members were impaneled as judges when circumstances warranted. There were no juries selected from the population at large to hear cases. Instead, litigants presented their arguments to the judges, witnesses were called, and evidence (a written contract, for example) was examined. Trials were often held on the grounds of temples and those who testified were required to swear an oath on a sacred **symbol** of the local god. Perjury was punished not by law but by divine retribution..."

Another cuneiform series—the *surpu-tablets*—is treated in our original Mardukite "Liber-9"† concerning cultural "taboos" referred to as *mamit* in the Akkadian language (Old Babylonian). Lengthy lists of "taboos" or "sins" appear in the series, all of which are actions potentially "causing" an illness or affliction (which might otherwise be religiously treated as "demons"). The tablets also reassure that "*The MAMIT of any kind that afflicts man, MARDUK, Priest of the Gods, can attend.*" The list is fairly extensive, detailing numerous "causes of headache, disease and possession" that we might otherwise treat as common-sense in the Western World (concerning health and cleanliness), whereas the remainder appear to illustrate a *Code of Ethics* that is suggestive or implied, rather than imposition strict rules.

An individual is warned (on the *Surpu tablets*) about causing themselves trouble, for example, if they have:

> "...sinned against their god or goddess; ...slighted what is due to the gods; ...caused obstruction between family or friends; ...held hatred toward an elder; ...propositioned their neighbor's spouse; ...used a false balance in business affairs; ...stolen or caused another to steal; ...unjustly entered their neighbor's house; ...spoken of what is unholy; ...promised pleasure and joy but not giving it; ...offended the righteous; ...pointed at the holy fire; ...struck the young of an animal; ...torn up plants and trees; ...eaten from an unclean cup, plate or dish."

Mesopotamian-oriented Anunnaki Traditions—ancient or modern—place particular emphasis on themes of "Cosmic

---

† The text of *Liber-9* is incorporated into "*The Complete Anunnaki Bible*" (or "*Necronomicon: The Anunnaki Bible*), in addition to the Grade-II Master Edition textbook "*Necronomicon: The Complete Anunnaki Legacy*" and a 10th Anniversary reissue of *Liber-R+9* titled: "*Novem Portis: Necronomicon Revelations and Nine Gates of the Kingdom of Shadows.*"

Ordering" or "The World Order of... this god or that one"; essentially anything along the lines of order, structure, sequence and systematization in place of "chaos." Even the notorious "Eye for an Eye" rhetoric is really relaying a cuneiform version of "*karma*" (or "Causal Law") more than anything else—especially when we discover that most "Free Citizens" were, in actuality, charged significant monetary fines or required to "repay in kind." The "Code" required a "victim" be "made whole"—in some cases, the offender would have to work for them.

Nowhere among Hammurabi's "282 Laws" do we find mention of imprisonment. In fact, such methods of "correction" are not effective for anything other than getting an individual further "spun in" to the **Human Condition.** The experience restimulates existing unresolved "**fragmentation**" and makes it more "solid"—further separating an individual from their potential to experience a basic state of "***Self-Honesty***" (*Beta-Defragmentation*); And we expect *Seekers* to have achieved a basic state of *Self-Honesty* after using *Grade-III* and *Grade-IV*—in combination with *Liber-Three* (*3E*), this present volume—before approaching "*A.T.*" ("*Actualization Tech*") in *Grade-V* as *Wizard Level-1*.

* * * * * * *

NOTES ON EPISTEMOLOGY

"Epistemology" is a school of philosophy containing theories about the basic structure of **knowledge** and reason. An understated, misrepresented and much misunderstood field, epistemology is actually the heart of every other philosophy and science because it pertains to how we might know anything about anything with any certainty. "Logic" offers a means by which we can analyze **semantic** reasoning —later divided into subjects: physio-logic, meteor-logic, even sciento-logic... But, epistemology is where our study of knowledge, reasoning, knowing, and truth interacts directly with "metaphysics" and what we hold true about the appea=

rance of "reality."

Essentially every bit of knowledge—every belief, every idea or concept—is a *bit* of data an individual carries and supports as their view of "reality." Regardless of its **actual** or *factual* truth, logic or reasoning, this personal **agreement** (as data) affects how an individual "sees" and interacts with the "world." The materialist interpretation by Rene Descartes led academia to the standard "scientific method," which became something of a stumbling block for postmodern sciences, such as quantum and string theory. Materialist science would have us believe that everything is separate and that reality is something that **exists** "out there" completely independent of the observer. Yet, we find in our Systemology that reality is quite dependent on personal cognition, "observation," sensory **perception** and realizations for it to actually "exist" and persist "*As-It-Is.*"

When we consider all of the partitions of knowledge—the "-ologies" and "-logics"—by their own classification, each "school of thought" is entirely dependent on its own closed-**circuit "paradigm"** of semantic vocabulary in order to functionally operate. Although an individual might examine observable "causality" within a particular "field" of science, only consequential end-results are **apparent** from standard-issue **levels** of observation. Any supposed "absolute knowledge" objectively yielded from such observation does not reveal the true nature and/or source-cause of what is observed. This is one reason why Descartes originally put "God" into his epistemology. With "God" in the equation, all models work—so long as they are *dualistic* models. [Of course, an emphasis on God also protected Descartes from persecution as a "heretic" during the era of Galileo.]

Personal interpretation of any system's language or vocabulary (**semantic-set**) can be objectified and then later "agreed" upon (or accepted) as "reality" by mainstream society. In essence, we generally and socially call "truth" really results from "**authoritarianism.**" The authoritarian scientist and/or reality **engineer** wants you to accept knowledge that you cannot personally verify outside the boundaries of the paradigm (and its use of language) specifically created to **identify** and prove the very knowledge in question. Most specific paradigms are self-serving and self-supporting in exclusive isolation.

French philosopher Rene Descartes (*1596-1650*) is credited with originating some significant modern contributions to epistemology, which he demonstrated to be the basic general philosophy back of all other "modern" scientific thought. From within his entire literary work, only a few simple key principles distinctly stand out, although thousands of words and multiple essays were composed to offer additional explanations and clarification to the era and audience he wrote for. During his time, as humanity emerged from its "Dark Ages," this was revolutionary thinking. Descartes caused the very foundations of modern science to tremble with his new "epistemology." But, he is accused (by some critics) of overly generalizing to a point of incompleteness. A closer examination reveals that rather than attempt to persuade the reader to "buy" a particular **patter** "sold" as "Absolute Truth," Descartes is more interested in uncovering a route by which an individual can discover this for themselves.

In "*Discourse on the Method of Rightly Conducting Reason and Seeking Truth in the Sciences*" (1637), Descartes describes—

> an intensive process by which the operator must attempt to clear their **slate** of all knowledge that can be doubted; which proves to be essentially everything determined through sensory perception and "human" experience in the Physical Universe.

Descartes suggests that these things can be added back into a personal paradigm later on, after vigorous scrutiny and in a logical order of certainty. First and foremost, *Self-knowledge* is given priority, proved by the *Self-Aware* **consciousness** of an individual; then *God*, the perfect **encompassing** generative force and source in the Universe; and finally *mathematics* and *geometry*, the means in which one might measure and quantify existence in the Universe. However, pursuit of mathematics necessarily loops a seeker back toward contemplation (or interpretive use) of symbols and language. Descartes even illustrates that as a model of observable (empirical) materialist science—even if we are certain of what our senses tell us about a causal "how"—no absolute knowledge of "why" can be determined by the same methods.

"*Meditations on the First Philosophy in which the Existence of God, Reality and the Real Distinction of the Mind and Body of Man are Demonstrated*" (1641) is Rene Descartes most famous work, though many readers have found "*Discourse on Method*" more practical. "*Meditations on First Philosophy*" does, however, reveal the thought progression distinguishes his epistemology. It also presents his most famous **axiom** of "*a-priori*" knowledge [the "*Cogito*"]: "I think, therefore I am." This is famous, though flawed; and logicians point out that it is not a true propositional proof—simply a statement. We can apply the most basic rule of "inferential logic" ["*modus ponens*"] to create a simple "if A then B; A, therefore B" conditional proposition: "If I think, then I exist. I think, therefore I exist." But, this does not solve the entire issue, which is a point directly addressed in the text for *Liber-3D*, "*Imaginomicon*":—

> "Descartes... wrongly **identified** the 'thinkingness' with the 'beingness' of *Self*. Although it received far less **attention** [than the original '*cogito*'], eventually this error philosophically earned a correction in Jean-Paul Satre's insight: The consciousness that says '*I-AM*' is not the same consciousness which *thinks*."

The *Being* is *Aware* that *it* is "thinking"
—that ***Awareness*** is not a *part of* the "thinking."
The *Being* exists independent of the "thought."

Perhaps the least cited, but most concise discourse by Descartes is "*Principles of Philosophy*" (1644). The work composes over one hundred propositions, each with an explanation, as well as significant **axioms** and other clarifications of his unique paradigm. Its demonstration style of Axioms and Logics has influenced and inspired many more recent "New Thought" presentations in the past century. Though the title might suggest some all-encompassing resolution or textbook for a broad study of general philosophy, this slim volume reduces philosophy to only two main aspects:

—the nature of human knowledge (*epistemology*) and

—the nature of material existence and reality (*metaphysics*).

Descartes puts forth the idea that "the senses deceive; and all that we can determine of material existence is accessed by material senses, then processed cognitively." What's more: when rigidly fixed to the *Human Condition* as a *Point-of-View* (*POV*) for *Awareness*, anything "beyond the physical" (or "meta-physical")—such as cognitive **faculties** and the "Mind-Body" connection—cannot be determined with material senses; therefore it lies beyond the domain of "empirical" science. Development of future "meta-sciences" (such as our *Systemology*) must also take into account the "spiritual" factor of *Self* (the actual 'I-AM') and the other Universes and alternate levels of existence not directly experienced from the POV of a "Human Body."

Standard models that radiate **apparent** truth may be overturned by new developments of understanding in spite of public/mass acceptance of the prior knowledge. The *Human Condition* is **implanted** to resist accepting large changes in paradigms or methodologies. As creatures wired by experience and habit, most common knowledge is taken for granted, but based on former knowledge foundations previously adopted. Many philosophers suggest a comparison of one's personal belief (paradigm) against the objective or social world-at-large. On the other hand, *Wizards* are more concerned about the effects of beliefs on reality. In the end, the knowledge we receive from the **external** world must still be processed through various sensors and relays and then weighted against some existing form of established knowledge.

Descartes also inspired German philosopher Immanuel Kant (*1724-1804*). He set forth to revise his own revision of a similar epistemology, which he describes in "*Critique of Pure Reason*" (1781). With rising interest in "empirical objectivism," Kant's *Ethics* requires the existence of an "abstract moral agent," what he called the "Good Will"—and which we might identify as the "*conscience.*" An equally abstract "**maxim**" exists as a driving force or core **imperative** that Kant tries to impress as a Universal. It, of course, fails to be Universal if personally subjective, like a "conscience." While it may be actually true that "you" and "I" exist, proving the existence of one does not necessarily prove existence of the other.

> True **premises** carried to a false conclusion and
> true conclusions drawn from false premises
> are both **invalid** usages of logic and reasoning.

Kant's emphasis on "reasoning" and "logic" circled around *Ethics* as "the purest **evaluation** or practical application of epistemology." Reason—or rather, "Pure Reason"—is the pot-of-gold at the end of Kant's rainbow. Using the propositions of Descartes as a base, Kant determined that "reasoning" is the "highest cognitive ability **capable** to man." It is from this faculty that humans possess ability to obtain "self-knowledge"—by which all other understanding and judgment about reality is formed. "Reason" can be used to describe what is observable, communicable within the **Beta**-range of action and causation; but it may not adequately explain its underlying nature or true source. And that's all there really is to say about famous high-ranking founders of contemporary epistemology.

The standard-issue *Human* uses experience as the essential **catalyst** for interpreting knowledge. Experience is describe-ed in terms of "**sensation**" and "**perception**," which are often confused with each other:—

> —*Sensation* involves receipt of *external* stimulus and "**internal**" **communication** from sensory organs.
> —*Perceptions* regard internal **processing** of data received and communicated from the senses.

For example, your senses pick up and receive the light off of this page, revealing *form*. Perceptually, however, you have abilities to distinguish symbols as coherent letters—and their meaning as *words*. Humans are predominantly programmed (encoded) with audio-visual cues. This makes it quite easy to implant impulses to *label* all *forms*. This means that in addition to a communicable language (to objectively describe a **concept**), sensory experience is dependent on light and/or other detectable *Electromagnetic* (*EM*) **vibrations** in order to distinguish or **differentiate** its "reality." The primary limitation in this method is the "ladder of abstraction," where our words do not share a *one-to-one* (or *A-for-A*) relationship with the forms that they describe.

* * * * * * *

NOTES ON ETHICS

Ethics is the social science or study of moral philosophy, which is to say the extent to which one's actions are objectively "right" or "wrong." Most arcane mystical and esoteric systems operate on the **premise** that an individual is primarily responsible for everything that happens to them in life—everything they experience and the manner in which that experience is treated. Wizards study *Ethics* to better understand how to actively handle personal **responsibility** for their lives. Though a fragmented individual is not necessarily knowingly *Aware* of all processes taking place, their consciousness is constantly (and often compulsively) building and rebuilding their position in reality to have an experience.

Total responsibility for *Ethics* as **metahumans** also includes *ethically* handling matters pertaining to the organization, function and representation of **Mardukite Zuism** and the Systemology Society.

> A "true" *Ethic* requires "*true knowledge*" for "*knowing*"
> what is "right" and what is "wrong"
> —moral philosophers are often also epistemologists.

Semantic debates regarding this perceived knowledge are called "moral arguments." If we were forced to label it, a Wizard's *ethic* blends "objective rationalism" with "Utilitarianism" using set premises regarding *Creeds* and *Codes* of Mardukite Zuism. Some consider this effort "***Utopian***" idealism; yet quite simply, personal systematic **defragmentation** increases an individual's "clear vision" (and reality or understanding) on the highest ideals and levels of *knowingness* regarding ethics.

An "individual" (or for purposes of general philosophy, an "ego-conscience") has the ability to go beyond considering what is *only immediately* "good" for Self; they can see the entire **"holistic" dynamic** system of existence. An individual is certainly capable of interpreting "objective laws of the Universal Imperative" governing the *Prime Directive* of this *Beta-Existence*, which is implanted *sixty times* over with the **command**: "TO SURVIVE." The **Alpha-Spirit**, as an eternal being, has no need to be concerned with its own "survival"—because that is one thing it is innately doing already (by the nature of its *Beingness*) in **Alpha-Existence**. The "I-AM"-Self is carrying out an entirely different (upper-level) "directive" or "imperative" for the Spiritual Universe, which is "TO BE" and "TO CREATE." [A more detailed relay of these concepts is communicated in "*Imaginomicon*" (*Liber-3D*).]

In his discourse, "*Grounding for the Metaphysics of Morals*" (1785), Kant introduces semantics for two different types of "imperative": the "**hypothetical** imperative" and the "categorical imperative." He argues that the Universal Imperative (of Universal Law) must be a "categorical imperative." To clarify, a "hypothetical imperative" appears conditional and relative, or perhaps not universal toward survival of all people. These are the *"if"* statements that are subject to an individual's own personal inclinations—however much **Self-determined** these may be. The effects are consequential or hypothetical: "If you do 'A', then 'B' could happen to you." In contrast, Universal or "categorical imperatives" are typically *"you ought"* sentiments, emphasizing that they are not solely motivated by inclinations or personal **considerations** of subjective consequences and conditionals.

Wide-angle (systematically holistic) consideration of objective effects and subjective consequences—getting the "whole picture"—is an integral part of effective *Utilitarianism* as a moral philosophy; and this is as good of a time as any to begin introducing the subject of *Utilitarianism* directly. [Although the subject will be treated further in the next section *"On Utilitarianism."*] Many individuals claim to have already discounted "Classical Utilitarianism" as a flawed system of ethics—so our organization apparently has very little modern competition for its application.

For the first act of *"**Ethics Processing**,"* a *Professional* **Pilot** (of Mardukite Systemology) would inquire *what* the Seeker's idea of "Classical Utilitarianism"*actually "is."* Whatever answer is given with, the *Pilot* responds with a "Thank You," **acknowledging** the *Seeker* for **participation** in the "**communication** cycle" (and "**processing** session"). The *Pilot* directs a similar acknowledgment after each *"**Processing Command Line**"* (*PCL*) or question, once answered. A *Pilot* doesn't **evaluate** content of the response directly. A note is made, especially if the answers are "way off base" or "coming out of left field." (This example illustrates the basic fact no system of "Classical Utilitarianism" exists...) [Systemology of Communication (as it relates to basic practices of systematic processing), is described fully in material for *"**Metahuman Destinations**"* (***Liber-Two***). These "basics" served (for nearly two years) as a placeholder in *Grade-IV*, substituting a much greater disciplined and complete "Course" for standardizing *Professional Piloting Procedure.*]

In most cases, a *Seeker* is processed toward "defragmentation"; and this means, by *definition*, that some of their own *definitions* are actually "fragmented"—regardless of how reasonable they may *seem* to the individual. As with other fields, areas and subjects of *knowingness*, philosophical debates often erupt from lack of semantic clarity regarding that subject, its vocabulary, and/or varying interpretations of the same... All because a word, concept or idea was not understood properly as intended—which is why the statement (phrase) "A-for-A" or "One-to-One" is used to describe perfect duplication of communication.

The two individuals most famous for its propagation (Jeremy Bentham and John Stuart Mill) each had their own slant on the philosophy called "Utilitarianism." Understand that we are treating applications of "philosophy"—a **facet** of learning that most individuals are likely to be either disinterested in completely, or else carry very specific emotionally **charged** opinions (which are actually *their* "beliefs") on the matter. There could be many factors present to **incite** this, but more often than not it stems from the fact that philosophy, mathematics, history and physical or natural sciences have all been mishandled in modern contemporary education systems. This strongly affects an individual's ability to study and learn beyond their formal education—and this affects Systemology, because we have never pretended that the pursuit and relay of this work did not appear somewhat on the "nerdy" side of the **spectrum**.

> Utilitarianism is actually a consequential ("*teleological*") moral philosophy rooted in a belief that ethical actions in nature (physical phenomena, *Beta-Existence*) are dependent on consequences of these actions as a determinant or explanation, as opposed to a "rule" or "law."

An emphasis on end-goals and consequences is what provides the concept (and namesake) of "utility" for Utilitarianism. Some philosophers in the past have had difficulty "reading between the lines" or even taking a position other than one extreme side of a **dichotomy** or another. In most instances of philosophy, our "excluded middle" becomes the "path less traveled by." It provides workable concepts that probably better represent the "Truth" of things far more than those positions taken in the past by the "better-known" extremist philosophers. The present author finds no contradiction to incorporating "objective reasoning" into *our* "Mardukite" version of *Ethics* as Utilitarian Systemology. "Thought" and "Reasoning" actually do apply to Utilitarianism. When combined, our meta-paradigm allows an individual freedom to rise above mundane/material (man-made) laws, if those laws are deemed unjust or destructive toward the "greatest number" or more specifically: the highest inclusive (or affected) "Sphere of Existence."

* * * * * * *

NOTES ON UTILITARIANISM

John Stuart Mill (1806–1873) launched his philosophical literary career from London (England) when he completed writing his two-volume set, titled: "*A System of Logic, Ratiocinative and Inductive*," published in 1843. However, the work he is best known for is "*Utilitarianism*"—a title based on the concept derived from Jeremy Bentham, a close friend of Mill's father, James. His treatment of ethics is clearer and more readable than Immanuel Kant. Mill was even once the editor for the "*Westminster Review*," which had provided the very first English translations of Kant's "*Metaphysics of Morals*," but Mill was extremely critical of "German Metaphysics," claiming it had a tendency to "deprave one's intellect."

Mill illustrates faults of "*a priori*" moralists; for example, Kant's "first moral premise" (or "golden axiom"), which suggests a person should act as if such actions should be "the rule" for all men. Mill remarks that there is no logical contradiction found in that philosophy (as there should be) that would prevent a person from simply seeing or accepting that all other "**rational** beings" adopt a similarly "outrageous" immoral rule of conduct. This means that conventional "golden rule" ethics is flawed, because a person can act "unethically" using the excuse that others could also just act similar. Such a view is held by contemporary society in many ways. This has actually led to environmental destruction, wildlife abuse and capitalist fascism.

> Jeremy Benthem states that "the greatest happiness of the greatest number is the foundation of morals and legislation." Benthem's philosophy focuses on "quantitative" amounts of happiness—known as "Quantitative Utilitarianism"—not "quality." But according to John Stuart Mill, right and wrong should be connected to "pleasure" and "pain," employing faculties an individual innately possess.

"Pleasure" and "Pain" are frequently treated by humans as valid determinants of "Good" and "Bad." In our Mardukite Systemology we recognize (and treat) a "*Reactive Control Center*" (*RCC*), a primitive survival mechanism installed in the "Mind–Body Connection" for a **genetic vehicle**. The "*RCC*" emotionally encodes experiences of "pain" and "loss" as "*Imprints*." This mechanism is responsible for all "fight-flight" and "stimulus–response" reactions. Such "*Imprints*" are more easily restimulated into action, when an individual maintains a low-level of **Awareness**.

While these terms—*pleasure*, *pain*, *good* and *bad*—all seem highly subjective and encourage ideas of "value hedonism." On the surface most will agree that *pleasure* and *pain* do play an important role in what an individual deems "good" or "bad" as based on personal "experience." This form of experience is sometimes called "conditioning" or "reinforcement" in traditional social sciences. Those outside of our

Systemology paradigm will understand (using their own semantics) that through an action's consequential reinforcement, emotional states (response-reactions) are developed
concerning a cycle-of-actions or **Imprinting Incident**.

> These emotionally **charged** imprinted recordings
> develop into what some refer to as a "tendency"
> *toward* or *away* from particular actions in the future.

We cannot demean our statement by calling it a "preference," as such implies only a weak subjective moral
premise. "Preferences" can also be *implanted*; so, much like
reaction-response "tendencies," these "**personality**" traits
do not necessarily remain under full (*Self-*)*determinism* of an
individual This does not make an argument based on preference completely untrue; simply weak. A rational being
prefers to endure "pleasure" and avoid "pain" whenever
possible. If a "*facet*" from an *Imprinting Incident* (when
"pain" or "loss" had occurred) is present in the environment while an individual is maintaining low-Awareness,
then automated mechanisms ("**Reactive Control Center**"/
RCC) may take over considerations ("**control**") of the Physical Body ("*genetic vehicle*"), removing the "**Master Control
Center**" (*MCC*) from the **circuit**—and likewise removing a
clear "Self-Honest" "line of communication" between *Self*
(Alpha Spirit/"I-AM") and *beta-Existence.*

> A *tendency* automates **willingness** to "*reach* or *withdraw.*"
> Additional validation makes the tendency more demanding
> until the response is operating automatically (reactively)
> to yield positive results and avoid those that effect poorly.

On the surface, Utilitarianism might not appear very "spiritual" since most individuals only recognize its hedonistic
views—where "pleasure" and "pain" become the only
"ends" in material life. However, Mill disuades propagating
this inaccurate generalization by explaining that "*spiritual
inclinations*" of an individual are what ultimately contribute
to their supreme happiness and highest optimum experien-

ce of existence. Material "things" and worldly "goals" are not generally desired as the "ends" in their own right—but instead as a means to promote greater pleasure and happiness in the Physical Universe.

All persons must be held accountable for consequences of their actions. This does not require libraries worth of laws and precepts to understand. In *Utopian Philosophy* (explained in the next section), Thomas More considers it morally unjust to subject people to so many laws and of such obscure language that no one—except their authors and lawyers continuing to propagate their reality—actively knows or understands them all.

Given a choice between two options, a Utilitarian is encouraged to choose the path that "employs the highest faculty" and this is where we see a strong connection between Mill's philosophy and the *Pathway*—the "Right Way to **Ascension**." Intellectual pleasures are obviously of a higher quality (value) than physical ones alone.

> Mill warns, however, that those who learn to operate on these higher faculties will require a higher quality of life to remain happy and can potentially have greater suffering than a person driven only by physical mundane inclinations. In other words, the higher you fly, the greater the distance of a potential fall.

According to Utilitarian philosophy there are two main causes of unhappiness that can be more detrimental to life than just the physical pain and emotional loss alone:—

Firstly, there is "selfishness"—acting as though the individual is the "*only one*"; that the *only* Sphere of Existence is the *first.* This completely goes against the basic tenets of Utilitarianism.

Secondly, and perhaps more importantly, there is the "want of mental cultivation." Serious emotional depression often results for an individual not making use of their "higher faculties."

Mill frequently used "intelligent appreciation of music and art" as a primary example of high-value intelligence in *"aesthetics."* In fact, *music* and *art* were the two specific facets of life that his father had forbidden him to take interest in as a child.

A Wizard-Level Systemologist [*Grade-V* and above] is earning critical data regarding the Spiritual Systemology of Alpha Existence—all previously experienced **condensations** (versions) of shared common-agreement Universes. This is particularly relevant in this instance, because it is during the "Wizard Grades" that we turn our **attentions** toward understanding the Standard Model from a "higher-level" *point-of-view*—turning around 180-degrees to **confront** *Gateways of Infinity* as opposed to the "Veils" of a "low-level" (*Beta*) existence.

Upper-level *Gateways of Infinity* represent even higher **"Spheres of Existence"** (though they are better defined as curves or arcs of the "infinity-loop") that are not critically aimed at "survival in *beta-existence*" so much as they are balancing the *Infinity of Nothingness* equation with potential *Infinite Creation.* The "dynamic systems" demonstrated as "Eight Spheres of Existence" in our Standard Model repeat at a higher resonance with **Alpha** qualities. The ninth and tenth, harmonizing with the first and second, are: *Ethics* and *Aesthetics.*

Mardukite Systemology, is an applied spiritual philosophy and "high-level" spirito-intellectual pursuit. It qualifies as a "higher pursuit" for Utilitarian purposes, operating toward the highest Sphere of Existence a *Seeker* holds a reality on. Our Systemology not only provides increased happiness and certainty in *this* lifetime (**incarnation**) and *this* version of *Beta-Existence*, but it also provides "lasting gains" that significantly assist the *Seeker, Master* and/or *Wizard* while "between" "lifetimes" and into the "next."

This hybrid neo-Utilitarian *Ethic* was first developed for "Wizards" during the early-2000's, while the present author still operated under the name "Merlyn Sone." Its earliest version appeared in the 2008 publication: "*The Great Magical Arcanum*" by Joshua Free. Refinement of the "greatest number" concept applied to "Spheres of Existence" on our "Standard Model" is the newest application. Its appearance now in Systemology erupted from necessity; out of a need to resolve a way through a critical barrier **confronting** those that have reached far enough on the *Pathway to Self-Honesty* to seek clear passage up and across the *Fifth Gate.*

Considering the nature of the *Fourth Gate* ("*The Sun*") and the *Fifth* ("Mars"), we are now dealing with a lot of *FIRE*—purging emotional mass, dissolving fragmentary parts, immolating **iniquities**. In view of what is required for this part of the journey, it is clear to those of us—such as the present author—that have dedicated 100-hour work weeks to the "Gatework" for over a decade, there are few others that are likely to brave their way completely through this *wall of fire*, successfully passing through Sacred Flames that wash away all that is Human, leaving only Self to remain unscathed.

> A Wizard seeks "greatest happiness" for all affected Life,
> and by incorporating our Standard Model of Spheres,
> this includes Planet Earth as an necessary organism
> for continuation of existence on the lower spheres
> —for too long slighted out of moral considerations.

There is no reason to quantify, weigh out and/or balance moral values, which is where neo-Utilitarianism (Systemology) greatly differs from its predecessors (inspired by Bentham and Mill). For example: If A and B are competitors, some interpretations of former outdated Utilitarianism would allow A to put B out of commission using any means necessary, assuming that A's happiness and gain is quantitatively greater than B's unhappiness, pain and loss. For this reason, many critics shot holes in Utilitarian paradigms traditionally given. Essentially, A initiates actions that cause pain, which is "evil," and A also violates the rights and free-dom of B. With a concise revision of Utilitarianism, we can prove this course of action to be unethical.

> Our society does not recognize that it can truly be stronger by having stronger, empowered actualized individuals. It instead creates and enforces a central-ized epicenter and seat of power that pushes itself down onto the greater population of individuals and workers; conceptually represented in the past by a "*pyramid.*"

Those uneducated regarding higher faculties of life are at an obvious disadvantage. Actually this is one reason that the New Age Movement grew so quickly. The mundane pleas-ures (and ideals) available to material-minded folk *will* actu-ally pale in comparison to higher pursuits of life, once recognized. Some argue that people naturally possess these actualized abilities. Yet we can see everyday that folk re-peatedly and blatantly compromise higher pleasures for lower ones. Some believe that our "standards" of **Self-Actu-alization** (or in Utilitarianism) are simply too high of a "standard" for present-day standard-issue humanity. Hence our Systemology **heralds** the arrival of metahumans—*Homo Novis*, the "New Human."

John Stuart Mill saw a possible Utopian world available to humanity if society could adhere to Utilitarianism. He stressed that law and order were important, but also ability to recognize when injustice is present in the mandates of supposed civic authorities. He often spoke out against cor-ruption in government and personally contributed to the English Reform Bill of 1867. Some consider Mill "ahead of his time," but the message he carried is important for all times and in all places. It **validates** on paper, using written words of a noted philosopher, the beliefs that most folk already carry about how the world *ought* to be.

* * * * * * *

NOTES ON UTOPIAN PHILOSOPHY

Here we address a social philosophy and ethic for (primarily) independent rural (country-dwelling or pagan) living communities adopting a neo-Utilitarian moral philosophy (as suggested by Systemology) to enhance "greater happiness" and "**Ascension**" of all participants.

"*Utopia*" is a little-treated concept in our vocabulary and contemporary academics. It is not easily definable, since each individual is certain to hold their own unique version of an "ideal" worldview. Some believe *Utopia* is a type of "Nirvana-on-Earth" free of any labor and suffering or tangible quality to experience. This is not a realistic view as the agreed upon Physical Universe presently stands. *Utopians* actually labor quite intensely when they are working, but such a society emphasizes only necessities of material happiness, and thus work is performed by necessity. No one labors needlessly. A typical workday consists of six hours divided by a meal and two hours to pursue individual inclinations at the peak in the day (when outdoor labor conditions are not always efficient).

A utopia requires all citizens earn proficiency in agriculture in addition to whatever other craft or trade they intend to contribute to the community. This means all folk take turns working the fields (or at least one complete cycle under direct supervision of a more experienced farmer). Some citizens also maintain agriculture as their sole trade, seldom trading off to work in other parts of the community (by choice).

Everything is manufactured from natural materials with an emphasis on longevity and value. Building structures and produced goods are not expendable; anything repairable or reusable is kept, mended or re-purposed. In most instances, "money" is non-existent within the community—though a store of "fiat currency" is kept for emergency dealings with the "outside world." In many respects, no one person has more "wealth" than anyone else. All necessary clothing and supplies are made, stored and dispersed as needed. It is each citizen's responsibility to maintain their own supplies in good order as well as the condition of any essential tools required for their craft.

There is never a short supply of what is needed. Tendencies to "hoard" are dissolved. No one has a need for more than what they can functionally use. As things eventually wear out or are destroyed, they are fixed or replaced. In most cases, an "expected duration" is set for replacing each type (a farmer will obviously require more durable clothing than a boot-maker) and as suggested, Utopians seek to reuse as much as possible. If a particular supply of something is deemed "surplus," then efforts are redirected toward other foreseen shortages or deficiencies. "Surplus" goods may also be exchanged in fair trade with other similar communities.

Traditional (academic) "Utopian Philosophy" emerged with Sir Thomas More's novel, "Utopia" in 1516; a treatise describing the "best form of commonwealth." [More was also beheaded for treason, refusing to swear to the "Act of Succession."] "Utopia" chronicles social philosophy of a fictional island—"Utopia"—named after its original settler, "Utopus." The island was previously called "Abraxas." He describes the living spaces on the island, divided by equally spaced cafeteria halls, storage houses and "buildings of industry." Retail outlet are not necessary, nor taverns and superlative office-space. Advertising, marketing and excessive packaging are non-existent in non-competitive industries. Essentially, even "leaders" in the community do not live more lavishly or possess more "wealth" than others. In fact, More suggests that the living quarters of each household could be rotated every ten years. However, an individual might accumulate more aesthetic craft-items or surround themselves with more of their own artistic works and inventions as they progress in years. Such would seem only natural.

Wizard-Level Systemologists are interested in *Utopian* models, like More's, as fundamental examples for esoteric study and practiced application. There is no continuing interest in failed New Age communal efforts of "quasi-hippies"—such as gained prominence several decades ago. More's vision of *Utopia* does not condone polygamous relationships, which actually "compromise the central family unit" that make a *Utopian* community so strong. Much as in ancient Mesopotamian law, sexual infidelity is essentially intolerable; even divorce is generally frowned upon (with obvious exceptions).

Specialization is a common factor of *utopian* visions. Inescapably, a person should contribute what they best can. *Utopian* ideals keep labor efficient, minimizing the actual time spent performing it. An individual is then left more personal time to pursue their own inclinations toward happiness, usually intellectual or craft-related—not to mention the ability to pursue spiritual freedom from this existence. This makes for a more productive "working man," one that doesn't feel like they have slaved for all their waking hours to primarily benefit another—or only toward care for and feed of a material body.

Idleness and sloth is, however, not tolerated and the primary function of a "chief" is to provide certainty and security by maintaining productivity in the community. The "head" of each household is responsible for making requests and obtaining the supplies for the house. Rotating *"guildmasters"* of each trade will report their own inventories and supply needs for (craft) production. Medical treatment and sick houses are offered to those who both need and want them. Services are not denied to those who request them, nor are they forced on those who do not want them. The same applies to euthanasia as a means of ending suffering during critical venerable periods.

All of this reflects the best of what *Philosophy* represents through the ages. It is, however, in no way a fixed criteria or standard for modern *Mardukite Zuism* and/or *Systemology*. The idea of *Utopia* has ever after remained a theoretical construct of philosophy. In the broad sense, most communes/communities are not nearly as efficient, or self-sufficient, as they would like to believe. At their operative size-level and with no other similar communities to network with, most cannot actually functionally employ the minimalist lifestyle described here. The question remains as to whether such a community would even be possible today based on the standard-issue Humans Condition—or, is the rise of a tyrant, operating outside the state of *Self-Honesty* always inevitable?

:: UTILITARIAN SYSTEMOLOGY FOR SEEKERS[‡] ::
– Systematizing Ethics for a Pathway to Self-Honesty –

When *Ethics* is applied to our Standard Model of Systemology—its *Spheres of Existence*—it should seem easy to classify the strongest Moral Philosophy based on observation of survival in *Beta-Existence*. What promotes the greatest conditions of survival would therefore be the highest good. Most ancient 'moral codes' and 'taboos' regard observable consequences—actions that had either promoted or **thwarted** survival; and naturally this is reduced to the most fundamental sensory experience of the Human Condition (pertaining to the *First Sphere*): "pleasure" and "pain."

The purpose of *Ethics* is to determine what is right action and wrong conduct universally across the boards, in all **times** and **spaces**, regardless of an authoritarian regime or what cultural paradigm-set is in place. This is what makes *Ethics* a high standard of thinking—"high thought"—for philosophy. It has perhaps only recently been perfected to any applicable extent. Given that our primary emphasis has been on "*Self-Honesty*" ever since the inception of the Pathway, it should come as no surprise that proper handling of *Ethics* is the Key to reaching true Metahuman destinations.

* * * * * * *

UTILITY AND THE SPHERES OF EXISTENCE

One of the challenges with using the Standard Model in relaying Metahuman Utilitarianism: it tends to emphasize the individual as identified in space-time of *Beta-Existence*. This

---

‡   Portions of this chapter-lesson are based on the "*Grade-IV, Freedom From*" lectures given by *Joshua Free* to the *Mardukite Academy of Systemology* (in July 2021) at *Mardukite Babylonia SLV Borsippa HQ*; remaining sections were issued as supplemental lecture handouts.

is the orientation point at "1.0" and why we are able to effectively use the Standard Model to navigate experiences of *Beta-Existence* and "rise above" it. The Standard Model is essentially the blueprint for lower Universes. Hence, the motivator of *Life* in "Beta-Existence" relates to perpetuating its own existence, or else "survival." Of course, this can *only* be the case while identified with *Beta-Existence*. By its own nature, an Eternal Spirit can only (or must) "survive" in "Alpha Existence" as an *Alpha Spirit*. An immortal spirit is implanted with the motivation to survive only when fixed to a particular identifiable "genetic vehicle" as a particular **Identity** (or *Self-Identification*). The individual is seeking to *Be* its own basic nature—as something to "*Do*"—applying efforts toward *Infinite Survival* (*Sphere Eight*) or else to achieve Immortality, but which is already its natural state in Alpha Existence.

After **succumbing** to present positions and considerations of the Human Condition, awakening as the Alpha Spirit, eternal in nature, is now something to *Do*. A Seeker then discovers *seven veiled layers* set between the two states. Infinite Survival *within* Beta-Existence still speaks nothing of conditions of the Alpha Spirit. There is no physical/material boundary of the Physical Universe that would deliver *Self* (using a *genetic vehicle*) at the doorstep of the next Universe beyond. To approach another Universe requires breaking the gravity of this plane as an Alpha Spirit, then knowingly having Awareness and ability to either create an appropriate form for the newer plane or simply take **command** of one that is bioengineered or birthed for communication at that range of existence. This is, of course, assuming the individual has not already mastered the art of *Beingness* without dependency on a "locatable body"—but, again, such vehicles can be useful for communicating within a particular "shared" Universe.

As relayed in *Unit-2* of "*Metahuman Destinations*" (*Liber-Two*) —then illustrated more clearly in *Unit-3*—the more recent the **implant**, the lower the Spheres (harmonic) it manifests on. This means that at "1.0" where Self is *Aware* of *Life* existing as a *genetic vehicle* or "material body," it now can be "hurt" and experience "pain"—whereas in higher existences, this is not possible. The fixed *Point-of-View* (*POV*) for Self had to fall pretty far down to reach such a state; but that also tells us that we have been imprinted on the idea of "pleasure/pain" for far less time on the **Backtrack** then the older a more deeply ingrained implant incidents. Yet, one can also see that they get more and more solid in their effect as you get down to "1" on our scale.

> There are four implant **patterns** for each Sphere. The (most recent) implanted platforms (or circuitry) appear on the *First Sphere* (1.0) and are, from lowest "frequency" (most recent) to highest "frequency" (earliest, happening further back): *To Endure, To Survive, To Eat* and *To Feel.**

Implants are patterned platforms on which other encoding and imprinting of a certain type (or experience) may be recorded. They are particularly significant in systematic processing and other advanced studies at higher-level Wizard Grades; but implants are mentioned in *Grade-IV* (*Wizard Level-0*) to prepare *Seekers* with a general idea of how all this imprinting and programming is actually involved (and/or entangled) with the Human Condition—and solidly fixed energetic "mass" that accumulates through countless lifetimes on the **Spiritual Timeline**. Such "mass" ultimately resulted in weighing down considerations of the individual to exclusively place themselves *here.* This is what we are to correct, if there is any hope in liberating the *Human Spirit* from the *Human Condition.*

The *Second Sphere* is traditionally labeled "Home (and Family)" because it extends directly from stable security maintained by *Self* in *Beta-Existence* (when identifying with a "genetic organism"). The *Second Sphere* also **correlates** with "2.0" on our Standard Model for *Beta-Existence*, which is to

---

*   This effectively updates the chart list from *Liber-Two, Unit-3.*

say the "Reactive Control Center" (RCC), which is emotionally encoded with imprints of "Havingness" and "Loss" (in addition to the lower scale of "Pain" and "**Biological Unconsciousness**" from "1.0"). These first two Spheres are treated for "survival" in Beta-Existence, but they share a harmonic quality resonating with the first two higher Alpha-Spheres (or arcs of Infinity, when treated as an extension of our Standard Model) of *Ethics* and *Aesthetics*. This is easy to understand if we consider the relationship between *Ethics* ("9") to a "Body" at "1.0" and the idea of *Aesthetics* ("10") as a higher-level equivalent of "human emotion" at "2."

beta	alpha
"SURVIVAL"	*"CREATION"*
8	16
↑	↑
7	15
6	14
5	13
4	12
3	11
2	10
1	9

The four implant patterns for the *Second Sphere* are, from lowest (most recent) to highest (earliest, happening further back): *To Protect (Care For)*, *To Satisfy (Cope)*, *To Reproduce* and *To Join*.*

Although we speak of "Home" and "Family," the encoding for the *Second Sphere* pertains to anything an individual can "*Have*" and therefore potentially "*Lose.*" Hence, an organism expands efforts to "survive" (or *enhance* "survival") by *having* certain things; and even continuing existence through a legacy, mainly children. This is also where we find heavy **emotional encoding** and other imprinting regarding the

---

* This effectively updates the chart list from *Liber-Two, Unit-3.*

"reproductive act" ("sex") itself.

> From our examination of basic fragmentation, it is logical to state: any action encouraging or causing *Pain* or *Loss* to any Sphere is unethical.

At the *Third Sphere*, the basic dynamic systems expand to concern "*Organizations*" and "Grouping." This applies to "organizational grouping of data" (**internal** to a Mind-System) as well as "organized groups of individuals" (externally) manifest in the world-at-large. It is from this "Sphere" that we derive our three circuits of imprinting/programming involving "others" (as treated in **SOP-2C** and **Route-3** circuit-processing): *Self* to *Others*; *Others* to *Self*; and *Others* to *Others*. Information received and encoded on these three circuits contributes to an individual's association (or grouping) of data (as knowledge) and calculation of effort (in *Beta-Existence*) to be "right" in their communication (including actions) in producing the appropriate (intended) effect.

Where systematic functions of the Human Condition pertain to the Mind-System, or "Master Control Center" (MCC), we treat the range between the RCC (at 2.0) and "4.0" on our Standard Model. This is the limited range of "Beta-Thought" relating specifically to the Human Condition. All remaining upper-level thinking (outside of **associative** and **experiential knowledge**) is for "Metahuman" consideration. In "Unit-3" (of *Liber-Two*, "*Metahuman Destinations*"), the *Third Sphere* of existence (and implanting) is precisely defined as: "Organization of systems and alignment of Self in groups; associative knowledge used to gauge efforts" all at "3" with "groups"—and "experience of failure and **erroneous** calculations; personal error as miscalculation from false knowledge" at "*minus*-3."

As the *Third Sphere* applies to "society," an individual is extending their reach into dynamic systems which are not restricted only to a "family unit" and "home-life." This means participating as a member of a group ("3") composed of representatives from many different families ("2") and, of course, the various individuals ("1") themselves. Whether we refer to various social circles, clubs, religious associations and even the community we reside in, an individual participates in the **existential** survival of the group. This correlates to a perceived value (or esteem) that contributes to their own survival on the *First* and *Second* spheres in Beta-Existence.

> The implant patterns for the *Third Sphere* are, from lowest (most recent) to highest (earliest, happening further back): *To Expand, To Participate, To Cooperate* and *To Organize.*[*]

An individual also tends to withdraw participation ("**presence**") in a *Second* or *Third* sphere, if they feel they have wronged the group (or partnership)—or feel wronged themselves—and this includes "*failed **help**.*" On the downward journey and trapping of the Human Condition, an individual does not "go out of communication" with all of existence at once. Such takes place gradually—knowingly at first—with a few lines selectively closed off or set on automatic. But eventually the avoidance is quite sweeping as the individual completely withdraws their reach and thereby becomes the total effect of environment.

As much as we would expect a *Seeker* to carry fragmentation concerning a *genetic vehicle* or "body" ("1") and even family life ("2"), we discover older experiences imprinted on a deeper laid platform of incidents involving "groups" ("3") and an individual's *participation* therein.

The *Fourth Sphere* **encompasses** all human individuals, human families and human groups—and thus is the representation of the entire "Human Condition" in its standard-issue Beta-state. In previous volumes of our material, the *Fourth Sphere* is given as: All Human Life. Each group, sub-group, family and individual is a component of "Humanity" as a

---

[*] This effectively updates the chart list from *Liber-Two, Unit-3.*

whole. The Human Condition is a dynamic system. It would make sense that any motivation or ethical action should serve the betterment of all Humanity and a healthy continuation of its material Beta-survival. When handled outside of *Self-Honesty*, this is where the "chain" breaks down. Upper-**echelon** "metahuman" understanding includes *utility* of the *Fifth Sphere* and above.

> Implant patterns for the *Fourth Sphere* are, from lowest (most recent) to highest (earliest, happening further back): *To Unite, To Control, To Share* and *To Establish.*[*]

Our "new ethics" is for Humanity (including present and future "metahumanity" or the "New Human"). It does not stop (or end) with a short-sighted consideration of only what pertains exclusively to one species of little beasties we often identify as *"humans."* Such *"Fourth Sphere"* limitations of the standard-issue Human Condition and low-Awareness handling of the Mind-System has led planet Earth (*Fifth Sphere*) to its ecological imbalance and brink of annihilation; the classic case of a species that never learned "not to shit in its own nest."

The *Fifth Sphere* is not only the Earth as a living organism, but also a composite of All Life on Earth—meaning not only plant-life and animals, but the very same **organic** *genetic vehicle* used for the Human form ("4"). As such, it encircles the boundaries of the Human Condition on our Standard Model. Since continued survival of a human-like species on Earth *is dependent on* an Earth to inhabit (both existentially and by semantic logic). An even higher ethic is necessary than standards formerly treated in modern civilization—and this necessarily must include the Earth (Planet) and its eco-systematic balance as the "greatest number" above (and *as*) all lower spheres.

Even an ego-centric worldview, if executed *in Self-*

---

[*] This effectively updates the chart list from *Liber-Two, Unit-3.*

Honesty, should have reached this same logical con-
clusion from the very beginning. Hence, the alleged
"best of **intentions**," when acted upon *outside of Self-
Honesty*, tends toward disaster. In a state of *fragmentation*, especially regarding *Ethics*, an individual cannot
possibly *Know* what is *Best* when operating on mortal
programming of "eat today; die tomorrow."

Not surprisingly, an examination of early-period esoteric
paradigms (such as *Grade-I, Route-D*[‡]) toward their own "metahuman" ideals (by some other semantic) are exceptionally
Nature-oriented. This focus on the natural environment
seems to increase the likelihood that an individual will "rise
up" out of their confounding Human Condition and gravity
of the systematic social structure impinged on that condition in civilization. Otherwise, too often we find the needs
of the *group* ("3") or even the *individual* ("1") given more
weight than the optimum survival of all humanity ("4"), all
Lifeforms on Earth ("5") and all existences in the Physical
Universe ("6").

> Implant patterns for the *Fifth Sphere* (pertaining to
> *Lifeforms*) are, from lowest (most recent) to highest
> (earliest, happening further back): *To Adapt, To Heal,
> To Live*[†] and *To Grow*.

While *ecological responsibility* is certainly not a "new"
concept for philosophy or "ecopsychology" (whatever that
is and for whatever it's done), it has not been properly introduced to *Ethics*, and certainly not in former "algebraic
utility" or "utilitarian calculus" inspired by Bentham and
Mill. Our Standard Model of Beta-Existence also considers
planet Earth ("5") as yet one component of an even larger
dynamic system—or *Sixth Sphere*—which is essentially all
Beta-Existence itself, or else, any Universe. As much as we
might like to gripe about entrapment within our own agree-

[‡]   See the Master Edition anthology "*Merlyn's Complete Book of
      Druidism*" by Joshua Free; additionally refer to "*The Complete
      Mardukite Master Course*" transcripts.

[†]   Possibly a better translation is "*To Experience.*"

ments *here*, there is a "cosmic imperative" where we seek to sustain continued existence of the Universe—for what would happen if it were to collapse short of our individualized achievement of *Self-determined Ascension* of *Actualized Awareness* back to "Alpha"?

When we consider "6.0" on the Standard Model (of Beta-Existence), we are at the theoretical point of Alpha-Thought and the ability to construct, create and participate in shared/common Universes in general. In most cases, however, we treat the *Sixth Sphere* as other-determined *Beta-Existence*, or else that which an individual *superimposes* onto their personal "Home Universe" ("7") by agreement/**postulate** (Alpha-Thought).[*] From the perspective of the basic Standard Model of *this Beta-Existence*, other "**Games** Universes," "Penalty Universes"—and even the recently previous "Magic Universe"—would all fall under the *Sixth Sphere*.

> Implant patterns for the *Sixth Sphere* (pertaining to *Universes*) are, from lowest (most recent) to highest (earliest, happening further back): *To Own*, *To Gather*, *To Locate* and *To Discover*.

Naturally, we not only label our philosophical approach due to its intended audience, but—

> "Metahuman Utilitarianism" (in our Systemology) is perhaps the only formal model of moral philosophy published (on Earth, anyways) that calculates entire universes and other non-Human *Lifeforms* into its ethical equations.

We are, in all seriousness, equally factoring in POVs for species *apart* from those which are "Human"—or even those exclusively "terrestrial" to Earth. We must consider the unspoken truth that our Standard Model of Spheres is *relative* to any *individual*, the *planet* they occupy and corresponding *universe*. The common conceptual perspective of "Humans on Earth" (in *this* version of Beta-Existence) is

---

[*] See also "*Imaginomicon*" (*Liber-3D*).

simply the most accessible example.

Realizing and calculating any higher Spheres of Existence requires, at the very least, a basic state of *Beta-Defragmentation*. Individuals carrying extreme fragmentation about *who they are* (at "1.0") are seldom in the best position to demonstrate certainty about the *Spiritual World* ("7.0") or the truth of *Divinity* or *Infinity* ("8.0"). And yet, we discover the majority of low-Awareness individuals professing a lot of knowledge about "God." What's more, such erroneous paradigms are often used as basis and justification for erroneous ethics. So, we end up with half-wits conducting harm with hostile actions (which they don't understand) in the name of a higher authority (which they also don't understand), under the premise that it will all "just work itself out" in the afterlife.

> Implant patterns for the *Seventh Sphere* (pertaining to *spiritual lifeforms*) are, from lowest (most recent) to highest (earliest, happening further back): *To Embody, To Collect, To Influence* and *To Predict*.

An individual's perception of a "Spiritual Universe"—or *Seventh Sphere*—does play a role in the "Ladder of Awareness" they are using to climb up out from the mire of *Beta-Existence*; it directly represents the "Other" or "greater than" *this.* However, in previous traditions, the *Self* as (Alpha) Spirit is not really emphasized until *after* an individual has "died"—for only *then* are they considered a "Spirit" in some worldviews. But the fact remains that:

> an individual *is* a Spirit first and foremost. Spiritual Beingness is the natural state of Self. The very idea of having "TO SURVIVE" as any other **Identity** is clearly an implant.

Our present survey of the basic Standard Model naturally concludes with "Infinity" as the *Eighth Sphere*—which is how it is classified throughout Grade-III and Grade-IV (and even in prior Grade-II presentations of *Mardukite Zuism*). From a

Beta-Existence POV, "Infinity" and "Divinity" are essentially synonymous. Using a standard-issue Human Condition POV, the concept of "Infinity" is "conceived of" individually based on a Seeker's state of Awareness. For some in a low-Awareness high-fragmentation state, the concept of "Infinity" is simply whatever the individual considers the "utmost" "topmost" or "ideal" aspect of all existence, simply extended to all points and spaces and times (for their Reality).

Very often, the specific identification made with Infinity/Divinity contributes to fragmentation. For others, it involves symbols representing "goals" that an individual is implanted to "work toward achieving" during their lifetime/incarnation. After a *Seeker* (or Pilot-in-Training or Mardukite Minister or Grade-III+ Mardukite Master, &tc.) has worked through the *Pathway to Self-Honesty* as outlined in the basic "Beta-Defragmentation Systemology Operating Procedure"‡ (which requires all of *Grade-III* and *Grade-IV*), these other matters of the *Backtrack* are treated in the "Wizard Grades" (otherwise referred to as the *Gateways of Infinity*).

> Implants for the *Eighth Sphere* (pertaining to *Infinity-Divinity*) are, from lowest (most recent) to highest (earliest, happening further back): *To Worship, To Commune, To Convert* and *To Enlighten.*

The implant patterns for Religious Conviction and Divine Worship are among the oldest and most basic in any *Beta-Existence*, constituting the primary "Pass-Not" boundary between the basic Standard Model (*Beta*) Spheres of Existence and their Alpha-Octave or upper-level harmonic qualities as "Arcs of Infinity." This upper-**band** of All-Existence (*Creation, Creativity*) is what balances out the "*Infinity of*

---

‡   "Beta-Defragmentation S.O.P. v.1.1" (*Grade-IV, Wizard Level-0 Metahumanism*) from *30, April 2021* is given in "*Imaginomicon*" (*Liber-3D*) premiere edition; "v.1.2" revised on *22, June 2021* with minor formatting changes.

Nothingness" equation—and likewise encompasses, enshrouds and encircles *All* "Beta-Existences" as a higher echelon of dynamic systems. These "Arcs" are treated further in our forthcoming advanced (*A.T.*) Systemology "*Wizard Levels*" (Mardukite *Grade-V* through *Grade-VII*).

* * * * * * *

UTILITY AND HUMAN BEHAVIOR

Humans primarily behave as a result of:
(1) personal Awareness levels; combined with
(2) implanted goals; and
(3) imprinted experience.

Apart form this, we can consider that all creation—anything that exists for *Beta-Existence*—relatively may be categorized with one (or more) dynamic systems represented by our Standard Model of Spheres. By understanding these factors, a Systemologist is able to glean the "utility" of our methodology and its real-world applications; both for increasing one's progress along the Pathway and for predicting behavior of others. By considering the existential dependency of all *Life* amidst our Model of Spheres, the *moral philosophy* of "right" and "wrong" is clearly illustrated and establishes a structure for our *Ethics*.

Calculating someone's reach and even predicting their actions is simple when based on data of how they associate or align personal understanding and prioritization of the Spheres. Whether pictorially demonstrated with nice tidy concentric rings or not, each person carries their own individual Awareness of "values" concerning all existence. For example, some will devote most of their energy and **attention** to "Family" (*Second Sphere*), whereas another may follow a lifestyle (or give preference) to "Environment, Animal Life and Pets" (*Fifth Sphere*) as their primary motivation. There are no spheres directly "against" any others—but it will be demonstrable that an individual favors certain

Spheres of Existence while opposing emphasis on others. It is possible that a person can misalign or misappropriate "**terminals**" and significances associated with these dynamic systems—and such is also a indicator of fragmentation.

> Using *Utility*, an action is more ethical the more/higher Spheres of Existence it promotes (assists survival of) and the fewer (lower) systems it harms or hinders.

An individual's relative condition of success and survival is primarily dependent on the relationship held with each Sphere of Existence. A *Seeker* that is systematically defragmented on each of the Spheres of Existence—thereby maintaining clear communication **channels** with each—is going to get along better and reach farther in *Beta-Existence*. This "reach" is part of the "ticket" *out*. The way *out* is *through*; not withdrawal and individuation into lonely caves and mountainsides—not fortification of the *First Sphere*. "Seclusion" is not wisdom; it's just "hiding." It's no different than an alcoholic that "solves" the issue by avoiding environments containing alcohol. Well, they haven't actually *solved* the issue of alcoholism that way; there is no increase in developmental faculties—there is no increased ability to *Hold-Back* with Self-determinism as such.

> In *Grade-III* ("*Crystal Clear*"; **Liber-2B**) we applied the "*Beta Awareness Scale*" to the first four "spheres" and "zones" of the Standard Model (of Beta-Existence) to illustrate dynamic systems composing the Human Condition. This is also valid data for determining how actualized an individual's reach is (in the Physical Universe), their *Ethics* (conduct and behavior), their ability to clearly communicate (or relay communication) and chronic conditions or level of optimum survival (success) in daily life. These are all elements for consideration that compose the total system of our Systemology Ethics.

In most instances, increased Awareness means an increased ability to "foresee" future results and act toward them. This includes maintaining a wide-angle view of the entire Standard Model at all times. Individuals that can only "think" or "operate" regarding the first few spheres have a tendency to be shortsighted. This is worse when an individual is not even Actualized (defragmented) regarding the *First Sphere* as Self. Such individuals are "Potential Dangers" to optimum survival of both the Systemologist and the community at large. The only resolution we have discovered is our systematic processing; making it the most important activity you can *do* for someone.[†]

A standard-issue (fragmented) Human being does not know to "process out" their perceived "problems" and thereby applies shortsighted actions to resolve them. Such efforts are referred to as "***Harmful Acts***" in Systemology, or more accurately "**counter-survival**" actions.

> ***harmful-act*** : a counter-survival mode of behavior or action (esp. that causes harm to one or more *Spheres of Existence*)—or—an overtly aggressive (hostile and/or destructive) action against an individual or any other *Sphere of Existence*; in *Utilitarian Systemology* —a shortsighted (serves fewest *Spheres of Existence*) **intentional** overtly harmful action to resolve a perceived problem; a revision of the rule for standard *Utilitarianism* for Systemology to distinguish actions which provide the least benefit to the least number of *Spheres of Existence*, or else the greatest harm to the greatest number of *Spheres of Existence*; in *moral philosophy*—an action which can be experienced by few and/or which one would not be willing to experience for themselves (*theft, slander, rape, &tc*); an iniquity or iniquitous act.

Fragmentation and energetically **charged** masses (sometimes called "ridges") are connected to *Harmful and Hostile Acts*. This includes what we have done to others, others have done to us, and what we witness others having done to

---

† Get trained to do processing, or refer to a "Professional Pilot."

each other. These are all "systematic processing" points (and **Hot Buttons**). These are critical for achieving "Wizard Level-1" and working through *Mardukite Grade-V*, where *iniquities* must be "incinerated" in order to rise above. Therefore, the *Ethics* (or *Liber-Three/3E*) portion of the *Pathway* is not an afterthought, filler or some arbitrary supplement—it is a detrimental factor for Ascension through the upper "Wizard Grades."

> There is a considerable difference between:
>
> —the individual that struggles to adhere to a *moral code* or *law*, doing so only for fear of civic/social punishment or for religious purposes (a belief in metaphysical punishment, karma &tc.); and
>
> —an *Ethical* individual that performs "right actions" and the "highest good" for its own sake.

Therefore, we note differences between a *moral* standard, as socially defined (by a particular group or society) and the "metahuman" observation of actual *Ethics*, which treats absoluteness of "rightness" and "wrongness" as it pertains to the Standard Model of Spheres.

> The individual, as "I-AM"/*Self* or Alpha Spirit,
> beneath fragmentation, is basically "*good*."

This truth about the "Spirit" (of *Lifeforms*) is what allows Systemology techniques (systematic processing technology) to yield positive effects in *defragmenting* veils of erroneous consideration clouding or distorting clear vision of what is "right" and/or (for) the "highest good." All individuals act in Beta-Existence to "SURVIVE" and thus, in their own fragmented POV (which they refer to as their "own right" or "opinion"), believe themselves acting "justly" for what is "best." None truly believe that they are acting upon "evil" or "false" fixated purposes for the sake of "evil" alone; not even the "villains."

An individual's "*Spiritual Timeline*" is explored in greater detail as they progress through the Wizard Grades. At this juncture, we can determine that the *Alpha Spirit* begins its existence with a very high *Ethics*, superior to even what is demonstrable within the Standard Model of Beta-Existence. Proper *Ethics* is actually an upper-level dynamic system, equivalent to a *"Ninth Sphere"*—or more accurately, *First Arc of Infinity*, carrying a "harmonic" with Alpha-Existence relative to the *First Sphere* in Beta-Existence.

The Alpha-Spirit seeks to operate and act in the most optimum manner, which is most evident with their original "Home Universe." Eventually, cohabitation considerations within "Shared Universes" and "Games Universes" (which are, themselves, superimposed over one's own personal "Home Universe")[*] results in more and more behavior that is less and less optimum—and from which a being may lose its ability to *Hold-Back* the *Harmful Acts.*

> **hold-back** : withheld communications (esp. actions) such as *"Hold-Outs"*; an intentional (or automatic) withdrawal (as opposed to reach); Self-restraint (which may eventually be enforced or automated) to not practice *Harmful-Acts*; not reaching, acting or expressing, when one should be; an ability that is now restrained (on automatic) due to inability to withhold it on Self-determinism alone.

Loss of high-level *Ethics* forms a perceived need for *moral codes* and *penalties* as a guide. This also leads to *Hold-Outs.*

> **hold-outs** : withheld communications; energetic withdrawal and communication breaks with a *"terminal"* and its *Sphere of Existence* as a result of a *"Harmful-Act"*; unspoken or undiscovered (hidden, covert) actions that an individual withholds communications of, fearing punishment or endangerment of *Self-preservation* (*First Sphere*); the act of hiding (or keeping hidden) the truth of a *"Harmful-Act."*

---

[*]   Refer to *"Imaginomicon"* (*Liber-3D*).

We selected the term *"Hold-Outs"* for our Utilitarian Systemology semantics, based on its application in professional photography—where numerous snapshots/pictures are *withheld* from final selections openly communicated to present an event, *&tc.* Oftentimes, an individual carries around many *Hold-Outs*—hidden, but occupying their attention. They are fed energy as compulsive creations. The individual participates in Reality with a constant anxious worry (problem) that someone else will "find out." Therefore, they are forced to *Hold-Back* their reach and communications **(energetic-exchange)** *outside* of *Self-Honesty*. And, as it turns out:—

> these *Harmful-Act–Hold-Out* sequences are what keeps a Spiritual Being entrapped within a Prison Universe.

Therefore, the Wizard's *Way Out* of Beta-Existence requires *clearing* the *slate* of what is emotionally and energetically carried as "mass"/"matter" by the Spirit: to be certain that the "heart" is "light enough" to be weighed against a feather.[‡] Many religions have established their own methodologies for confessional procedures. Yet, none seem to be effective for *systematically rehabilitating* the Power and Beingness of the Spirit. Former attempts simply enforced "guilt" and other enforced programming, fixing attentions on a *moral code* rather than a higher *Ethic*.

Ethics is the lowest *Arc of Infinity* for Alpha-Existence. Imposition of a *moral code* (and *penalties* when an individual *fails*) resulted in construction of "Penalty Universes" or "Prison Universes." The *Beta-Existence* (Physical Universe) we consider present, is actually a "Penalty Universe" created by those (once) occupying a previous manifested universe, referred to (in our Systemology) as the "Magic Kingdom." Even the "Magic Universe"—similar to *this* one, except that the "electron is free" (and able to be utilized without "wires")—was itself first constructed as a "confined

---

‡   Alluding to "afterlife judgment" in ancient Egyptian mysticism. See also *"The Vampyre's Handbook"* by Joshua Free for additional details.

existence" *beneath* an even wider encompassing shared "Games Universe." Hence, *Ethics* is no small matter once we consider how large a part it plays in why an individual consistently finds themselves "located" in (and "fixed" to) a *Beta-Existence* "space-time" as they do.

The I-AM-*Self* once experienced an essentially unrestrained existence as a *Free Spirit*, due to the naturally high *Ethic* "in" place. During accumulation of experience across a *Spiritual Timeline*, this deteriorated into rigid *moral codes* that promote imposing (or enforcing) restraints (*Hold-Backs*) on Self and others. **Validation** of "guilt" leads to further "*Hold-Outs*" due to regret—*Hold-Backs* and *Hold-Outs* being "no-action" *imprints*, or else of "regret" when one did not *Hold-Back* an action and now *Holds-Out* admission and responsibility for it. Just as *facets* of other types of *Imprinting* and *Programming* can affect the freedom of an individual Alpha-Spirit, so too will these energetically charged masses tied to *Harmful-Act/Hold-Outs/Hold-Backs*. These specifically affect ability to reach optimum states of *Self-Honesty* with our "Wizard Level" work.

Once a *moral code* is in place (or *Ethics* are implanted), a series of "hidden" restraints are agreed to and become Reality—even when an individual operates in opposition to this programming. In fact, when a *Seeker* negates *morality*, they are at once in **conflict** with their own true values (and nature) as Alpha-Spirit. In addition to *Hold-Outs* and struggles over *Hold-Backs* (personal restraint), an individual will also employ a sequence-"**pattern**" or programmed-circuit of "justification" to explain motivation for their *Harmful-Acts*. In many instances, this **displaces** personal responsibility onto some "other" *terminal*—which further **inhibits** one's own *Self-Determined* restraint. This creates mechanisms that automatically *Hold-Back* ability.

The present author has spoken ambiguously at length (amidst several **gradients** and volumes of "Gatework")— concerning a perfected state of *Self-Honesty* sought as "Beta-

Defragmentation." The standard experiential boundary of *Beta-Existence* is fixed at "4.0" on the Standard Model; also relative to the "Beta-Awareness Scale."† But it is a true solid "4.0," elevated solely by an individual's freedom of *considerations* and handling of *Self-Determinism* that is apart from, or outside of (***exterior** to*), any POV held rigidly as the "Human Condition."

The ultimate state of *Self-Honest Beta-Defragmentation* requires going above and beyond the Human-Mind or "MCC" (4.0) on the Standard Model. Hence, *Grade-III* and *Grade-IV* include emphasizing actualization of "Will-**Intention**" (5.0), "Creative **Imagination**" (6.0), and "**Alpha Thought**"/"**Postulates**" (7.0), to the extent that a *Seeker* is able at a given level of **realization**. These additional factors are correct concerning handling of the Mind-Body connection. They are still drawn from our Standard Model—one developed using a POV (perspective) of Beta-Existence *looking outward* toward Infinity. However, once the **threshold**-cover was lifted on Wizard-Level "Alpha/Ascension-Tech" (*Actualization Techniques*/"*A.T.*"), it became quite clear that *Ethics* is the fundamental "keystone" for accessing (and surviving) the "Fifth Gate" and its *immolation of iniquity*.

A "charge" on *Harmful-Act/Hold-Outs* may be "confronted" and "flattened" by a *Seeker* using (*pre-A.T.*) Self-processing before they are certain to surface for *Piloted A.T. Processing*.

* * * * * * *

UNDERSTANDING THE SYSTEMOLOGY OF ETHICS

Many individuals are likely to consider "Ethics" and "moral philosophy" as serious intellectual studies that only apply to the most serious criminal cases or social offenses. An individual is not always *Aware* enough to *realize* the *actual* consequences of their actions. Much of the time, the accumulated actions that breakdown clarity of (or "frag-

---

† Introduced in *"Crystal Clear"* (*Liber-2B*).

ment") a communication line (whether for "SURVIVAL" or "CREATION") are not blatantly considered "*Harmful-Acts*" or outright overt attacks on a "terminal"—or against some "Sphere of Existence." In most cases, the responsibility and acceptance, coupled with realization and ability to confront, all increase as a *Seeker* peels away more layers of "*Hold-Outs.*" Our methodology of *Ethics* (toward "spiritual rehabilitation") is based on such observable progressive gains. For example:—

Let us consider a well-to-do productive office-worker; and one day they accidentally damage a piece of company equipment. At the time of this particular incident, no one else is around to know what happened. But the office-worker knows that what happened is "bad" and fears consequential repercussions, so they "*Hold-Out*" admittance of cause and responsibility—of any knowledge at all regarding the incident or the equipment. Because it is now a **Mental Image** of a "stopped-**flow**" (which the individual has to keep secret) an "energetic mass" forms and is suspended on the *Spiritual Timeline.*

In this situation, "*Ethics Fragmentation*" is compounded further by developing an automatic "*Hold-Back*" response-reaction mechanism. This is because, while a "*Hold-Out*" remains in suspension: free reach (expression, communication, &tc.) within the "organization"/"company" (*Third Sphere*) is now restricted; and the individual may later experience "*pings*" when encountering *facets* of the experience (such as in the location of the incident or in the presence of similar office equipment). This is just one illustrated example of how easy it is to fall away from "high-power" *Self-Honesty* when operating as standard-issue "Human"— even when one has no blatantly malicious or "hostile" intentions at the start.

The same systematic principles for *Imprinting Incidents* (described in *Grade-III*[*] apply to processing *Harmful-Acts*, *Hold-Outs* and *Hold-Backs*. In fact, "*R1R*" (**Route-1** *Revised*)[∞] is a preferred processing method for incidents on the *Backtrack*—particularly during *Pre-A.T.* work in Grades *IV* and *V*. But any systematic processing serves an individual better than allowing the standard-issue (pre-programmed) tendencies to take over. Humans often attempt "intellectual negation" or "Self-determined forgetfulness" of an *Imprinting Incident*. Rather than confront the *Mental Imagery* with full *Awareness* —and dissolve any charge on its *facets*—the reflex is to make nothing of it; to more easily stop its existence (communication) from reaching others. Of course, we know from Systemology that imprinting is made more solid if treating it— responsibility for its cause, its nature, its mass, &c.—as anything other than what it *Is*.

> Although "*Harmful-Acts*" have their own ethical considerations to analyze (in addition to treating the *Imprinting Incident*), it is the resulting "*Hold-Backs*" and "*Hold-Outs*" that accumulate and really reduce *Actualized Awareness*—prompting an individual to withdraw their reach from "higher" *Spheres*.

This very sequence of actions results in an individual breaking off more and more relationships and closing communication channels with increasingly greater *Spheres* of a "Beta-Existence." Experience of a fragmented *Life* continues. The being succumbs to the effect end of the scale via their un-**willingness** to *Be* or *Do* anything, then alone be in communication or social fellowship with anything. If uncorrected, this spiritual and physical atrophy often marks the (relatively) nearing collapse of any tolerable POV maintained by the Alpha-Spirit with an **extant** Universe. An individual does not suddenly "go out of communication" with an entire Universe all at once; nor is "intending to" a necessary condition for it to gradually happen. For example:—

---

*   "*Tablets of Destiny*" (*Liber-One*); "*Crystal Clear*" (*Liber-2B*).
∞   Formerly RR-SP-1; "*Tablets of Destiny*" now revised in 2022.

Let us consider a well-to-do productive postal-carrier delivering mail daily to residences; then one day they find themselves encountering a painful experience with a stray tomcat. Without warning, the cat leaps out from the bushes and begins savagely attacking the mail-carrier's face. A blur of feline tooth and nail flail about wildly frantic—as if the cat were deliberately designing an art-doodle in blood-drawing scar lines. The mail-carrier freezes in place stunned, hurt and embarrassed: a *Mental Image* of the cat preparing to pounce is suspended in time, emotionally encoded with *facets* of the environment, and of course, the searing pain.

From a *Grade-III* (*Master-Level*) perspective, record of the event seems typical of an *Imprinting Incident*—and, of course, there are several systematic "Routes" at one's disposal to remedy the light **degree** of *fragmentation* that ensued. But who is to say in this case (other than the postman) how "light" the experience may have actually been. Emotional and analytical "charge" on the incident itself may be rather "light"—but without *Self-Honest* exploration of the *Backtrack*, we cannot be completely certain of how this actually "stacks up" with an individual's existing *Implants*, *Programming* and *Encoding.*

A *Grade-IV/V* (*Pre-A.T. Wizard-Level*) Systemologist has a much wider view and understanding of *Life* and *Existence* than even a "Master." In this example, our mail-carrier is the recipient (or "effect") of a "*Harmful-Act.*" We know that the incident is stored with a *Mental Image* and associated with environmental *facets.* This is recorded (along with the registry of pain) as a survival-mechanism by the "Reactive Center" (*RCC*) so that it may issue "warnings" when restimulated in the future.

Embarrassed by "losing a fight" to a cat, our main character establishes a "*Hold-Out*"—or unwillingness to communicate the incident to others. The longer this is maintained in suspension, the more solid the "*Hold-Back*" becomes until the individual no longer feels comfortable extending their reach at work (*Third Sphere*) or in the presence of cats (*Fifth Sphere*). **Affinity** for (or "liking") cats and similar animals is likely to fall away, blocking and/or fragmenting communication channels with the *Fifth Sphere*. This is likely to continue so long as the individual remains fragmented with the subject/terminal "*Cats.*" Additionally, the "*Harmful-Act*" is registered as "motivation" to justify future considerations of action. When left unchecked from this point onward, the matter becomes a *slippery-slope*.

Ethical fragmentation occurs via *Imprinting* and *Facets*, meaning we are again in the domain of the "RCC"—or "Reactive Control Center" (a *Zu-line* relay point at "2.0" on the Standard Model). It wasn't until the Systemology Society had worked beyond this point once already in *Grade-III*, and into higher faculties through most of *Grade-IV*, when the "*RCC*" reared up on us again and threatened to undermine an individual's preexisting gains on the *Pathway*. In brief: *Ethics Processing* experiments began July 2020 synchronous with our *Grade-IV Professional Piloting Course* given for "*Liber-Two.*" [*Ethics Processing* is also a remedy for *Seekers* that made slower gains in Grade-IV and/or had difficulty previously achieving basic Beta-Defragmentation (after using the combined texts: **Liber-One**, *Liber-2B*, *Liber-Two* and *Liber-3D*).]

A considerable amount of attention is given in our Systemology toward resolution (or proper handling) of the "Reactive Control Center." Whether the mechanism first evolved genetically or spiritually, the RCC is a "mental construct" inherently attached to the "Mind-System" of all *Lifeforms* on planet Earth (at the very least). Its original purpose is to automatically (and non-analytically) "record wrongness," then display the data (when restimulated) to "increase survival by minimizing pain and exposure to dangerous facets." Of course, the RCC seems to produce the opposite experience at this present evolutionary stage of civilization and the Human Condition. Any supposed benefits once obtained from this "safety system" became obsolete a long time ago—and yet the (standard-issue) "mechanism" remains "operationally" in place.

> Although *Ethics* is an "analytical" endeavor, any
> *Imprint Charges*, *Hold-Outs* and/or *Hold-Backs*
> keep the RCC actively involved (if restimulated).

Both examples (*office-worker* and *postal-carrier*) involve a "*Hold-Out*" concerning a previous "*Harmful-Act*." This begins with a small amount of withheld communication, but then results in a growing series of personal "*Hold-Backs*" on *ability* and *reach*. The employee (in both examples) starts appropriating their "workplace" (*facets*) as a dangerous environment. This causes a decline in performance (productivity) and increased separation (or fragmentary individuation) from the organization (job), social groups—the *Third Sphere* in general.

Not only is personal energy (*Awareness* "units") spent compulsively keeping a "*Harmful*" or "*Hostile*" incident (*Mental Image*) suspended, but the individual also perpetually maintains (creates) a highly-charged "worry" (fragmented energetic "ridge") about "others *finding out*." This is referred to as "*Missed Hold-Outs*" in our Systemology Ethics.

missed hold-out : an individual's *Hold-Out* that someone else nearly found out about, or which leaves the individual wondering if they did actually find out or not; undisclosed event when someone else's behavior (or speech) restimulates emotional-response-reactions ("worry" &tc.) about potential discovery of withheld data, a *Harmful-Act* or *Hold-Out*; also less often referring to, in *systematic processing*, a Seeker's "held-out" (hidden) data that they expect (or "worry" &tc.) to be discovered during a *session*, but which is *missed* by the Pilot.

Where a "*Hold-Out*" involves the Seeker's own undisclosed actions (which should still be addressed in *Ethics Processing*), a "*Missed Hold-Out*" involves someone else's actions. It is possible that the "*Hold-Out*" was not even treated as such by the Seeker—may not even be thought about ever—until the energetic charge on the incident is nearly found out and then missed. This directly restimulates any charge on the energetic-mass. Since the Seeker is erroneously left with an *uncertainty* to "wonder" about (thereby reducing Awareness and presence), the whole sequence-chain is a source of present-time fragmentation.

For this specific application, the nature (or contents) of the "*Hold-Out*" itself is quite secondary in significance (by comparison) to the primary fact that: "*something* was almost found out"—contributing to the fragmented state of a *Seeker's* present condition. Unlike systematic methods for processing-out *Imprinting Incidents*, the exact moment of uncertainty (or Mystery) should be "spotted" on the *Backtrack* (and realized/discharged "*As-It-Is*"). Otherwise, a *Seeker* risks accumulating additional "*Hold-Backs*" due to a perceived confusion and/or **degree** of (un)willingness to act or reach.

Mardukite Systemology, insofar as it relates to the "Power of Choice," frequently references the logic of **Games Theory**, supplementary to standard/academic "*systematology*," which is crossed with knowledge from the *Arcane Tablets* and 20th Century American New Thought. The "*Harmful-Act–Hold-Out*" sequence is comparable to the "Offensive/Defensive" *dichotomy* of "play" in standard *Games*. An individual can certainly be bogged down with "things" in *Beta-Existence*. There is a general sense (implanted) that a "**player**" is meant to gather and accumulate energy-masses, while simultaneously minimizing losses. This is why a Seeker practices physical (objective) processes of "reaching" and "letting go" on Self-determinism. Otherwise, the challenge is how to override tendencies that "hold a person back" from adequately "releasing" their grip on "things."

> An individual needs only to "*consider*" a *reality* that
> they are "weighed down" or "stuck" in order to feel
> "entrapped" and *actually* restrict their own actions.

The Mind-System buffers direct experience (projection and reception) of energy between the Alpha-Spirit and its perceived Universe. Where it concerns *Beta-Existence*, direct **manifestation** of *Alpha-Thought* (*Will-Intention*, *&tc.*) is reduced to physical *Effort*. Therefore, the original intention of a Mind-System is estimation of *Effort* (to be applied toward a particular result). Fragmentation affects this estimation, and considerable emotional **turbulence** is connected with the "misses" and "close calls" of life experience. An "accident" might be an *imprinting incident*, but this goes on to include further situations with potentially deeper emotional encoding. It doesn't only concern times when we were impacted from a car, but the nearness of an accident—a missed accident—that seems to incite the greatest reactive-response. Or, for example: a *test* that is only missed by a "point" or two. So, in this application of *Ethics Processing*, we are also interested in what others have "nearly found out."

All "circuits" are applied to *Ethics Processing*. Failure to do so proved to be a shortcoming in the original version of Route-1.[*] "Processing-out" each circuit or POV on an incident (or event type), even if one or more has to be *imagined*, provides opportunities for optimum energetic release on that channel. This means for any *Harmful-Act* you have committed and then *Held-Back* ("**circuit-1**"), you would also *run* the concept of having someone else commit it against you ("**circuit-2**"), and of course, another/others to another/others ("**circuit-3**"). This will remove enough residual energy from a channel to prevent incidents from restimulating "*automated motivation*" or considerations for future actions and responses.

---

[*] "RR-SP" given in the First Edition of "*Tablets of Destiny.*"

hostile-motivation : an *imprint* of a counter-survival action (*"Harmful-Act"* or *"Hostile-Act"*) committed by another against Self, stored as data to justify future actions (retaliation, *&tc.*); any *Sphere of Existence* (though usually an individual) receiving the effect of a *"Harmful-Act"*; an *imprint* used to rationalize "motivation" or "justification" for committing a *"Harmful-Act"*; in systematic *games theory*—the *modus operandi* concerning "payback," "revenge" and "tit-for-tat."

The "Mind-System" records and stores all parts (*facets* and *POVs*) of similar incidents on an associated-knowledge chain. As a result, there are some instances when fragmentation remaining from incidents of "being the effect" (something happening *to you*) will not "process out" (or reduce in charge) until similar incidents of "being the cause" (doing something *to others*) are fully confronted. If not resolved systematically, these "action-motivation sequence-chains" can actually remain suspended (actively awaiting restimulation) across many lifetimes/incarnations.

Along the course of an Alpha-Spirit's long existence on a *Spiritual Timeline*, many patterns of harmful behavior are recorded and stored. Therefore, it is also necessary to **flatten** "Circuit-3" turbulence in *Ethics Processing*, which is frequently overlooked. Witnessing the actions of other "beings" (even when imaginary or fictional) has a tendency to restimulate energetic charge and/or solidify fragmentation of the first two *circuits*.

Metahuman Wizards maintain a higher actualized Power
and higher degrees of Awareness
through Acceptance and upper echelon Responsibility,
demonstrated by a superior Ethic
rooted in Spiritual Utility, Self-Honesty and Forgiveness.

[**"Route-0"**/**"Circuit-0"** emphasizes *Responsibility* (*"Power"*) and *Self-at-Cause.* This is applied during an additional advanced *pass* through all basic processing from *Grade-III* and *Grade-IV* as a "check-out" for completing *Beta-Defragmentation Standard Procedure (Version-1)*‡ and prerequisite for employing *Wizard Level-1 (Grade-V)* as "A.T." (*Actualization Technology*). If there is no energetic-charge on a particular "line" or area, then there is no need to process it again. Listing and checking for charge does not restimulate *Imprints, Incidents* or *Implants*; but, "over-processing"—for example, something that has already been *reduced,* **flattened** or *resolved*—can cause a Seeker to **inadvertently** apply Alpha Thought (postulate) "compulsively create" the same energy-mass again.]

* * * * * * *

BASIC ETHICS PROCESSING: "SPHERES-ASSESSMENT" (PRE-A.T./GRADE-IV, WIZARD LEVEL-0, ROUTE-3E)†

This present volume (*Liber-Three/"Ethics"*) extends a continuation of processing given in "*Metahuman Destinations*" (*Liber-Two*). That volume concludes (in Unit-3) with systematic processing of "**HELP**" on "circuits" to channel-*terminals.* An individual's concept or definition of "*Help*" shifts with *Awareness* levels and degrees of *Self-Honesty.* So, for present purposes: "HELP" is defined as assisting (continuation) of optimum survival. ["Help" and "Failed Help" are processing "*hot-buttons.*" Personal realizations that "Help is Needed" and "Help is Possible" are fundamental conditions for effective application of Systemology techniques.]

The "Spheres-Assessment" may be Self-processed∞ using the PCL:—"...ASSIST SURVIVAL OF..." (rather than "*Help*"). **Assessments** may be expanded with prepared standard lists of ter-

---

‡   Instructions appear in "*Imaginomicon*" (*Liber-3D*).
†   For additional systematic processing instructions, a *Seeker* should
    refer to both "*Crystal Clear*" (*Liber-2B*) and "*Metahuman
    Destinations*" (*Liber-Two*).
∞   As a *Piloted Procedure*, professional assessments are a prerequisite
    for admittance to *Wizard Grades* when following the official structure
    of our Systemology organization (or Mardukite Academy).

minals. It is sometimes much more effective—assuming a *Seeker* has heightened Awareness at this gradient of the *Pathway*—to apply basics at the extent of understanding that an individual actually realizes with each "pass" through the material. We do not expect a *Seeker* to become a winged saintly angel overnight—or perhaps ever. We recognize that personal reach—and ability to confront—is increased gradually with continued study, meditation (***thought experiments***) and systematic processing in a specific "area" of focus.

A complete assessment treats all *Eight Spheres of Existence.* It may require a *Seeker* multiple session periods (or sittings) to work through all eight sufficiently. Although this is classified as an assessment, it is systematically processed, which means new realizations and actual defragmentation can occur. The simplest application is a **Route-2** PCL format using the most basic "terminal" for each Sphere. In fact, many processes (from previous publications) concerning "terminals" may substitute treating entire *Spheres of Existence*—assuming the *Seeker* appropriates correct understanding of what each Sphere represents.

When first starting out, a *Seeker* scans through each ascending *Sphere of Existence*—starting with "1. SELF"—spotting and listing whatever "terminals" ("things" or "masses") **resurface**, or are recalled, which appropriately represent that particular *Sphere.* For this example, we would at the very least assume an individual would correspond the "body" or "*genetic vehicle*" as a *terminal* for *Self* (*First Sphere*) in *Beta-Existence.* [An individual may prepare worksheets or record data in a "processing journal." In any case, the PCLs (used) and responses should be written down.]

> *Self-processing* a standard "Spheres-Assessment" requires alternating PCLs (until a new realization or absence of further answers is achieved). Apply "Route-0" or "**Route-3**, Circuit-0" *Pre-A.T.* commands to *Self* as "YOU" for *Solo-Piloting*—such as (for the *First Sphere*):

> A.)
> How could (your physical body) assist your survival?
> B.)
> How could you assist survival of (your physical body)?

This continues through each successive Sphere:[*] "2. HOME-LIFE" (Family, Children, Partner, Sex...); "3. SOCIAL GROUPS" (Organizations, Job/Workplace, Religious Groups, Church of Mardukite Zuism, Clubs, Systemology Society...); "4. HUMAN SPECIES" (Nations/Society, Civilization, Mankind/Human Condition...); "5. ORGANIC LIFE" (Lifeforms, Plants, Trees, Animals, Planet Earth...); "6. PHYSICAL UNIVERSE" (Beta-Existence, Matter, Galaxies, Extraterrestrial...); "7. SPRITUAL UNIVERSE" (Alpha-Existence, Alpha-Spirits, Creative Beingness, Decayed Entities...); and "8. INFINITY" (Infinite Creation, Supreme Beingness, Divinity/God).

> When *Professionally Piloted*, the correct PCL for a basic assessment is: "What are some things that would represent (*sphere* or *terminal*)?" or "Tell me some things that could represent (X)." [Be consistent with PCL wording once a set patter is found most effective or deemed best understood.]

When a *Seeker* is familiar enough to refer to (and understand) the *Spheres* by number, then do so. Otherwise, this data (above) may be used to prepare a "word-association" list suitable for newcomers. As usual, a *Pilot* is especially interested in any particular *Spheres* or *terminals* that incite "reaction-responses."[‡] If a *Seeker* misappropriates associations ("items") to Spheres/terminals (that do not analytically/rationally make sense), this is also noted. "Items" that *stand out* as "fragmentary" are given additional processing attention, once the assessment part is completed.

---

[*] A script for all eight will not be given here, but may be included in "procedure manuals" released/published in the near future.

[‡] Skilled use of "*GSR*"/"*Biofeedback Technology*" is particularly useful here—and becomes necessarily essential for processing upper-level *Wizard-Grades*.

Ethics Processing is introduced in systematic sessions with basic PCLs given above. At *Wizard Level-0*, the *Seeker* can begin to recognize and personally "process out" or "discharge" energetic stores (*Hold-Outs/Hold-Backs*) connected to fragmented *Spheres* or terminals (which typically also have *Harmful-Acts* and *Hostile-Motivators* associated). Even at *Grade-IV—Wizard Level-0*—the key to opening a channel is still "Willingness to Confront" (or "face up to"); and to "increase horsepower" on the upward journey, the emphasis is still on "*Responsibility* as *Self-at-Cause.*"

Standard "**Route-3E**" Procedure is introduced by running a basic "confront" PCL on all three "*circuits*" of a channel using Route-3 methodology. [During an additional Route-0 (*A.T.*) pass though all basic procedures for a *Beta-Defragmentation Check-Out*, Circuit-0 is also included: "What part of yourself..." *&tc.*]

A.)
What part of (*X.*) could you confront?

B.)
What part of (*X.*) would you prefer to not-confront?

Systematic processing is applied to any noted "items" with:

A.) What have you done to (*X.*)?

B.) What have you held-back from (*X.*)?

The other *circuits*—"What has (*X.*) done..." (*&tc.*)—also apply. This PCL wording is overtly direct. It is most effective for advanced *Grade-IV/V* applications (when a Seeker already maintains higher-than-average *Awareness*). However, if applied *earlier* on the *Pathway*, a "stepped-gradient" approach is necessary to reach a better (more certain) reality on the process, all "*circuits*" may be run through using a more accessible (alternative) PCL, such as "Think of something you have..." or even "Recall something..."

* * * * * * *

ETHICS PROCESSING: "SELF-HONESTY: SOLO PURGE"
(GRADE-IV ETHICS, PRE-A.T. SOLO, 3E)[†]

Unknowingly or naively "following" the "**command**" or programmed *Implant* patterns has a tendency to cumulatively lower one's *Awareness* (and state of *Beingness*) further away from *Self-Honesty* like a dwindling spiral. Not only will increased *Harmful-Acts* and *Hold-Outs* fragment continuous communication shared among participants in a Reality/Universe, but heavily charged weights and energetic-masses accumulate and keep an individual's spiritual aspirations ("Ascension" *&tc.*) out of reach.

As with other types of fragmentation, the co-creation and fragmented participation with dynamic systems of *Life, Universes* and *Everything* binds an individual to their own rules and contracts—subsequently and unknowingly making them the *Effect* of their own *Cause.* The most recent (lower) Universes are increasingly solid-state as "thicker" agreements add to previous structures. In this present *Beta-Existence*, agreements of "restriction" were made to balance the equation of any "force" applied to act (action) in the Physical Universe. Here we see an inevitable condition of *Hold-Backs* placing limits on ability.

The more an individual demonstrates inability to *Hold-Back* on their own judgment and Self-determinism, the greater the restrictions (enforcement and denial) are imposed by the agreed-upon systems. For example, "**Cosmic Law**" or "Causal Law" governs a system that is commonly understood as "*karma.*" However, the idea of *karma* as a individualized punishment via Divine intervention is not altogether true.

By an **insistence** and agreement that "all actions must be balanced," the individuals themselves—those

---

[†]   For additional systematic processing instructions, a *Seeker* should refer to both "*Crystal Clear*" (*Liber-2B*) and "*Metahuman Destinations*" (*Liber-Two*).

occupying Beingness/POV within these systems and Universes—impose their own criteria for "backlashes" and "kickbacks" when acting in a common environment. In short: an individual "does it" to themselves based on:

(A) what they have done; and

(B) what they will not confront.

These Universes are shared by other participants, each *implanted* to uphold a similar enough "reality agreement" to combine and make the apparent structure experienced as *Beta-Existence* even more solid for all concerned. Logic behind the *"hostile-motivation"* factor is rooted in "balance"—although it never actually leads closer to a balanced equilibrium. An individual is harmed; data is recorded; then data is used as motivation to "do unto others." Of course, one can also find themselves at cause for many "unmotivated" *Harmful Acts*, each carrying their own charge—an equation that must be balanced. After which:—

energetic charge from a *Hold-Out/Hold-Back* accumulates enough mass to "pull in" necessary conditions for a *"hostile-motivator"* to manifest in the individual's future. A *Hold-Back* is essentially a "pull back" from a terminal, strong enough to "pull in" undesired phenomenon as a *motivation* for previous *Harmful-Acts.*

To be completely and systematically clear on this point:

Hold-Outs are a "social" variety of *Hold-Backs.*
Thus, all *Hold-Outs* are *Hold-Backs*;
but not all *Hold-Backs* are (known) *Hold-Outs.*

It is possible an individual may not even be *Aware* (as in "consciously""knowingly") of the many *Hold-Backs* subtly restricting and defining **parameters** of their own tendencies and personal inclinations. A *Beta-Defragmented* state of total *Self-Honesty* lifts the "bars" or shackles, allowing further *reach* on the *Pathway*—upward to *Gateways of Infinity*. In combination with *Grade-III* and *Grade-IV*, our present systematic *Pre-A.T.* resolution of "Systemology Ethics" (or "Metahuman Utilitarianism") is the "hidden key" to reaching a stable basic state as **Homo Novus**—the "New Human." This is the ideal direction and destination for humanity's present (and future) "spiritual evolution" (or *revolution*, if you prefer).

On our *Route to Ascension*, this refined culminated library of published "*Mardukite Systemology*" material (spanning several volumes since the "*Original Thesis*" by Joshua Free, published in 2011) now represents the first necessary (prime) milestone achievement—of which there is no substitute for; not even at "higher levels." Such "upper" *Wizard Grades* are dependent on a Seeker having already reached a basic state of *Self-Honesty* (*Homo Novus*) to be most effective.

> The purpose of our Systematic Ethics Processing is to rehabilitate an individual's willingness to be at Cause.

As an introductory application, the first basic step of a "Self-Honesty Solo-Purge" is for a *Seeker* is to actually *spot* the things they've done on the *Backtrack* (in the past). Prior to any additional treatment or consideration of these things, an individual must first take responsibility for action —being at Cause for the doing of things. A retraction from this point results in *Hold-Backs*. As an additional step, we would want to *spot* points of *Hold-Back*—actual instances of inhibited (*Held-Back*) action. The more "charge" can be taken off the *Backtrack* with preliminary "Solo" work, the easier and more effective a *Piloted Check-Out* for the "Wizard Grades" will be.

Ability to spot and confront these actions increases on a gradient scale; as more is lifted, more becomes available within reach. It is suggested to begin with an area of life (partner, family, work, *&tc.*) that they are commonly having difficulty with—and which is most accessible for recall, *&tc.*

[One would also note which *Sphere of Existence* it pertains to.] A *Seeker* is then prompted to *write down exactly what action(s) they did.* Such confessional-style "therapies" are common to many traditions and religions, but we are concerned with a specific systematic approach here. For example, we are not interested in attaching any reflections, rationalizations, thoughts of shame or regret and so forth. At this stage, we want to emphasize *actual physical actions done by Self*, regardless of any considerations, justifications or additions.

> An individual raises *Awareness* to free themselves from a "*Harmful-Act—Hostile-Motivation*" sequence cycle by taking responsibility/confronting what Self has done without feeling regret, guilt, shame or a need to blame.

This first part (of listing) treats the nature of the actions systematically. Then afterward, if necessary, the process may be cleaned up (specific charges "flattened") further by a second part: writing confessions; letters of "admittance" (admitting *doing* actions). These are directed to persons and groups that the *Seeker* maintains "*Hold-Outs*" (and "*Hold-Backs*") from—often times even related to *actions* formerly listed. The letter should include *all details on display with nothing hidden or withheld.* This is continued until there is a noticeable sense of "release." These letters are generally *burned* afterward; not retained or sent anywhere; although they may increase ability or prompt interests in opening a closed-off channel of communication. As a personal choice, this does not actually have to happen afterward—but a *Seeker* should not continue to experience any automatic "flinch" or "withdrawal" from (communicating/connectivity with) that terminal (and its Sphere).

The standard (*Piloted*) layout of Systematic Ethics Processing (Route-3E) of a specific "*Harmful-Act—Hold-Out*" sequence may be applied to the form or method of Solo/written processing. Some *Pilots* have practiced this in training sessions by recording the *four points of data* on note (index) cards. It is more common to use a "steno-book" or appropriate journal/log to record full *systematic processing sessions.* However, the *Wizard Level-0* application of Route-3E often involves what many individuals consider "sensitive information." To be fully effective, a *Seeker* must both understand the value (personal gain/benefits) of *Ethics Processing* and feel safe exploring it without fear of punishment (guilt, evaluation or judgment of any kind) from others. The more critical or sensitive "3E" (*Ethics*) records are generally only kept long enough to qualify a *Seeker's* transition to *Wizard Level-1* proper.

Much like *systematically processing* an *Imprinting Incident,* the act/action must be specifically located in the "Space-Time" of the *BackTrack* and confronted "*As-It-Is.*" At a *Pilot's* discretion, the *Seeker* may be prompted to follow up basic data listing with a more formal and complete "confessional letter" written and read out loud in session (to resolve heavily charged fragmentation) and then is destroyed. The *four pieces of data* collected for each action are:—

HEADING : Short description of *"What"* as a title.

A.) WHEN (TIME) : The *"Exact Time"* the event occurred; time, date and duration (how long was spent carrying the action out). This distinguishes/separates entanglement of a specific time from the reality experience of all other times (including how the "present time" is treated).

B.) WHERE (SPACE) : The *"Exact Place"* where the event occurred; including not only location, but also unique facets of the environment. This distinguishes/separates entanglement of a specific location (and environmental condition) from the reality experience of all other locations (including how an individual's "immediate surroundings" are treated.

C.) CONSIDERATION : The *"Exact Considerations"* in which the event occurred; including what kind of law, code, rule or social convention was violated, and whether it was an error/mishap or civic crime. Essentially, answer the question of "What were you *thinking* 'at the time' (or 'immediately prior')?" Another standard PCL is "What problem 'was it' (or 'might it be') a solution to?"

D.) WHAT IS (DETAILS) : The *"Exact Event"* actions that occurred; an account or script of activity detailing exactly what the individual has physically done, step-by-step, as if viewed by a third-party observer. Only actions the individual has done and not what others have done or anything that would fall under *'Considerations'* (above). This also distinguishes/separates entanglement of the physical event actions recalled from personal considerations.

If a *Seeker* is unable to achieve any sense of "release" using *systematic 3E-processing*—or significant turbulent fragmentation is still restricting free-**flow** on a channel—there is likely to be a *"Missed Hold-Out"* connected to that area, or else all critical information has not yet been recalled and addressed (confronted *"As-It-Is"*). As an additional safeguard, it is standard practice for *Pilots* to end any 3E-session by applying PCLs that remedy these conditions.

* * * * * * *

ETHICS PROCESSING: "SELF-HONESTY: FORGIVENESS"[*]
(PRE-A.T. WIZARD LEVEL-0, ROUTE-0, SOLO 3E)[†]

"Forgiveness" is a much misunderstood subject, influenced by religious connotation and other social applications among standard-issue Humans. When treated conventionally, the concept accepts and validates the *Harmful-Acts* of another. At a low-level of application it says, "I see you've cause me harm and it's okay." But, of course, *the hell it is*

---

[*] Based on the *"Freedom From"* lecture series for *Liber-3E*.
[†] For additional systematic processing instructions, a *Seeker* should refer to both *"Crystal Clear"* (*Liber-2B*) and *"Metahuman Destinations"* (*Liber-Two*).

okay. So, here we find a kink in trying to be "right" while occupying the Human Condition. Someone with low-Awareness bumps into you and presses "play" on an automatic circuit to apologize and you're supposed to say "it's fine." Society has actually run this circuit into the ground where we all have come to accept that "it's fine" actually means "it isn't fine," you know?

In our *Systemology Ethics*, "Forgiveness" is treated at a higher order of meaning, next to "Understanding." It suggests a *Seeker* "Understands" something "*As-it-Is.*" In systematic processing, "Forgiveness" is a *concept*, not a *terminal*, because it is not a "mass" (object) or "energetic-mass." It is, however, descriptive of the quality of a channel (to a terminal) or personal significance given to an "energetic-mass" by consideration. Therefore, when applied in processing:—

The *concept* of "Forgiveness" *may be run on* a terminal.

So, in the end, what we are really dealing with is another semantic for "release" of "emotional encoding" and "freedom from" fragmentation. It is, essentially, letting go of the hold on, or a rigid fixed attachment to, the space-time-event that has already passed and survived. Meanwhile, the unprocessed fragmented state tends to stick one's POV in treating experience of a present time environment as if the previous conditions are still present in it.

"*Failed Help*" and "*Betrayal*" are the two aspects contributing greatest to the collapse of communication channels with any relevant terminal—and further to entire *Spheres of Existence.* They are detrimental to Ascension. They individuate a person away from higher Spheres and put them in a position to think and act as if they are the only one in Existence—hence the *First Sphere* of *Self.*

Technically, the person will still feel as though they are operating toward the "greatest good" (for "SURVIVAL") even if the extent of that realization is reaction-responses born from hatred or revenge. Such a mode of operating will generally "stick" the person right in the middle of the fragmentation they would rather avoid. But, they base willingness to act solely on an accumulation of *Hostile-Motivators.*

Grade-IV methodology is used for training not only *Professional Pilots* of the Systemology Society, but also the *Mardukite Ministers* of the Church of Mardukite Zuism. In addition to materials already released, *Liber-3E* is an integral part of "pastoral" or "spiritual" advisement available to *Seekers*—either to get along with a happier life, or to continue further and achieve *Self-Honesty* as a "Meta-Human Condition" and access *Gates of Infinity.* Our applied methodology is an advancement and improvement on how the concept is used by religions in the past. So, whether applying solo-exercises or receiving formal *Piloting*, an individual should get a sense of "relief" by confronting their actions—and should understand that they are *forgiven.* If this acknowledgment is not positively received, or a *Seeker* is still feeling heavy emotion, it is likely that only part of a *Hold-Out* or *Harmful-Act* has been confronted or processed. Acceptance of "Forgiveness" is then an excellent monitoring tool regarding the completeness of Route-3E applications.

> In order to pursue upper-level Wizard-Grades with full effectiveness, a *Seeker* simply cannot have attentions still rigidly fixated on *guilt, Hold-Outs* or low-level *justification cycles* of any kind. Thus, we are impressing achievement of *Self-Honesty* in *Liber-3E* more strongly than ever before.

The most Basic "Route-0" *forgiveness* PCL (*Routine-3E* circuitry) include:

> A.) IMAGINE you are treating others with *forgiveness.*
> B.) IMAGINE others are treating you with *forgiveness.*
> C.) IMAGINE others treating others with *forgiveness.*

An advanced (*A.T.*) "Circuit-0" application would include the concept of *Self-Forgiveness*, or else "treating *Self* with *forgiveness*." Ultimately this is really what it all leads up to: each individual having to fully let themselves *off the hook* from stored/charged energies of what has happened in the past.

When we consider how long the Alpha Spirit has existed—how many Universes it has occupied, how many roles it has identified with—it is not surprising that each of us has *done* virtually all you can possibly think of *doing*—both good or bad. It is also not very surprising that many of us would rather choose to forget a lot of the misdeeds. Apparently, there even are *Hold-Outs* we *Hold-Back* from ourselves. But, of course, these accumulate—building up energetic-mass over time—and often conceal or close off channels with various Spheres of Existence and even entire Universes. Somehow or another, this is the case for each and every one of us involved with this whole mess of operating (or entrapment to) the Human Condition in the Physical Universe.

> An individual decides "I don't want to know"
> and winds up on the effect end of a Mystery.

Unlike *Analytical Recall* (*Route-2*), application of *Imagination* and **Creativeness Processing** (*Route-0*) to *Ethics Processing* allows a *Seeker* the freedom to consider a wider range of possibilities that are not restricted to *known* (consciously recalled) events from this lifetime. Often times there are some nearly-automatic practically-reactive "ideas" that one has regarding personal events on the *BackTrack*. Without need of validation or concern about whether one's speculations are accurate, *Route-0* may be used to treat real matters that remain just below the surface of *Awareness*. If the imagined event is fictitious, *Creativeness Processing* will only add greater fluidity to considerations a *Seeker* maintains on the line. However, if the imagined event does, in fact, include facets of an actual event (even if "out of sight") than the processing can actually assist in resurfacing more of what is hidden—or at the very least, provide a very real sense of relief and release. So, either way, there are gains; but this process can also be applied to known events.

FORGIVENESS (PRE-A.T. ROUTE-0 ETHICS/0E, BASIC 3E)[‡]

Circuit-1 — What *Harmful-Act* "might" you have done?
\ IMAGINE[*] yourself being *forgiven* for it.

Circuit-2 — What *Harmful-Act* "might" others have done to you?
\ IMAGINE them being *forgiven* for it.

Circuit-3 — What *Harmful-Act* "might" another have done to others?
\ IMAGINE them being *forgiven* for it.

Circ-0/A.T. — What *Harmful-Act* "might" you have done to yourself?
\ IMAGINE you *forgiving* your Self for it.

[‡] Refer to a later section ("*Metahuman Ethics: Entering the Wizard's Way*") for additional processing enhancements.

[*] *Conceptual-Certainty* (*Route-0E*) may be substituted for *Route-0*, if a *Seeker* has not yet worked on *Creative Ability.*

:: UTILITARIAN SYSTEMOLOGY FOR PILOTS ::
— Professional Processing to Bridge Grades IV. & V. —

Historically, social and civic use of Ethics for justice, religion, medicine and penal systems, all impresses the Human Condition with concepts regarding "apparent dangers" of *Truth* and *Honesty*. In fact, we find no shortage of examples describing coerced confessions, enforced communication (under duress) and interrogative interviews for thousands of years—and that's just including our "most recent" version of *Earth Civilization*. Essentially, all relevant *Mental Images* and considerations are "imprints" encoded to "fear"— *facets* of punishment and pain, guilt and shame, potential loss of property, personal freedom or even one's own *Life*.

There is also a more deeply implanted *Fear of Discovery* or *Fear of Being Discovered* present among all Life-on-Earth— and once we find out why, we release ourselves from it.

Using our established semantics and systematic logic to understand: this low-Awareness "fear" point of Beingness is synchronous with the "Reactive Control Center" (of the Mind-System) and what some would call the "Fight-or-Flight" survival-response-mechanism of the standard-issue Human Condition. Therefore, the *BackTrack* is likely to have entire chains of encoding from assuming various Identity "*Phases*" as both "interrogator" and "interrogated"—"executioner" and "executed" *&tc*. Naturally then, the concept of *Truth* is easily fragmented by association as-equal-to "pain" and "**unconsciousness**" or even "death."

Piloting systematic processing for "Route-3E" requires a higher level of skill and training than former Routes. To be certain there are no "hidden communication channels" in the Systemology Society, details from our *Professional Piloting Course* for *Ethics Processing* are given here alongside other chapter-lessons better directed to all *Seekers.* There is every reason to believe an individual that worked through all four former "Routes" (and primary texts) can understand and benefit from *Pilot* information—or even enhance *Self-Processing* efforts. The official "*Pre-A.T.*" Wizard-Levels (particularly *Grade-V*) are *Piloted*; after which, much of the upper-band of higher-grade prep-work for *A.T.* ("*Actualization Tech*" or "*Ascension Tech*") may be resumed *Solo.*

> The primary methodology of *Ethics Processing* (*Route-3E*)
> is to *Confront* something *As-it-Is.*
> The "RCC" (if active) prevents someone from "*confronting*"
> by doing all looking, **computing** and evaluation for them.

When processing *Seekers*, a *Class-3E Pilot* must operate at high-Awareness with ability to *confront*—face-to-face handling and proper management—of "discreditable" and "hostile" *Hold-Outs* by certain individuals using the "*phase*" of a malevolent personality-package. An Alpha-Spirit does not directly set out to occupy a POV from an "evil" *phase-personality.*

A being will often times start out on this part of the pattern as a high-Ethics enforcer of some kind, essentially minimizing the "Evil"; and so, it gets to where you start having to classify what is evil and hating it and it's that thing *over there*, so to speak. Naturally, we participate in creating solidity of this part of our Reality. The Enforcer is trying to do everything right—everything by the book—and suddenly there are enough *Harmful-Acts*, *Hold-Outs* and *Hostile-Motivators* on their path, that they suddenly "drop down" a notch on the scale, or in *Awareness*, so to speak. So now, they are an Avenger, using force to balance the "evil acts" they are faced with; and all the while they have been creating this "Mental Image" of the "evildoer" and making ir more solid and more solid until ultimately in the end, the Avenger crosses over and into the "phase" of his nemesis, the **Malefactor**. Therefore:—

we do not need to judge and chastise our fellow Seeker;
we defragment the view of the path which led them there.

* * * * * * *

BASIC APPLICATION OF ROUTE-3E ETHICS PROCESSING

Many systematic *Grade-IV* PCLs introduced for "Route-3"
and "Route-3C" within SOP-2C[‡] also apply to "Route-3E" for
Ethics Processing. [If the language used in the former sentence is confusing in any way, especially to a newcomer to
this paradigm, be certain to spend additional time review-
ing the vocabulary given in the glossary and/or supplemental materials preceding this publication.] If a Seeker has
already received and successfully flattened a complete run
through that processing, it may be left alone until the *"Pre-
A.T. Personal Integrity Check-Out"* required for Grade-V.[*]

However, during *Piloted systematic processing,* if a *Seeker* is
painfully struggling to achieve *Grade-IV* realizations, has not
effectively achieved any, or is not progressing forward on
the *Pathway,* it is only due to one or more of the following,
with a slight push to considering the latter:—

— the *Seeker* is feeling hungry, thirsty, tired or restimulated by the environment;[†]

— the *Seeker* is maintaining a misunderstood word/
concept;

— the *Seeker* is not applying presence to the session,

[‡]   Refer to *"Metahuman Destinations"* (*Liber-Two*).

[*]   Until the org be certain that training, skill, ability, technology and
equipment is properly duplicated by independent practitioners, the
full "Check-Out" to access upper Wizard-Grades (as of January 2022)
is administered exclusively at the "Borsippa HQ" (*Colorado*) for
Mardukite Academy & Systemology Society.

[†]   In substance abuse/chemical dependency ("twelve-step") programs,
the acronym H.A.L.T. is used to remind an individual to stop and
evaluate if they are experiencing any of the main conditions that
hinder rehabilitation: Hungry, Angry, Lonely, or Tired. If these are
left unattended, personal progress tends to *halt.*

due to attention fixed on an outside problem;

— the *Seeker* is not trusting of Systemology methods, or has been mishandled by a Pilot;∞ or

— the *Seeker* is suspended in place, maintaining *Hold-Outs* and *Hold-Backs*, or with attentions directed at *Harmful-Acts* and even *Hostile-Motivators.*

It is detrimental to successful application of our methods that these conditions be determined or resolved. This list should be briefly checked-out before starting *any* systematic processing session, *Piloted* or not.

Whether or not a *Pilot* (or *Seeker*) utilizes mechanical **biofeedback** tools (described later) to assist, the ability to provide high-power processing in Systemology requires high-level intuition and proper application of this applied philosophy. The keyword here is *"applied"*—that means you're supposed to *do* something with it. When it comes to *Wizard-Grades*—when it comes to *Actualized Alpha Ascension*—you won't be able to just *think* your way up and out. Handling the *"Way Out"* requires a high-tone ability to *Confront*; as does the gradient of *Gatework* we are presently treating.

In some situations, an early emphasis on *Ethics Processing* is necessary just to get an individual *moving* at all on the *Pathway.* It is not for us to judge a *Seeker's* misdeeds. Our only interests concern improvement of their own ability and spiritual freedom. Progress on the *Pathway* is the importance here—and some *Seekers* find the weights they have burdened themselves with in this material existence, prior to pursing this *Pathway*, are already too much for them to *Confront* and resolve at their present *Awareness*-level.

For this reason, Route-3E (and *Liber-3E*) is introduced for

∞   This includes actual or imagined events. Mardukite Systemology—as a concept and group entity—also has a tendency to restimulate fragmentation, especially connected to "education" and "religion."

Grade-IV rather than Grade-V. It may be introduced immediately as an integral of Route-3 (described in *Metahuman
Destinations*). Therein, we process *Three Circuits* regarding
channels of *Communication*, *Interest* and *Agreement* (in that
sequence). The emphasis of those series regarded *Recall* and
Analysis of "demands" (enforced, coerced, &tc.) and "rejection" (withdrawal, inhibition, &tc.) on those lines. This is
quite similar to our present focus on what someone "*has
done*" and what they have "*held back*." When an individual
rejects some thing, they are *Holding-Back* on those lines, and
essentially withdrawing responsibility.

To our existing array of PCLs, we have but to add "*Hold-
Outs*" to each of the series. For example: where we have
Communication Demanded of others, of us, and cross-flow;
then *Communication Rejected* by others, by us, and cross-flow;
we then add *Communication Held-Out* on others, on us, and
cross-flow. A Grade-III or early Grade-IV *Seeker* may need to
have explained that a "*Hold-Out*" is an intentional inhibition, withdrawal or refusal to reach, communicate or connect. PCLs are not effective if a *Seeker* is uncertain of a
word's meaning, or if the meaning they associate is misap-
plied.

> Initially, we are not as concerned with targeting jus-
> tifications (or excuses) in basic "Route-3/3E" as
> much as we are interested in distinguishing imprin-
> ted considerations (and *facets*) of a particular space-
> time event as separate from present-time and
> present-environments. Personal computations and
> justifications are often revealed when properly pro-
> cessing (more accessible) considerations.

HELD-OUT SUBJECTIVE COMMUNICATION
(EXPANDED RECALL, BASIC 3E)

Circuit-1 — RECALL a time you *held-out* communication
on someone.

Circuit-2 — RECALL a time someone *held-out* communication on you.

Circuit-3 — RECALL a time someone *held-out* communication on another.

Notice that some existing *Grade-IV* PCLs already cover similar ground. "*Inhibited Objective Interest in Communication*,"
where an individual is demanding that someone *not* communicate with someone or some thing, is the same as "*Enforced
Hold-Outs*"—though at the time of initial development, these
were not considered as a matter of *Ethics*.

HELD-OUT SUBJECTIVE EMOTIONAL INTEREST
(EXPANDED RECALL, BASIC 3E)

Circuit-1 — RECALL a time you *held-out* on liking
someone.[‡]

Circuit-2 — RECALL a time someone *held-out* on liking
you.

Circuit-3 — RECALL a time someone *held-out* on liking
another.

HELD-OUT SUBJECTIVE REALITY AGREEMENT
(EXPANDED RECALL, BASIC 3E)

Circuit-1 — RECALL a time you *held-out* on agreeing with
someone.

Circuit-2 — RECALL a time someone *held-out* on agreeing
with you.

Circuit-3 — RECALL a time someone *held-out* on agreeing
with another.

These are just a few examples of appropriate PCL. While a
Pilot (or *Seeker*) should not vary wildly from those PCL given
in previous material, it requires the "intuition" and a great
deal of "listening" to apply the right sequence or series that
actually creates a change in *Awareness*. There are actually
more processing examples given throughout *Grade-III* and
Grade-IV than would be critically necessary to resolve *Self-
Honesty* for a typical *Seeker*. The remainder are given so that

---

‡ Or "something"; or a specific charged terminal, if applicable.

a *Professional Pilot* can apply a complete intensive **Systemology-180** rundown for any *Seeker* at their existing level of understanding (or *Awareness*) and produce results—which is to say a positive change in a Seeker's *Awareness*.

But *Grade-IV* is separated from *Grade-III* for a reason—and we should expect that a solitary *Seeker* has minimally completed a *Grade-III* understanding prior to applying *Grade-IV* to Self-Processing. Furthermore, a *Pilot* should be trained on all relevant professional materials (ideally up to *Grade-V*) prior to applying *any* of the methodology to others. The *Systemology Society Professional Piloting Course* for Metahuman Systemology minimally includes the texts "**Tablets of Destiny**" and "*Crystal Clear*" for *Grade-III*; then "*Metahuman Destinations*" and "*Imaginomicon*" for *Grade-IV*.

There are also *Grade-III* supplements, including "*Systemology: The Original Thesis of Mardukite New Thought*" and "*The Power of Zu*" which are available as stand-alone titles or in the *Grade-III* anthology, "*The Systemology Handbook.*" The first distinguishable *Grade-IV* supplement is the present volume, "*Liber-3E.*" An expanded version of the "*Basic Course*"* that appeared in the premiere edition of "*Imaginomicon*" (but which was removed from the Mardukite Academy Revised Edition) is also in development as a stand-alone title, in addition to the complete Pre-A.T. *Beta-Defragmentation* procedures manual, "*Systemology-180.*"†

"Route-3C" (in *Metahuman Destinations, Unit-3*) closed with considering various persons, places and terminals (even *Spheres of Existence*) with the aspect: "HELP." We considered "willingness to help," "help given" and "help not given," but focused on mostly "positive" expressions. We did not touch upon more serious detrimental imprinting regarding "*Failed Help.*" This *facet* (or aspect) and "*Betrayal*" are the two key *hot-buttons* from *Grade-IV Processing* that **correlate** most to *Harmful-Acts* and *Hostile-Motivation* in *Ethics*. In turn, these

---

*   "Principles of Systemology" (*Published in 2022*).
†   Forthcoming publication by Joshua Free in 2022.

are the avenues leading to close-off reality channels (total "*Hold-Back*") in an existing Universe. There are a few more aspects of this subject that require defragmentation for *Self-Honesty*. These may be used during the earlier series of "Help" if the individual is not gaining new realizations with that aspect; otherwise they are standard practice for a *Route-3E* Ethics-cleanup prior to Grade-V.

HELP—PROBLEMS AND HELP (EXPANDED 3C, BASIC 3E)

Circuit-1 — How has your *help* been a *problem* to another?
　　　　　　\ Tell me about it. (*Two-Way Communication*)

Circuit-2 — How has another's *help* been a *problem* to you?
　　　　　　\ Tell me about it. (*Two-Way Communication*)

Circuit-3 — How has another's *help* been a *problem* to others?
　　　　　　\ Tell me about it. (*Two-Way Communication*)

C-0/A.T. — How as *helping* yourself been a *problem* to you?
　　　　　　\ Tell me about it. (*Two-Way Communication*)

It is important for a *Seeker* to realize that there are *no real problems* with actual *Help*. A basic systemology of problems itself is treated in "*Metahuman Destinations*" (*Liber-Two*), to which we can state that it is two *flows*, postulates, goals, modes, considerations (*&tc.*) directly in conflict with one another. We are mostly concerned now with flattening any turbulence on the lines of *Help*, correcting and defragmenting a *Seeker's* willingness to reach at terminals that they have had difficulties with. This includes general *facets*, those similar terminals that are tangled up a cross-association with a "past failure." This happens all the time, for example, where an individual has difficulties with their "mother" and then displaces considerations on all reflections of "Mother," *&tc.*; issues with a specific "boss" or "employer" is processed as a general terminal encompassing *all* "bosses" or "employers" after it has been run on the specific.

> By processing general terminals rather than only specific names, the range of consideration for application is increased to include other earlier similar aspects that could be contacted. Early on, this is also one of the keys to tapping into memory of "past-lives"—or even other "hidden data" that has not yet resurfaced about *this* lifetime.

The following are processed by running alternate PCLs of each circuit repeatedly to a satisfaction or realization before treating the next circuit.

FAILED HELP—REJECTED HELP (EXPANDED 3C, BASIC 3E)

Circuit-1 — How might you reject another's *help*?
  \ How might you fail to *help* another?

Circuit-2 — How might another reject your *help*?
  \ How might another fail to *help* you?

Circuit-3 — How might another reject *help* from others?
  \ How might you fail to *help* others?

C-0/A.T. — How might you reject *helping* yourself?
  \ How might you fail to *help* yourself?

> Experiencing "*Failed Help*" and/or perceived "*Betrayal*" promotes (or prompts) *Hold-Outs* and *Hold-Backs*— fragmentation, "*justifications*" (*illogical computations*), "*Self-created disabilities*" and "*motivations*" (*hostility*).

In the systematic process below, make note of all names and terminals that surface. If any carry an energetic charge, incite reactivity or represent difficulties and problems, they may be run appropriately on "*Help–Defragmentation*" following second below, which is an expanded version of a standard process given in "*Metahuman Destinations.*"

INTENTION TO HELP (EXPANDED 3C, BASIC 3E)

Circuit-1 — Who have you intended to *help*?

\ Who have you intended not to *help*?*

Circuit-2 — Who has *helped* you?
\ Who has intended not to *help* you?

Circuit-3 — Who has *helped* others?
\ Who has intended not to *help* others?

C-0/A.T. — How have you *helped* yourself?
\ How have you intended not to *help* yourself?

HELP–DEFRAGMENTATION (EXPANDED 3C, GENERAL 3E)

Circuit-1 — How could you *help* a ___ ?
\ How could you fail to *help* a ___?

Circuit-2 — How could a ___ *help* you?
\ How could a ___ fail to *help* you?

Circuit-3 — How could a ___ *help* others?
\ How could a ___ fail to *help* others?

C-0/A.T. — How could you help yourself concerning a ___ ?
\ How could you fail to help yourself concerning a ___ ?

The previous should be run on all "trouble terminals" and all *Spheres of Existence.* It may even be run on a list of various terminals for each *Sphere* to determine remaining charge or fragmentation. Based on information provided in "*Imaginomicon*" (*Liber-3D*), we discovered a "final touch" *should* be added to a series or cycle (and this is not exclusive only to the "*Help*" series): the **conceptual processing** command

---

* A direct approach considers doingness and actuality, such as: "..have helped" and "have not helped" rather than intention, but in "*Route-3E*" we must gradually "draw the *Seeker* out" from their darkness and concealment to the extent that they feel safe and secure in reaching. Another advanced application for "Route-3E" is "have given" and "have not given." These are called "direct" because they allow a *Seeker* to directly treat what has actually happened "As-it-*Is.*"

line ("get the concept of")‡ or even "*Imagining*" (Route-0).†

> By prompting the *Seeker* to assume responsibility and control of intentionally created *Mental Images* without emotional reactivity or cross-association, the level of defragmentation (*Self-Honesty*) and effectiveness of a series-run can be determined. The following is an example for "*Help.*"

HELP–DEFRAGMENTATION (CONCEPTUAL ROUTE-0E/3E)

Circuit-1 — IMAGINEᐃ *helping* a ___ .
\ IMAGINE not *helping* a ___ .

Circuit-2 — IMAGINE a ___ *helping* you.
\ IMAGINE a ___ not *helping* you.

Circuit-3 — IMAGINE a ___ *helping* others.
\ IMAGINE a ___ not *helping* others.

C-0/A.T. — IMAGINE yourself being a ___ and *helping* you.
\ IMAGINE yourself being a ___ and not *helping* you.

* * * * * * *

ETHICS PROCESSING: STANDARD SPHERES-ASSESSMENT (PRE-A.T. WIZARD LEVEL-0 STANDARD R-3E CHECK-OUT)

The following PCL-skeleton (SP-R-3E) is a systematic formula for applying *Ethics Processing* to all key areas and any applicable terminals representing *Spheres of Existence.* It may be used as a general assessment, as a check-out, or specifically targeting charged "turbulent terminals." We are concerned most here with *Confronting* all actions, *Hold-Outs* and *Hold-Backs* that are accessible.

---

‡   *Conceptual-Certainty Processing* (*Route-0E*) is treated further in a forthcoming section of this chapter-lesson.

†   *Route-0, Imagination* and *Creativeness/Imaginative Processing* are described in more detail within "*Imaginomicon*" (*Liber-3D*).

ᐃ   "Get the idea" or "Get the concept" can replace "IMAGINE" for *Seekers* not yet officially processed on "*Route-0.*"

> The systematic logic we have applied here is:
> "Defragmentation via Direct Confront As-It-*Is*."

It may be that lighter more reachable answers must be pulled off the channels before deeper heavier incidents (and imprinting) can be contacted and released (knowingly and willingly).

> The method applied here introduces "R-3E"—literally the Standard Procedure for (back of and beneath) all *Ethics Processing* as "Route-3E." It differs from traditional "*Expanded Route-3*" because this is intended to resurface key points of specific data, rather than analyzing and distinguishing intertwined or entangled *Communication Circuits*, which is the systems logic behind "Route-3." This is a Wizard-Level Procedure, systematically intended to not exclusively restrict answers to this lifetime or incarnate-body when run extensively at high-Awareness levels.

ETHICS PROCESSING FOR STANDARD PROCEDURE R-3E
(PRE-A.T./GRADE-IV, WIZARD-LEVEL, ROUTE-3E, SP-R3E)

Basic Terminals (as Sphere-Representations) for Ethics Processing —(1) "YOUR BODY"; (2) "SEX" "CHILDREN" "FAMILY" "HOME"; (3) "WORK" "COMMUNITY" "A 'TYPE' OF PERSON"; (4) "SOCIETY" "HUMAN SPECIES"; (5) "ANIMALS" "NATURE"/"ENVIRONMENT" "PLANET EARTH"; (6) "A 'TYPE' OF OBJECT OR MACHINE" "SOLAR PLANETARY SYSTEMS" "GALAXIES" "PHYSICAL UNIVERSE." Treating higher *Spheres* such as (7) "SPIRITS" *&tc.*; (8) "RELIGION" *&tc.* are also important, especially given the 'religio-mystical' backgrounds many *Seekers* have before finding the *Pathway* with our Systemology.

Advanced Wizard-Level Applications—this same formula may be applied to upper-level work to handle terminals representative of the "*Arcs of Infinity*" (the upper-Alpha *Spheres* beyond "8" on the Standard Model of Beta-Existence for the Human Condition) which concern a truer Alpha-Directive, primarily with "SURVIVAL" of *Creations* and *Universes*, rather than an already "ETERNAL" *Alpha-Spirit* that is only convinced of its need to survive through a body after heavy implanting and entrapment in *Beta-Existence* systems.

** When using a **Biofeedback** *Device*, it is important to check each individual word of a PCL for an existing charge prior to use in session processing. Every series or process should begin with communication between *Pilot* and *Seeker* regarding what process is about to be run and the words used for it. It is possible that a particular button or concept carries a *charge* on its own; it is also possible to get charge-reads on a misunderstood word. **

[*Ethics Processing* is a *Seeker's* best chance to get everything out in the open—to confront, handle and discharge everything accessible *As-it-Is* prior to upper-level *Wizard Grade* check-outs and further ("*A.T.*") *Actualization-Ascension Tech.*]

— What *Actions* have you done involving ___ ?
\ What have you *Held-Back* from doing involving ___ ?
— What *Actions* has another done involving ___ ?‡
\ What has another *Held-Back* from doing involving ___ ?
— What would you permit others to do involving ___ ?∞
\ What have you *Held-Back* others from doing involving ___ ?
— What could you allow others to find out about you involving ___ ?Δ

---

‡ Or "*have others*"—based on an agreed upon PCL patter that the *Seeker* understands to mean "circuits other than 1."

∞ Alternative patter to "*permit*" (preferred) includes firstly "*allow*" and secondly (if needed) "*find acceptable for.*"

Δ "*Find out*" implies discovery or a revealing, as opposed to another version of this: "*What would be acceptable for others to know about you?*" A *Professional Pilot* may have to work, or rather "*word,*" a PCL around an individual's acceptance level (reach and understanding) as discussed prior to simply running a series of command lines out of the blue. There is an exchange of direct communication during the setup of each process or series. Lack of such communication will limit the success rate of our applied philosophy.

\ What have you *Held-Out*[*] on about yourself involving ___ ?
— What could others allow you to safely find out about
themselves involving ___ ?
\ What have others *Held-Out* on about themselves
involving ___ ?

* * * * * * *

CONCEPTUAL PROCESSING FOR ETHICS ("ROUTE-0E")

Conceptual-Certainty Processing is applicably effective for any
Seeker at any gradient; however, its refinement at the Systemology Society was reserved for experimental developments at Wizard-Levels. It is part of the original "*Route-0*"
research series, beginning years prior to the publication of
"*Imaginomicon*" (*Liber-3D*). Starting with *Grade-III*—as an
early precursor to *Imagination* and "*Creativeness Processing*"—
it was discovered that:

a "*Concept*" of something can be systematically processed
even if an actual *Recall* is difficult to obtain or
a specific memory unavailable.

However, in late 2019 (and throughout developments of
2020), newly apparent shortcomings suggested it not be re-
commended as a direct or primary route to *Beta-Defragmentation*. Where it came to treating terminals, the actual
"energetic-mass" (fragmentation) did not always fully resolve because the "Source"/"Cause" was still *not-known* and
often remained *non-confronted*. Difficulties found in processing certain *computations* with *Conceptual-Certainty* led us
directly to the existence and subject of *Implants*—yet this
would require further investigation that surpassed the
scope of the "***Master Grade***" (*Grade-III*) and *Wizard Level-0*
(*Grade-IV*). [In fact, this upper-level experimental research

---

[*] This assumes a seeker understands the intended systematic meaning
of the phrase "*Hold-Out*," otherwise alternative patter would be "*kept
hidden.*"

and development cycle is still ongoing at the Systemology Society and Mardukite Academy through 2021.]

"*Route-0*"—as specifically treated in "*Imaginomicon*"—became our *Grade-IV* solution (or alternative) to *Conceptual-Certainty Processing.* "*Route-0*" is applied to our first official completed version of *Beta-Defragmentation Standard Procedure.*[Σ] However, for systematic practice-drilling personal ability to freely or fluidly manage *Alpha-Thought* (*considerations* and *postulates*) fully on Self-Determination, the formerly given "*Route-0*" methods are either like using dynamite where shovels are needed, or else quite the opposite if a *Seeker* is still in preliminary stages of systematically developing "*Creative Ability.*" *Conceptual Processing* also makes some *Ethics* processes accessible/workable earlier on the *Pathway,* rather than only waiting until after a *Seeker* has officially worked with *Imagination* and *Creativeness* at the end of *Grade-IV.*

Wherever a PCL reads, "Get the sense of..." "Get the idea of..." "Think of..." and even the more blatant "Get the concept of..." we are treating considerations of a *concept* (as a thought or consideration, *&tc.*) and not a "feeling" or "sensation." Much like proper use of "IMAGINE" PCLs, processing *concepts* is useful for defragmenting *Imprints* and automation at a reactive (RCC) level; mainly because understanding and handling *concepts* is not restricted to associative-analytical thought levels. Many "computations" an individual makes about life are based on implanted *concepts* used as a foundation to encode relative *Imprinting* later on. And this is also where a *Seeker* comes around to face the nature of *Alpha-Thought* (*considerations* and *postulates*).

> *Concepts* may be run, but they do not represent "mass"
> —and therefore are not "terminals" themselves.
> But, "*Conceptual-Certainty*" may be run on "terminals."

Conceptual-Certainty was among the first methods used to

---

handle "automaticities" during early days of the Systemology Society. The logic is rooted in very ancient spiritual practices pertaining to consciously "making" the body/mind *do* what it is doing on an automatic circuit, and thereby taking control. When a concept is run long enough (or high-power enough) for *certainty*, then total command is resumed by *Self* determining a change to the nature, motion or speed of the tendency, *&tc.* For example, if you are sitting down while reading this now:

> —*Get the concept of you making that body sit in a chair.*
> Or, alternatively:
> —*Think of you making that body sit in the chair.*
> Compare to an objective application:
> —*You make that body sit in the chair.*
> Or, a command postulate:
> —*Sit in the chair.*

"Route-OE" is not exclusively intended to handle physical behaviors. However, Mind-System response-patterns often promote obvious or observable reactions, **compulsions** and behaviors. The behavior exercised as physical effort in *beta-existence* begins as a thought—even if a programmed one; and if so, it most likely has emotional encoding or some other facet of sensation associated with it that might "***ping***" the *Seeker.* It is important to continue through the process completely, even if a given concept, subject or consideration is causing physical discomfort. Safeguards and system-protections exist embedded into the basic foundation of fragmented Implant-programming patterns. These may then be encoded by some related event to have a "physical response" where a *Seeker* withdraws their reach on handling them due to an automatic "*ping*" or reoccurring chronic ailment that flares up each time.

Using these methods, a *Seeker* reclaims "energy-bits" of their past attentions that have been suspended on the *Backtrack* in connection to a particular area, subject or terminal.

Typically, these units of our attention—or **AttEnergy**—were either *rigidly fixed* or *widely dispersed* by some "other-determined prompting" (communication and social activity with others).

> Whatever impinging or obsessive thought an individual has, they would systematically process (or "run") the concept of having that thought (as *Self-Determined*). If the obsessive thought is, for example, a worry over buying a house; the *Seeker* runs the concept of worrying over buying a new house. Eventually, the "worry" can be turned off or changed into a "healthy interest" or even "enthusiasm" (on the *Beta-Awareness Scale*). Preferably, a *Seeker* runs the process until not only is there no automatic obsession to worry about buying houses, but no intrusive compulsion to think about buying houses at all. Afterward, the individual is free to more clearly think about, or not think about, buying houses as they choose—and without attached misemotional facets of anxious worry.

There is also the other side to consider. We have mentioned the obsessive circuit, but—what about a desired or intended thought or idea that is not surfacing? Rather than being compulsively fixed, there are matters that an individual finds difficulty "thinking on" by choice. If a *Seeker* finds that they are unable to "think" on a certain line or channel, run a process on the concept of being *denied* access to that line or *Held-Back* from reaching a certain *Sphere* (of existence or actions)—since that is what is automatically taking place.

> *Hold-Outs* and *Hold-Backs*, by semantic definition, "hold" *Attenergy* to an incident on the *BackTrack*.

Even if the exact mechanism qualifying this condition has not yet been "spotted" in space-time on an individual's *Spiritual Timeline*, just work with what is readily apparent at this stage of the *Pathway*—and do your best. As standardization of our *Beta-Defragmentation* procedure is reaching completion, we still seek to handle management of any accessible response-tendencies inhibiting a *Seeker's* total freedom and ability to knowingly "reach" and "withdraw" their attention, energy and personal power on their own determinism.

ETHICS PROCESSING FOR CONCEPTUAL R-3E PROCEDURE (PRE-A.T./GRADE-IV, WIZARD-LEVEL 0/1, EX. RT. 0E/CR-3E)

Key Concepts (Hot-Buttons) for Route-OE Ethics Processing—"**IN-VALIDATING**" "BEING CRITICAL" "WORRYING" "ATTACKING" "HOLDING BACK" "FAILING TO HELP" "LOSING CONTROL" *and* "MISCOMMUNICATING."

** When using a *Biofeedback Device*, it is important to check each individual word of a PCL for existing charge prior to use in session processing. Every series or process should begin with a communication between *Pilot* and *Seeker* regarding what process is about to be run and the words used for it. It is possible that one of these buttons or concepts carries a *charge* on its own; it is also possible to get charge-reads on a misunderstood word. **

** *A point-of-fact for training* :: This PCL makes an excellent example of demonstrating the systematic relationship between the *Circuits* (in most of our "Route-3" processing methods) and the *Spheres*. **

[Run the entire process inserting the same "*Key-Concept*" in the blanks. Flatten any significant turbulence on a *circuit* before leaving off of it for another. Record notes regarding any contacted or surfacing thoughts, memories, realizations or additional *Harmful-Acts*, *Hold-Backs*, *Hold-Outs* and other charges discovered on channels to terminals, communication-circuits, **phases**/identities, *Spheres*, and so on. *Ethics Processing* is a *Seeker's* best chance to get everything out in the open—to confront, handle and discharge everything accessible *As-it-Is*, prior to upper-level *Wizard Grade* check-outs and further ("*A.T.*") *Actualization-Ascension Tech.*]

Circuit-1 — Get the concept* of ___ *something.*‡

---

* If needed, the alternative standard patter is "Get the idea of..."

‡ The PCL can be left general ("*something*") unless there is a particular

\ Get the concept of not ___ *something.*
\ Get the concept of *something* being ___ .

Circuit-2 — Get the concept of another ___ *something.*
\ Get the concept of another not ___ *something.*
\ Get the concept of *something* being ___ to another.

Circuit-3 — Get the concept of others ___ *something.*
\ Get the concept of others not ___ *something.*
\ Get the concept of *something* being ___ to others.

C-0/A.T. — Get the concept of ___ yourself about *something.*
\ Get the concept of not ___ yourself about *something.*
\ Get the concept of *something* being ___ to yourself.

After running *Expanded Route-0E Conceptual Processing* (above) to a completion, the next step is to run the same "*Key Concepts*" with *Basic-Conceptual Route-0E* (below). Emphasis here returns specifically back to *Self*—what has *out-flowed* "from" and *in-flowed* "to" the *First Sphere of Existence*, representing the perceived position and POV of *Self* experiencing *Beta-Existence.*

Circuit-1 — Get the concept of ___ .
\ Get the concept of not ___ .

Circuit-2 — Get the concept of another ___ *you.*
\ Get the concept of another not ___ *you.*

Circuit-3 — Get the concept of others ___ *something.*
\ Get the concept of others not ___ *something.*

C-0/A.T. — Get the concept of *you* ___ *yourself.*
\ Get the concept of *you* not ___ *yourself.*

* * * * * * *

terminal (person, animal, place, thing) that is assessed as heavily "charged"—preferably "reading"/"indicating" as such on a mechanical *'Biofeedback'* device.

METAHUMAN ETHICS: ENTERING THE "WIZARD'S WAY"

The WIZARD **archetype** represents an individual's highest echelon of *Beingness* attainable as a persona-phase or identity-role for *'Players'* in the *'Game'* of *Beta-Existence*. This computation is so deeply ingrained in consciousness that it doesn't even originate in *this* Universe, but the one preceding it—the *Magic Universe* or *"Magic Kingdom"* as it is often called in our Systemology. Of course, implanted or imprinted data, while logical in **syntax**, does not always result in the most rational computation of reality for present spacetime. A logical evaluation of *this* present *"Mech Universe"* might suggest that an "advanced superpower alien race" might be the ultimate; and there is good reason for this, in view of the fact that some such superpowers in *this* Universe are *"High Wizards"* prior to crossing-over from the previous **condensed** "**continuity**": the *"Magic Universe."*

In many ways, establishment of the *'**Ancient Mystery School**'* served as an *Implant-Reinforcement Station* for those brought into this current incarnation of *Human Civilization* on Earth prior to formal systematization of the present *Human Condition*, which began during the first era of Mardukite Babylon over 4,000 years ago. A minimal amount of the original "magical" and "mystical" regalia, symbolism and philosophy crossed-over into this present cycle-phase of *Beta-Existence* via the *'Ancient School'*. Essentially only enough to restimulate *facets* of "hidden memory" and personal implant programming that most individuals continued to carry with them on their descent from the *"Magic Kingdom"*—the minimum critically necessary to "seem innately and intuitively familiar."

    ** Flattening the concept of being the effect of *"magick"* and *"mysticism"* (using *Grade-I* material and the volume titled *"The Complete Mardukite Master Course"*) is highly suggested for all Master-Level (or higher) *Seekers.* **

Inciting a sense of the "unknown" or "not-known" equally incites computations that "there is something to be known about"—hence the obsessive "pursuit of the *Great Mystery.*"

A Wizard-Level Systemologist is processed toward a realization on the *Great Mystery* of the Universe, which reveals itself to be that: *there is no Great Mystery of the Universe*. All of *'that'* has been imposed by the individuals themselves and is dependent on others to be in agreement with it enough to a point to where it becomes a 'thing' duplicated in all realities within its reach. The higher the Awareness-level, the greater the scope on exactly what is going on.

At one level of *Existence*, we "knew" (and still "know") what *'Is'*—and on a level of Truth that expounds far and beyond a sense of *'words'* and *'definitions'*. But then we agreed that it would be more interesting—more of a *"Game"*—if we could "not know" all these things, so we might have something 'new' to *Do* in trying to *'find out'* again. Hence, the Human Condition sets out to *create things* to *know* about. But in *Beta-Existence*, this hardly reflects the state of *Knowingness* that was once maintained. And the individual has sunk fairly low in the not-know to be meandering about blindly in the Human Condition, enough to where it has to remember to *'find their own way out'* again.

The "Way of the Wizard" represents access to the upper-routes leading to *Gateways-of-Infinity*, which is to say "Ascension," far and beyond the scope of what it means to be *"Human."* Fields of technological science and mechanical development usurped concepts of "**transhumanism**," so the Systemology Society settled on the terms "METAHUMAN" and "HOMO NOVUS" to denote our "spiritual" applications of techniques that elevate the *Knowingness* and *Beingness* of an individual toward their optimum states. It is difficult to even consider this a new "evolution," since we are peeling back layer after layer of artificial programming that ultimately returns an individual to their true, basic and original position prior to entering the Physical Universe and its implanting. And this is what the "higher" *Wizard-Grades* represent. The way out... The way back... *The Way...*

> Even at *Wizard Level-0*—as introduced with *"Imaginomicon"*—a *Seeker* discovers that the *Reality* being experienced may be an illusion, but it is one that is projected by *Self* as part of a shared or common agreement. We are still, in essence, creating our own personal universe as we always have been—but as we take on more layers of agreement with others about what *Reality* '*Is*', such become part of the postulates and consideration for how we design our Personal Universe. These layers each become cumulatively more convoluted, restrictive and solid until we either *clear the slate* or become the total *Effect* of our own *Cause.*

In the simplest systematic terms, we remain an individual fragment of the ALL within our own Universe that we are projecting in order to have an experience, but we superimpose a '*duplication*' in that Universe of whatever we are in communication with. For this reason, we emphasize defragmenting the channels of communication with systematic processing as a primary step toward *Self-Honesty.* The underlying blueprint of *Reality* is formed by communication-circuits and the continuous flow maintained between *Self* and all others acting as "*terminals*" in this Universe.

We maintain some level of reality agreement with whatever we identify or are in communication with. In any situation where there is actual contact or flow, both sides must 'duplicate' the full cycle of communication as *Reality.* A person acknowledges, recognizes or identifies a certain individual as the *Source* of the communication just as much as they must '*duplicate*' the content communicated by willingly being a receipt point. The entire '*Cycle-of-Action*' must be projected as *Reality* and '*duplicated*' by each each party "*A-for-A*" in order to have actual communication. And all of these *Mental Images* (and subsequent encoding from the content) are stored along each appropriate channel and contribute what we "take away from it" or register as "experience."

> Our "experience" is not a source of "fragmentation"
> until we find ourselves not-confronting it "As-It-*Is.*"
> That means not only the "acceptance" of what is done
> but also the "willingness" to be at either *Point-of-View.*

Ethics Processing is introduced on the *Pathway-to-Self-Honesty* to systematically resolve this issue. It is gravely overlooked or directly left out of what former basic systematic methods targeted. There are some individuals that do not seem to earn any stable gains from the *Pathway* until this area is resolved. It is not so much a matter of the actions themselves, but the significances assigned to them and other considerations attached. Most encounters are not permanently fragmentary, but that which is not-confronted directly will hang up on the *Spiritual Timeline* as a confusion—a fragmentation of the certainty, muddying the clear vision and experience of *Reality.*

> During a *"Harmful-Act"* there is
> a 'duplication' of all **viewpoints**
> by all persons, easily allowing
> a *"Phase-shift"* with the others.

There is a tendency for an individual to **dramatize** what has happened to them—or solicit assistance and support from others—with the old "look what they've done to me" while occupying a *Victim-phase.* This is derived from a basic survival tactic that projects "I am already wounded; please do not attack." The tendency is validated and strengthened by memories and imprints of when others might have "taken care of the individual"—such as with a childhood illness or injury. This tends to apply mostly to encounters with other friends and loved ones, where one might earn "**sympathy**" as the sole means of remaining in communication.

There are other environments throughout the greater

World-at-Large where this computation of victimization is highly counter-survival mistake to employ. In such instances, the individual is likely to take on the (more aggressive) *Malefactor-phase*, based on a completely separate computation that *"that one* is the winning position to be in," or the mode one must operate with in order to achieve a surviving position. So we have the issue of a fragmented personality-package that has "turned Evil" solely because of being on the receipt (*enforced effect*) end of too many non-confronted "Evil" acts.

We already began treating *Victim*-fragmentation at the very beginning—starting with *"Route-1."* Unfortunately long-term use of our original* *"Route-1"* methods—in exclusion to all others—tends to reinforce being the *Effect* or what we later consider *Circuit-2* (*"in-flow"*). *"Route-1"* is still a valid stepping-stone and place to begin for many *Seekers* that haven't yet regained control of enough *"AttEnergy"* or "attention units" (*Awareness*) to progress forward on the *Pathway* with higher studies and other *Routes* of processing. However, it does overlook other important aspects of fragmentation, such as what the individual, themselves, has done as an *"out-flow."* The total sum of these aspects contributes to later "acceptance levels" or *Hold-Outs* on free-flow communication and the *Hold-Backs* that Self-impose a restriction or unwillingness to act, or else *reach* thereafter.

|Whatever is non-confronted becomes a "hidden influence."|

The *malefactor* committing a *"Harmful-Act"* carries just as much, if not more, fragmentation at *Cause* as their "victim" does at *Effect.* Keep in mind that the experience of both POV is recorded by both. This means that when an individual is unwilling to confront their own created effects or completely unwilling to experience the "other side" of the situation, the event and all of its facets will be registered and carried as a fragmentary energetic-mass suspending *Aware-*

---

* Given in the premiere first edition of *"Tablets of Destiny"* (*2019*) and inclusion of that text in *"The Systemology Handbook."*

ness and attention on the *Spiritual Timeline.* It is simply wait-ing to be "pulled in" and manifested against themselves as a "*Hostile-motivator.*" Subscribing to the balance of all action in this Physical Universe, the *malefactor* has an incident hap-pen to them "after the fact" that would seem to justify or motivate the former action—but it is happening afterward. This phenomenon is misunderstood as *karma.*

We have briefly mentioned "sympathy" as a means of main-taining low-level connectivity or communication. There is also the matter of "empathy"—or else the ability to experi-ence another POV apart from one's own: to literally see what it's like "in someone else's shoes." This should be practiced as a *Pre-A.T.* exercise—and since it is related to use of *Imagination*, it may even be incorporated or cycled into the *Pre-A.T. Wizard-Level* "*Creative Ability Training*" (CAT) regi-men.[‡]

Before treating more significant Ethical concerns, "em-pathy" may be repetitively practiced (or "drilled") with a partner free of the inhibition that may be applied to casual contact in public or with strangers.

>—Entire instruction behind the exercise is simply: to attempt a *'duplication'* of sensations from another POV.

>—If you are even just speaking with someone, *Imagine* the impression you are projecting (how you appear and sound) from their POV.

>—If there is physical contact, *Imagine* the feeling or sensation of touch received by the other POV.

When we refer to "*Harmful-Acts,*" we are not exclusively treating physical violence. All manners of projected unkind-ness apply to *Ethics Processing*, particularly where the effect is a reduction (any perceived "*Loss*") in an individual's *Be-ingness* and/or *Awareness*-level. "*Pain*" and "*Unconsciousness*" are simply two common examples of more violent acts. We

---

[‡]   Refer to "*Imaginomicon*" (*Liber-3D*).

are reaching for genuine ability to face-up to the *BackTrack* as we increase progress on the *Pathway*. To ensure "wins" for a *Seeker*, the "lighter" incidents should be treated masterfully prior to tackling "bigger" *Ethical* hang-ups in one's past.

| Empathy may be applied to "supercharge" effectiveness
| of *'Forgiveness'*—as given in the previous chapter-lesson. |

In fact, an ability to actually confront environmental facets and personal experiences from all POV of an incident "As-It-*Is*," is a high-power key to discharging accumulated turbulent energetic-masses that restrain (or *Hold-Back*) true freedom of the Alpha-Spirit.[†]

* * * * * * *

ETHICS: "SEARCH AND DISCOVER (ON THE CIRCUITS)"
(GRADE-IV, PRE-A.T. WIZARD LEVEL-0, EXPANDED 3E)

Standard and Conceptual methods of *Ethics Processing* usually reveal quite a bit of material for resolve. It may be, however, that at a certain stage of release (or even at the very start) some significant attention must be given directly to a "search and discovery" effort. Although no specific instructions are given to restrict its application to *this* lifetime, there are also no specific instructions given as *Wizard Level-0* (*Grade-IV*) for targeting a *Seeker's* "past lives" directly.[∞] [This is an experimental formula directly distinguis-

---

[†] When processing an incident (or running "*Forgiveness*"), also *Imagine* the experience from the opposing POV. The Mind-System tends to classify and group imprinting incidents on a "chain." If a your sense of an incident is becoming stronger (more solid) in its restimulated charge (rather than releasing), spot a similar non-confronted incident "parked" earlier on the *BackTrack*.

[∞] An exception being the note regarding incidents that do not readily discharge because they are linked to a larger, stronger, *older* "chain" requiring a *Seeker* to "scan for" and "spot" a similar type of incident earlier in "time." This sometimes inspires *Seekers* with a "*sense*" of something that is only logically connected via a former incarnation.

hing communication-circuit energy-flows as treated throughout *Ethics Processing.*]

> NOTE: Energetic discharge and sense of release only takes place if what is discovered is fully confronted "As-It-*Is*" using methods and instruction given throughout our present *Liber-3E* text. "Discovery" and "Discharge" processes may be more effective when conducted by a *Professional Pilot* and/or using a mechanical biofeedback device to assist (as explained in the chapter-lesson: "Utilitarian Systemology for Wizards").

"Search and Discovery on Circuits" is worded very directly for use by experienced Systemologists. It is originally intended as a *Pilot's* "tool" for accessing layers of significance surrounding *Ethical* fragmentation. Each circuit is treated separately. The four PCL are run alternately in sequence repeatedly (1-2-3-4; 1-2-3-4) for a single circuit until a *Seeker* has no more readily available answers, they are interested in the discovery process and optimistic or relieved by the results. [If a *Seeker* reaches this point on one PCL of a circuit before the rest, that one part may be omitted from repeated runs.] This process may be run *Solo* as a personal data-inquiry toward *Self*, but its function is primarily to "root out" information—a list of which should be recorded for later use.

Circ-1 — What have you made another *Out-Flow*?
What have you made another *Hold-Out*?
What have you made another *In-Flow*?
What have you made another *Hold-Back*?

Circ-2 — What has another made you *Out-Flow*?
What has another made you *Hold-Out*?
What has another made you *In-Flow*?
What has another made you *Hold-Back*?

Circ-3 — What has another made others *Out-Flow*?
What has another made others *Hold-Out*?
What has another made others *In-Flow*?

What has another made others *Hold-Back*?

Circ-0 — What have you made yourself *Out-Flow*?
What have you made yourself *Hold-Out*?
What have you made yourself *In-Flow*?
What have you made yourself *Hold-Back*?

:: UTILITARIAN SYSTEMOLOGY FOR WIZARDS ::
— Advanced Tech Toward "Wizard Level" Processing[‡] —

> "AHA, A LOOKING GLASS INTO THE UNCONSCIOUS!"
> —*Carl G. Jung* about GSR-Meters

Research supporting application of a *GSR-Meter* for *systematic processing* includes: Volney Mathison's *"Manual of Electropsychometry"* (*1951*) and *"Super-Visualization: The Duplicative Techniques of Applied Creative Energy"* (*1956*); Mark L. Gallert's *"Electropsychometry: A New, More Effective and Faster Psychotherapy"* (*1955*); Peter Shepherd's *"GSR-Meter Course: Biofeedback Monitoring Skills in the Context of Transformational Psychotherapy"* (*1994, 2001*); Inna Khazan's *"Biofeedback and Mindfulness in Everyday Life: Practical Solutions for Improving Your Health & Performance"*; Dr. Michael Apter's *"Reversal Theory"* and *"Personality Dynamics"* among others; Frank A. Gerbode's *"Beyond Psychology: Traumatic Incident Reduction"*; and, of course, Carl G. Jung's *"Studies in Word Analysis"* (*1908*). Additional controversial sources were also explored—as cited in this chapter-lesson. Various different applicable "Meter" models now exist with several "patents" filed and on record for the same.

"Wizard Grade Systemology" optionally incorporates *GSR-Meters* to assist many upper-level *Systematic Processing* applications. If used, success depends on a *Pilot/Seeker* carrying a working knowledge of, access to, and certainty in ability to use, such a device.

---

‡   This chapter-lesson is based on *"Wizard Level-1 Experimental Research and Demonstrations for Ethics Processing and Beyond"* as overseen by *Joshua Free* in August 2021–January 2022 for the *Mardukite Academy of Systemology* at *Mardukite Babylonia SLV Borsippa HQ.* It is compiled from the notes prepared by the author in addition to those Staff members already participating at these levels/Grades of the organization.

"Psycho-Galvinometers" (or *GSR-Meters*; *Galvanic Skin Response*) measure electrical resistance of the skin surface. Experimental use of *GSR* for "transpersonal psychology" is as old as "psychology" and "psychoanalysis" itself. It has been little more than 150 years—since the field of Psychology separated itself from general Philosophy. [All sciences are originally "breakaways" with Philosophy—including such as **physics** and **physiology**. That the surface of skin is electrically active—and that detectable resistance changes occur based on emotional stimulation—dates back to the mid-to-late 1800's. Early "word association" investigations by Carl Jung compared measurable "critical arousal" (**"electro-dermal activity"**/*EDA*) to the "emotional charge" held by an individual regarding key words and concepts.

By the 1930's, the field of criminology applied *GSR*-equipment as a key component of the "polygraph," which also measures heart-rate, temperature, blood pressure and breathing. For both legal and practical reasons, a *full* "polygraph" is not employed within our Systemology—the additional measurements being quite unnecessary. However, it is no surprise that *biofeedback* devices and instruments used to gauge our *Ethics Processing* for *Personal Integrity* are also associated with what is commonly referred to as a "lie detector." We are, again, dealing with something called *"Self-Honesty"*—so...

For our purposes, a *GSR-Meter* (or *EDA-Meter*) detects *emotional fluctuation*, measures *energetic fragmentation* and monitors changes in *Awareness* whenever a *Seeker* contacts "charged" terminals, *imprints* or *implants* on a particular channel. Although design improvements (transistors, amplifiers, adjustable range/magnification, &tc.) expanded potential applications after the 1930's, the basic technology remains stable and relatively unchanged since intensive experimental research of "New Thought" movements emerging the 1950's and 1960's.

A *Systemologist* (*Pilot* or *Seeker*) does not require an extensive background-education in electricity/electronics in order to understand and operate a *GSR-Meter.* As with taking up an exploration, study and practice of any other new pursuit— much like when the *Seeker* started up on the *Pathway* with our Systemology—we will accomplish all that is necessary for transition into *Grade-V (Wizard Level-1)* by relaying a basic introduction to *Electronic Biofeedback Technology*, combined with concise communication of fundamental vocabulary and appropriate examples.

GSR-METER DEVELOPMENT FOR DEFRAGMENTATION

Research suggests that infamous Swiss psychologist Carl Jung was first to employ *GSR-Meters* in psychotherapy and psychoanalysis. He conducted "word association" experiments and "interviews" (asking questions, much like our *PCLs*) while measuring "galvanetic skin responses"—meaning observing, detecting and measuring change in electrical resistance across the surface of the skin (or Electrodermal Activity/EDA). It is important to note that such meters do not literally "read the mind."

An example GSR-Meter

One or two "electrodes" are held by, or attached to, a *genetic vehicle* and only *reflects* conditions of the Mind-System to the extent that it is affecting the body. Early meters were little more than the "*Ohm-Meter*" you might find inexpensively on the market today; they lacked amplifiers and range control, making them difficult to use. [A traditional "*Ohm-Meter*" is not suggested for modern practice.]

Various book publications (and patent records) from the mid-20th Century "New Thought" era suggest that two men in particular were primarily responsible for standardizing modern *Electro-Psychometers* ("*E-Meters*")—and even systematically applying them toward *defragmenting* the Human Condition:—

• Volney G. Mathison (1950, *Patent #2684670;* "*Mathison Electrometer*"—using a single electrode held in one hand) –and–

• Lafayette Ronald Hubbard* (first version filed 1961, revised in 1966, *Patent #3290580;* "*Hubbard® Electrometer*"—"a device for measuring and indicating changes in the resistance of a human body"—using two electrodes, one held in each hand).

Dissatisfied with existing "*polygraph*" experiments Volney conducted in the 1940's, he invented his own type of *GSR-Meter* that included transistors (an electronic switch with no moving parts) for the first time in 1950. At least by 1951 (possibly even 1950), he began regularly attending (and was significantly impressed by) Lafayette's "New Thought" lectures. He worked on perfecting his device, which detected

---

* In an effort to maintain a monopoly on his work, legal complications allegedly prohibit reference to "*Lafayette Ronald Hubbard*" by his more commonly recognizable name, which is apparently trademarked by "The Church" he established in 1953/1954. Elsewhere in the paragraph, the device name is printed ("*Hubbard® Electrometer*") in the style given on copyright pages of "Church" literature written by him. Usage of the name appears in the present text for educational purposes only, to describe historical development of GSR technology and is not intended to infringe on any legal trademarks or organizations that hold them.

and measured the type of "personal energy" (*Zu*) "*reads*" and "*fluctuations*" that Lafayette described. This allowed their brand of "*Pilot*" (called "*auditors*") a greater certainty toward "*Clearing*" an individual of their emotional and mental fragmentation. For several years after—until circuitry of the "*Mathison Electrometer*" became too convoluted for Lafayette's practical use—the two men sporadically collaborated on improving the equipment; all the while following very specific premises:—

• "Matter" is the physical appearance of "Energy" (*Zu*) as visible or detectable within the normative range of the *Human Condition*.

• "Energy" (*Zu*) is a "super-frequency" visible or detectable to Humans as "matter" or else manifest as the "stuff" of "*Mental Image Pictures.*"

• "Energy" (*Zu*) may be directed by the (*Alpha*)-*Spirit* or *Self*; "raised," "lowered," "released" &tc.

• Improperly directed (misdirected) "Energy" (*Zu*), "reduced flows" and "stuck flows," influences personal illness and disease.

• An individual can modify "Energy" (*Zu*) flows, selectively redirecting and applying attention, by intentionally duplicating "*Mental Image Patterns*" at the level of conscious *Awareness*.

• "Psycho-Physical" Energy (*Zu*) flows of the *Human Condition* register on, and may be relatively measured with, an "*Electro-Psychometer*" ("*E-Meter*").

"*E-meters*" received most public attention as "religious artifacts" of Lafayette's "Church"; but the "*Hubbard® Electrometer*" was not the first one developed and used for *defragmentation*—nor is it technically the only option now available today for a *Seeker* or *Pilot* of our Systemology. In the past few decades, several versions of this device have been constructed and marketed to "*Clearing* practitioners" independent of "The Church." They currently own a commercial (proprietary) trademark for the word "*E-Meters.*"

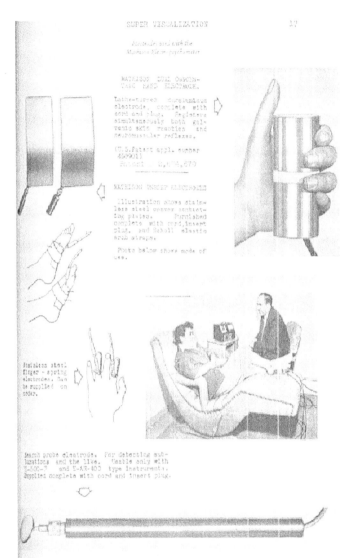

An illustrated sample page from
Volney Mathison's *"Super Visualization"*

Alternatively manufactured biofeedback devices (applicable for *our* Systemologists) are not presented or referred to as *"E-meters"* either, as per—carrying names like: "Ability Meter" (*UK*); "Clarity Meter" (*US*); "Clearing Meter" (*generic term*); "C-Meter" (*Austria*); "Delta-1 Meter" (*Germany*); "Freedom-2 Meter" (*Russia*); "Mindwalker" (*UK*); "OM-Meter" (*Russia*); "Phoenix Meter" (*US*); and "Theta-Meter"—to name a few commonly used ones.

A more recent design trend involves computer software, requiring minimal expense for hardware—typically two hand-held electrodes connected to a "black-box" that is then read and displayed on a personal computer rather than the device purchased. A brand new computer-based setup is a few hundred dollars, which is comparable in price to a quality second-hand refurbished/reconditioned *"Hubbard® Electrometer"* (perferably from a source in the *FreeZone*‡ that can check out the equipment before you get it; as opposed to the cheaper garage sale finds that have questionable pasts. This is not the area you'll want to 'skimp' on.

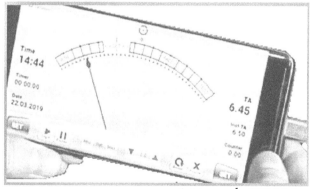

An example GSR-Meter
using cell phone technology

ELECTROPSYCHOMETRIC BIOFEEDBACK: HOW IT WORKS

> "Volney Mathison[†] was a pioneer in the discovery that all fears, feelings and resentments—all thought and emotion—were electrical in their nature. He found through experiments with lie-detectors during the 1940's that when a person was reminded of certain past events, or when a change of mood was induced in him, the needle in the meter would jump erratically; the degree of jump was in **proportion** to the strength of unconscious reaction. In skilled hands, the meter could be used to locate particular mental content, the nature of that content, the location of that content in space and time, 6and the amount of force contained within it."
>
> —Peter Shepherd, *GSR Meter Course*
> *Tools for Transformation, 2001*

Electrical "current" is electrical energy "flow"—meaning a *flow* (motion or action) of *electrons*, usually through a conductive wire; much like a flow of water moves through pipe or a hose. A "closed-loop" where electrons circulate is called a "circuit." We quite often treat personal energy "flows" and "circuits" in our Systemology. However, when referring to "electrical resistance" of a circuit, we quite literally mean: an "energetic-mass" (material) with an ability to "restrict" (slow down) electron flow. Larger or greater resistance in a circuit indicates greater or denser "mass" *resisting* free-flow of electrons in that circuit. And unless an individual intends on constructing their own Meter, this is really the extent of traditional electrical knowledge that a *Seeker* or *Pilot* needs

The basic electrical circuit used to measure an unknown (or variable) value of electrical resistance is called the *"Wheatstone bridge"*—named not for its original inventor (*Samuel Hunter Christie* in 1833), but for

---

† Volney Mathison (*1897-1965*) psychoanalyst, chiropractor, writer, inventor.

Sir Charles Wheatstone, an English scientist that improved and popularized its application and notoriety in 1843.

When a *Seeker* holds *electrodes*[Σ] ("*sensors*") of an *Electro-Psychometer* in their hands, they are part of a closed-circuit. A small unnoticeable amount of electrical current (usually no more than 2 volts) is passed through the body, which now acts as one "leg" of "resistance" in the circuit. To determine the unknown value of resistance from the body, a "*potentiometer*" ("*variable resistor*" and "range adjuster") is attached to the other "leg" and controlled externally by a rotating "knob" or "arm." This "balancing arm" (or "baseline control") is manually rotated to a position where the "display-dial needle" is visibly at the "set" point, indicating a "balance point" is reached for the circuit. While the "needle" is at the "set" point, the circuit is balanced: the "balancing arm" (or "baseline control") position on one "leg" or "side" of the "circuit bridge" is indicative of the electrical resistance value present across the surface of the skin on the other "leg" or "side" of the circuit.

This fundamental action compares to applying weights (with known values) on one side of a "balancing scale" in order to determine an unknown, but equivalent, weight (value) of mass on the other side.

Bringing attention out from the inner workings and mechanisms, it is more critical that all operators (*Pilots*, *Co-Pilots*

Σ   Although semantically and scientifically accurate, a few experimental participants at the Systemology Society found terms like "electrode" and "probe" to personally carry reactive association with something *invasive*. If not applying physics vocabulary, as above, to introduce a proper electrical-education ("*how they work*"), a preferred day-to-day name (and for sessions) is "*sensors.*" Another acceptable term is "*cans*"—which is part of the original terminology found in this practice. It simply references the fact that metal soup-cans were actually the first standard "*electrodes*" applied—attaching to the meter wire-leads with alligator-clips. Even after specially manufactured "electrodes" were designed, the term "*cans*" has remained in use among practitioners all the way up to the present.

and *Solo-Seekers*) are familiar with the external controls and dials of whatever model/type is chosen for use. Basic functions and controls of an *Electro-Psychometer* have remained standard for at least half-a-century. Whether using older styles, where every detail is represented by an analog knob, or newer models that employ digital technology—and even computers, the operation is the same. External appearance of some newer models is different than what will be described here, depending on how many analog functions (on older/standard models) are now "automated" (internally), such as "*balancing action.*"

[Our *Systemology Society* 'covert' 2020-2021 planned project was originally: "to design and produce (in-house) a 'SELF-HONESTY METER' or 'DEFRAGMENTATION METER' (preferred names for our *Systemology* application) and/or develop an instructional course pertaining to inexpensive manufacture of the same for practical personal use" Well, we fel short on thateon *every part of it*!—*Time*, *Results*, and so forth. By Autumn 2021 it became clear that attentions should be redirected back toward *Grade-IV* completion: finalization and release of "*Liber-3E*." If so desired, education materials exist 'out there'—primarily from or linked-through the *FreeZone*—to assist constructing your own Meter.]

There is one particular anomaly worthy of mention here—because all meters directly inspired by designs and operative uses from the Volney and Lafayette models continue to carry a misnomer forth. In the early 1950's the two men were giving a lot of attention to their *New Thought* concept of "emotional tone" or "tone scale"—similar in purpose to our "*Beta-Awareness Scale*" introduced in "*Crystal Clear*" (*Liber-2B*). The "range adjustment arm" that controls the "balancing action" (meaning the needle "balance point" or "set" position) was thought to indicate an individual's emotional tone level on the scale. Well, *it didn't*—but once labeled as a "tone arm," the name stuck.

Rather than indicate a display of the actual "electrical resistance"—measured in "*Ohms*"—by the Meter, Volney and Lafayette used basic numbers "1" through "6" (sometimes even up to "7"). The balance-set position is indicative of some things, but it is really the needle motion and pattern characteristics that become the critical reads during a process. While they do not necessarily indicate an individual's "emotional tone," the simple single digits aren't arbitrary and may have perhaps made the Meters easier to apply and interpret from memory, rather than actual "*Ohms*" values.

For example: up until release of Lafayette's *Professional Mark-VI* (in 1978), the "2" also had an "F" next to it and the "3" had an "M" next to it. This originally denoted target "clear readings" for each bio-physical sex. According to the story given by Lafayette in late-1950's lectures, skin resistance measurements were tested on dead bodies. Therefore, at *basic*—meaning emotionally and reactively defragmented; unaffected by any turbulence from the Spiritual Self—the meter-reads on the bodies were consistently 5,000 *Ohms* (*5000 Ω* or *5kΩ*) for females and *12,500 Ω* (*12.5kΩ*) for males. These figures are actually simplified on the standard Balance-Arm as "2" and "3" respectively. These set values are also useful to know for calibration before each use.

In many respects, it may actually be easier and more efficient for these application to use simple representative numbers. Otherwise, again, we are left with the hard figures —for example, the way the information just given is relayed in a **Traumatic** *Incident Reduction* (*TIR*) manual (Frank A. Gerbode's "*Beyond Psychology*"):—"...in most people, under ordinary circumstances, the resistance will be found in the range of 5,000–15,000 *Ohms*." Some *GSR-Meter* models do display actual electrical resistance in *Ohms*. To be consistent across the boards, we want to have the 'big picture' as a reference—if our *Systemology* is to have 'Universal' application as intended.

Balancing Arm	Electrical Resistance
1	400 Ω
2	5000 Ω
3	12,500 Ω
4	25,800 Ω
5	56,500 Ω
6	190,400 Ω

An *Ohm*-meter, such as you would find in a hardware store, does not work well for detecting *fragmentation*. Usually the display-dial will cover such a large range that you are not going to see precise movements, if at all. On the other hand, *GSR-Meters* allow an individual to display a smaller portion or range—and generally have controls that increase or decrease amplification (sensitivity). Although we can cover basic theory and technical information in this text, there is really no substitute to actually working with an operative model to gain personal experience, familiarity and certainty with these devices. This doesn't mean experience in memorizing a lot of data—we mean practicing with various individuals to see patterns and differences and feeling certain about the device before utilizing it as a *systematic processing* tool. If you're not certain in your general handling of *GSR-Meters* for *processing*, then better to skip it.

UNDERSTANDING GSR-METERS FOR DEFRAGMENTATION

"It is a remarkable fact that the real sources of one's anxiety may be so deeply hidden in one's subconscious that one will go about believing all sorts of other things are causing all the trouble, and erroneously blaming these other things which are *secondary effects*, not *causes*. Meanwhile, the true cause remains hidden, growing ever more powerful in its effects."

—Volney Mathison, *Super-Visualization*
Manual of Electropsychometry, 1956

Prior to Carl Jung's incorporation of *GSR-Meters* for 'Word Association', the standard gauge of psychoanalytics primarily consisted of *"Comm-Lag"*‡ (*communication lag*), which is the amount of time it takes to get a question answered. When used for *Systematic Processing*, a *GSR-Meter* may be used to detect *fragmentation*, specifically information that is suppressed, but accessible—meaning, able to be *confronted As-It-Is*—by a Seeker. This is not only useful for achieving true *Beta Defragmentation* in *Self-Honesty*, but is almost necessary to achieve any certainty of *Alpha (Spiritual) Defragmentation* at higher-level Wizard Grades.

The intended purpose of *Systematic Processing*—as described in *Grade-III*—is to bring undesirable, implanted and artificial *programs*, *imprints* and *postulates* into clear view for a *Seeker* to analytically inspect. Suppressed *fragmentation*, *imprints* and *programming* are uncovered in layers—as some is taken off, more becomes accessible that previously might not even register on a Meter. This is elevation of *Actualized Awareness* in action and objectively on display.

> "When restimulated mental content is confronted, repression dissolves into Awareness. When not confronted, detachment may suffice, but if further involvement is enforced, then anxiety results."
> —Peter Shepherd, <u>GSR Meter Course</u>
> *Tools for Transformation, 1994-2001*

An individual that avoids "handling their stuff" runs the risk of having the *charge* restimulated by their environment in everyday life. Energy-flows encounter resistance from *mass*, just like damming up a stream of water. Hence, in most cases, the higher the resistance, the greater the *mass* encountered. Here we mean quite specifically and literally *"mental mass"* (or *"fields"*) surrounding certain 'ideas' and 'concepts'—or as Carl Jung was researching, associated with certain 'words' and 'memories'.

---

‡   See also *Unit-1* of *"Metahuman Destinations."*

> As *energetically-entangled mental masses* are brought up to the surface for a *Seeker* to confront, the resistance increases—or "*rises*." When the *mass* is actually confronted *As-It-Is* and disintegrated with the *Seeker's attention* ("*attenergy*")—*Actualized Awareness*—then the Meter reads a resistance reduction, or "*fall*."

GSR-Meter use is only introduced at our "Wizard Grades" to supplement higher levels of *systematic processing*, because the device is not a substitute for understanding. A *Seeker* would already have to be familiar with vocabulary and concepts applied to a *process* or *PCL*. For example, a misunderstood word given in a *process* can cause false readings. Therefore, it is also important to check each of the actual words used in a *PCL* prior to applying them in order to be certain they do not already have a "charge" on them. This goes back to the original Jungian application of *GSR* for "word association."

A Meter is particularly useful when *Piloting* a *Seeker*. Although they do not indicate exactly *what* the *Seeker* is thinking about or confronting, they will indicate shifts in attention and *how* the *Seeker* is handling it. They do not necessarily "read" the *Mind*—but they do register how the *Mind-System* is affecting the body as it operates. For example, by observing the *Seeker* and Meter, a *Pilot* can determine when a "*hot-button*" is 'pressed' or *reached* during processing—or when the *Seeker* is *withdrawing* (backing off) from the same. There are indications for when the *Seeker* is experiencing restimulation of an *Imprint*—and when there is no longer a "charge" of entangled energy remaining on a particular circuit or channel. The Meters are intended only as *tools* to assist *systematic processing* and should not be the ultimate focus of observation. A *Pilot* is processing the *Seeker*; not the Meter device itself. It is not a substitute for observing the reactions and behaviors of a *Seeker*.

In spite of the fact that excessively sweaty, cold or dry

hands can affect the baseline read from the electrodes (and should be remedied before a *systematic session* begins), use of a *GSR-Meter* as we describe and apply it does not have anything to do with perspiration—which is what many skeptics and critics suggest. The human body does not sweat and "un-sweat" rapidly enough to provide the kind of instant reactive reads and changes we look for an observe during systematic use. By reactive read, we mean literally within an instant or second of a *Pilot* completing a statement, word or PCL. Anything more than three seconds and you are dealing with latent thought.

Fragmentation, by nature, is a state of *confusion*.

The purpose of all *systematic processing*, at some level or another, is to increase the *certainty* that an individual has about themselves, the management of *Self* and the environment. This also falls in line with what we know about *Self-Honesty* and the honesty exchanged with others. By desiring or wishing to know something, but not knowing it, the individual is unable to realize what something is—*As-It-Is*—and therefore unable to confront it. One cannot face what is not known. And this is why forthright honesty is critical for *actualization*.

This is contradictory to the social **fallacy** that
"what they don't know won't hurt them."
In fact, it is what "they don't know"
that causes the greatest energetic turbulence.

This factor is particularly strong between individuals sharing "interpersonal" or intimate relationships. This is why infidelity—or "cheating"—in relationships carries such significant *charge*. It is a *betrayal* of the highest order.

E-METERS, LIE-DETECTORS & SELF-HONESTY, OH MY!
(& SOME COMMENTARY ON THE POLITICS OF TRUTH)

"Detection and recording of galvanic skin response

is often combined with detection and recording of other autonomic-[ANS *(Autonomic Nervous System)*]- dependent psychophysiological variables such as heart rate, respiratory rate and blood pressure. The device that detects and records these (additional) variables is called a *polygraph*—meaning *'many measures'*. Changes in emotion associated with intentional falsification of answers to carefully selected and worded questions involuntarily and subconsciously alters autonomic output in such a way as to cause recognizable changes in recorded physiological variables. Keep in mind that although the procedures and measures used are similar to a polygraph recording, this is not a 'lie detector test'. All you will do here is record the [*Seeker's*] physiologic responses to certain questions. Some types of physiological responses are typically associated with 'lying'—although under the best conditions, one-third of innocent people 'fail' lie detector tests."

—Pflanzer & McMullen, <u>Galvanic Skin Response & The</u>
<u>Polygraph</u>
Lesson 9, Biopac Systems Inc., 2000

The quotation above appears in a manual of *"Physiology Lessons for use with the Biopac Student Lab (BSL)"* produced by a California-based educational-technology company, BIOPAC *Systems, Inc.* Their aim is replacing former analog methods of collecting "psychophysiological" (how the mind affects the body) research data with more economical digital tools that rely on a personal computer rather than stand-alone hardware. This effectually enables academic-students an ability to experiment with areas of medical science that previously required costly *chart-recorders* (used for traditional "polygraph") and *oscilloscopes* (for example, the ECG/EKG).

"Old-school" analog *GSR-Meters* (as described throughout this chapter) maintain solid popularity and practicality. However, in the past few decades, *"spiritual clearing"* Biofeedback practitioners have developed newer more modern versions that frequently integrate computers and "smart-phones." This is likely to be the trend into the future. It is not surprising that we now have many alternatives to the original devices developed by Mathison in the 1950's, and of course, Lafayette's professional models. Cost and availability is another factor. For example, the particular model used exclusively by the author at Mardukite Systemology Offices for the past several years—a Blue-Diamond-Dust *"Mark-VII Super Quantum"* refurbished from the *FreeZone*—would have required the original owner make a $4,000 donation to "The Church" to possess it. This is usually not a widespread issue, since an individual (that is not training to be a professional) really only works with a Meter alone by themselves when processing the upper-most levels.[‡]

For several years during the mid-1950's, Lafayette's courses and lectures did not include use of Meters. And nearly a decade later, the FDA militantly raided "The Church" and, among other things, confiscated all the unsold *"E-Meters."* These were eventually returned with the requirement that a disclaimer[*] be placed on them—but, the American-Medical-

---

[‡] "The Church" completed mass manufacture of a *'Mark-VIII Ultra'* behind-the-scenes by 2004. These were not made available to general members for another ten years. However, some of the higher-level Staff *'swapped out'* electronics in their *Mark-VII* with the new technology.

[*] *U.S. v. An Article of Device*; September 29, 1971—No. D.C. 1-63. "In a seizure action by the Government against the Hubbard E-Meter, the court ordered, *inter alia* [Latin—"*among other things*"], condemnation of the seized articles, and release of condemned E-Meters and literature to claimant for the purpose of bringing the devices and literature into compliance with the law (*Federal Food, Drug and Cosmetic Act*). The court further ordered that E-Meters be restricted for use only in bona fide religious counseling. Each E-Meter shall bear a warning, printed in 11-point type, permanently affixed to the front of the E-Meter, so that it is clearly visible when used: *The E-Meter is not medically or scientifically useful for diagnosis, treatment or prevention of any disease...*" The strangely worded message actually found on devices—and on a plate found at the front of every book issued since 1971—reads: "*The E-Meter, by itself, does nothing.*" You could almost make that statement toward any piece of matter.

Gestapo had continued monitoring Lafayette's practices since 1951, when he was charged with "unlicensed practice of medicine" during an "auditing" demonstration in New Jersey. Even today, many books released under the "New Age" genre—including our own—carry a disclaimer that they do not diagnose ailments, treat disease or replace professional medical advice. Although this is taken about as seriously as selling tarot cards and psychic services as "for entertainment purposes only," it is a critical factor in today's world.

Many *Biofeedback* and *GSR*-devices are on the market that do not possess the same features as Meters described in this chapter. Really though, many of them should not be considered "Meters"—acting more like "monitors," like a smoke detector. Those sold as "meditation trainers" or "stress-relaxation aids" likely resulted from a completely different type of experimental research and their applications seem contrary to our own. For example, clinical tests in some fields of psychology will show that relaxation elevates skin resistance—as does entering meditative states. Yet, in our work, increase in skin resistance essentially denotes greater tension and stress. So, why then do we work in the face of contradictory data in our Systemology? The short answer: contrary examples concern individuals that are not engaged in a *systematic processing session.*

Observation of this "paradox" demonstrates a basis for "*Reversal Theory,*" as pioneered in the 1970's by Dr. Michael Apter,√ a university professor of psychology and author of several books on the subject. The full nature of this theory is well beyond the scope of the present discourse—but it is dependent on basic motivation as a dichotomy, treated differently between two different states. In one state, the individual is operating in the normal wakeful every-day physical reality of action; in the other, a state of contemplative or analytical thought. Another way it is presented is the "means/ends" dichotomy—or even "journey/destinati-

---

√   In collaboration with psychiatrist/psychotherapist Dr. Ken Smith.

on." In several papers on the subject, it is even reduced to "playful" versus "serious"—but in terms of doing enjoyable things for the sake of doing them as opposed to engaging in an activity purely to reach or achieve a desired goal. While this sounds all fine and good, how does it relate to our Systemology?

As high-level *fragmentation* is already a state of energetic suspension and confusion (yielding lower states of *Beta-Awareness*), when we increase involvement, reach or arousal (by triggering heavier traumatic experiences), it produces stress, tension, anxiety and discomfort. In what might be considered "excitement" under other circumstances, we are pushing limits of tolerance while *systematic processing.* When an individual is in a relaxed state, the detachment or withdrawal from worldly matters is invited and generally pleasant. But when the same reaction is applied in *systematic processing*, the *Seeker* is "dodging" or moving away from what should be confronted, which produces tension and stress. This is why, in session, we are most interested in points when a *GSR-Meter* indicates a sudden reduction of resistance—or "fall"—because it denotes something that the *Seeker* is able to handle, reach for and is ready to confront; it denotes an increase in *Awareness* applied and a willingness to take responsibility. An increase or "rise" would indicate the opposite of this.

Of course, in order to have "falls" during a session there must be points when the Meter reads a rise, or that the Balance Point is a higher resistance. But, we are talking about *processing* each individual item or terminal, *imprinting incident* or event. A particular area or focus is indicated for *processing*, the needle (display) will indicate a reduction of resistance when the *Seeker* is no longer resisting the handling of it. A *Pilot* will keep an eye on the Meter to determine that a question or item is "*reading*" before it is *systematically processed.* This goes along with the answers a *Seeker* gives as well. *Processing* a "charged" terminal or incident continues so long as there is still a "read" (change) taking place. If there was no indicator or "read" to begin with, there would be no real way to gauge this; there would be no way to determine when a *Seeker* had flattened that *wave-action* (or energetic *"ridge"*).

A "ridge" is perhaps one of the most *solid-state* **waveform** patterns encountered when an individual is working with energies. It is essentially an energetic-mass formed from two energy-wave flows, typically in opposition to one another. In some ways, all of "matter" could be considered a highly condensed and compacted energetic "ridge"—and in all likelihood, that is how it came to be so in *beta-existence.* But rather than dissolving solid matter, we are concerned with *flattening* the "solidity" of the **collapsed wave-functions** that form and collect as "energetic-masses" around the individual.

The "stuck" *Mental Image Pictures* and "reactive" *imprinting* are formed on and as such "ridges." And they have a tendency to build up into greater and greater "masses" when left improperly handled, or in many cases, not managed at all. Essentially, this is what is being described in all of our previous *Systemology* material, in one way or another.

> • In *"Tablets of Destiny (Secrets Revealed)"* we examined the *emotional* qualities of *imprinting* and its nature in general.

> • In *"Crystal Clear (Handbook for Seekers)"* and *"Metahuman Destinations"* we *processed* the effects of *imprinting* on our *considerations* and *thoughts.*

> • In *"Imaginomicon (Approaching Gateways to a Higher Universe)"* we treated *Mental Imagery* blatantly and directly.

But in every case, we are still dealing with the same *fragmentation* phenomenon. *Here* we see it for what it is as its observable electronic properties. And:—

> when a *Seeker* is truly able and willing to handle, manage and/or confront the nature of their "stuff" *As-It-Is,* that increased *Awareness* is enough to "blow" it apart.

There are many types of experiments and training drills that can be conducted to understand more about the function of a *Meter*—and also to understand more about your 'subject' or *Seeker*. For example, in the BIOPAC manual quoted at the beginning of this section, a student instructs their subject to concentrate on each of a square sheet of colored paper, which is held two feet in front of their face; and *Biofeedback* is recorded for each. Sequential order of the colors presented are: *white, black, red, blue, green, yellow, orange, brown* and *purple.* A pause between each is necessary to get the baseline read again. This could be incorporated with additional questions to have some therapeutic value, but mostly it is for learning (and gaining experience) of the Meter itself.

Another common experiment is to learn the "yes"/"no" *Meter*-reads and reactions by working with a list of questions (or generating them at the time) for which there is no mystery about the answers. For example: Are you sitting down? Are we presently inside/outside? Do you drive a car/have a license to drive a car? But nothing that digs to deep under the surface. To get an even further handle on what is taking place when using a *Meter* in session and for Ethics (or Integrity Checkups), you can instruct the *Seeker* to intentionally "lie" about an answer to a question that is otherwise obvious. If they are sitting down—if they are indoors—have them answer that they aren't to each and see what and how things *read*.

SOME VERY BRIEF THOUGHTS ON POLITICS OF TRUTH
(A PERSONAL NARRATIVE AND INTERLOGUE)[*]

> "If you can't tell the truth to
> the people you care about the most,
> eventually you stop being able
> to tell the truth to yourself."
> —*Cassandra Clarke*
> *Mortal Instruments: City of Ashes*

"Truth was truth, whether I darkened my eyes to it or not."

"This earth appears to be a hell,
  or at best a planet condemned—
  A sort of purgatory..."

"Hide what you have to hide
  And tell what you have to tell.
  You'll see your problems multiplied
  If you continually decide
  To faithfully pursue
  The Policy of Truth."

(*Also used by Depeche Mode for their song "Policy of Truth"*)

—William Batchelder Greene, *1819–1878*
Individualist anarchist, Unitarian minister, soldier, writer
32° Scottish Rite Freemason, Massachusetts (1871)
33° Sov. Gr. Inspector-General of Northern U.S. Jur. (1872)

"Our *Systemology*, first and foremost, began with a study of 'systems.' It was not a play on words or to relate to the work of an already existent organization with a similar name. It was not even entirely my own invention, because an academic pursuit called *systematology* had already been established nearly a decade ago—and apparently branched off to become *cybernetics* and work used to advance other material technologies. But, I was concerned with the spiritual tech-

---

* Based on and quoting a "New Year's" lecture given by Joshua Free.

nologies and philosophies that could actually be applied and not just debated and theorized by a handful of intellectuals for their own 'mental masturbation' as we used to refer to it as. I didn't believe that the material sciences and New Age spirituality was working well enough in solving the affairs on Earth or the problem of the Human Condition—if anything, they were sealing folks into the mess even tighter, furthering the entrapment of Self into the Human Condition. But as a teenager at the time, living during an apex of New Age revival in the 1990's, I questioned my own potential efforts too. I mean: would the work I wanted to do bring an individual their spiritual freedom—or would it just be more empty hope for an 'enlightenment' that never comes?"

"At the time, a lot of the individuals I was surrounded with really didn't believe I was going to be doing anything innovative or significant during this lifetime. To them the whole question being, who was I, you know —and who were they that they would have happened to be on a first name basis with me. It was also quite difficult to advance anyone beyond what had already been established. It was easy to design, publish and distribute occult books that were cultural and/or ritual based—for example, traditions of Celtic Druidism. It was far more difficult to present a colorful enough 'creative psychology' or 'New Thought' that these type of ceremonial magicians and such would accept. I mean, I would expect that these Celtic Druids would have been *Systemologists*—not necessarily calling it that, but we are talking about the high-born intellectuals of Europe, credited with "systematizing the Celts." I would expect that the first established civic Human systems in Mesopotamia were also the product of an intensive intellectual knowledge of *Systemology* that, until recently, has primarily gone unnoticed."

"Nearly all of the elements that are effective in our *Systemology* relate back to the fundamentals that I developed, but kept to myself, as a teenager—thus over two decades in my past, now. But, there was not much I could think to *do* with it in the late 1990's, and it would take an entire decade for me to really try to synthesize any working knowledge of it for print-publications. Even in saying this, it has taken *three* different approaches to the subject before it caught on. The first attempt—'*Systemology 1.0*'—is still with us, but it is given as '*Systemology: The Original Thesis.*' While all of the theories and goals were adequately explained, it still left a *Seeker* wondering what to do with the knowledge. I'll admit that for a couple years even my own hat was thrown into that group. It wasn't until a few years later that I developed '*Systemology 2.0*' and released the title "*Reality Engineering*' (portions still appear in the appendix for '*The Systemology Handbook*'). Most of the critical previous elements were given more substance, but the presentation still lacked a certain demonstrable edge toward practical actualization. I did, however, start to notice a lot more of the Mardukite Alumni using the lingo in their everyday life. They knew there was *something* about all this, but I still had not fully driven in the nail yet. It took many more years of behind-the-scenes development before '*Tablets of Destiny*' and '*Crystal Clear*' could be presented—but it was obvious that now we had finally arrived at something that we could truly launch from. So much had gone into its unseen development that almost the entire Grade-III core took only a few months to refine and publish—and the rest, as they say, is history."

Seekers may well find humor in kick-starting new higher-level Wizard Grades with *optional* but-highly-suggested incorporation of *GSR-Metering*. This applies a more certain time-saving *Biofeedback Tech* toward accessing higher-level *Self-Honesty*. Of course, contrary to fantasy and enchantment themes denoted by its title, our "Wizard Grades" (*V*, *VI*, and *VII*) intend to provide *Seekers* a much needed "booster" for reaching Metahuman destinations—a much needed evolutionary *disillusion* and *dissolution* of what is otherwise an outdated sub-standard model for the Human Condition.

Some individuals will undoubtedly be taken aback—or even unpleasantly surprised—by suggestion of *GSR* as given within Mardukite Systemology *"Liber-3E"* (*this present book*) based on how such controversial devices have gained public attention in the past and the types of non-medical organizations that employ them; to ensure the protection of ourselves and our fellows *Seekers*, we of course, won't name names—but one in particular even sounds like "systemology." Certainly, some reaction is considered normal whenever we introduce new material or new directions of work—and we get it; and we forgive that.

Many *Seekers* are getting seasoned to those mild shocks that accompany the work by now. Especially given the way a *Seeker's* attention is so masterfully routed, piloted and directed across the entire span of Systemology materials thus far; not even mentioning the Mardukite **Master Grades** which precede it. However, to prevent solidifying any Self-imposed barriers or road-blocks, any remaining reactivity (if present) should be *processed-out* (much like we did with the subject of "religion" in the *"Crystal Clear" Liber-2B* handbook) as erroneous considerations—those based on something which must have been heard or picked up along the way, but of which is nothing more than a baseless opinion assimilated from someone else (who was probably in no better condition to make a wide-sweeping judgment in the first place).

Needless to say that any subject, field, religion or group invoking the name of certain science-fiction author and spiritual pioneer is headed straight into a battle-zone for religious freedom. But, if one is *Self-Honest*—if one does not seek to retaliate against the Suppressors in kind; if one is willing to press onward naked to the world carrying only the *Sword of Truth* by their side—then that particular warfront is paper-thin at best, entirely dependent on certain interpretations of copyrights and a misguided infiltrated and usurped group with a bottomless pocket of means to pursue maintaining **fallacious** interests in holding onto a *Monopoly on Truth*. Of course, it all still requires managing things intelligently and with tact—two things that seem counter-intuitive to what it means to be a teenager, especially at the end of the 20th Century.

"But, wouldn't you know it... I was listening to this song... and—okay, keep in mind I was 'Class of 2000' and so were most of my best friends. We were—or are—primed as the oldest year of the '*Millennial*' generation, yet we had been looking up to the Gen-X and they seemed so cool, but there was a separation. Even if only a few years difference, we had more in common with someone several years *younger* than us than we did with those graduating even a year or two sooner than us. We were born in the 1980's, but just young enough to not have been able to fully appreciate being '80s kids' or 'punk' or 'old-school Goths' and while in high-school, they released a volume of singles by *Depeche Mode* and I was listening to *Policy of Truth* and it got me thinking about how convoluted the whole matter of truth really is. Because there seems to be a question of whether or not to speak the truth with each other—to admit the truth of things. And given how much this Universe is built upon lies, the truth generally cannot be hidden for long, even if we think we will get away with it. And the matter of who we are and what we've done is a big part of that. The manner of my own work, starting very intently and intensely as a teenager and continuing through to the present also falls under this category. Although, in my case, I have often found that hiding truth in plain sight can also work quite well. For some reason it is just not accepted factually. Now, you've got it to where you try and present some element and the other person goes, yeah yeah, I saw '*The Matrix*' too."

"Concerning the sources of 'New Thought' inspiration, there are many *Seekers* mostly unaware of the 'other side of Reality'—what has been taken place for 70-years. Much of what I refer to in these statements is but a cute sentiment, albeit poetic. Putting that aside, there have been other *pioneers* in the past that have taken up similar life-paths, but of a different flavor—for example, the route once forged in public view by Dr. Timothy Leary. While considerably influential to me in my youth, well, what I am about to say is an oversimplification that somewhat misrepresents true beliefs and ideals that Leary (and myself) maintained, but: I make no such promise to a *Seeker* that they—or any random person on the street—will find personal enlightenment at the end of a twelve-hour trip on five-dollars worth of LSD. You might as well be hunting for a pot-of-gold at the end of a rainbow. Yet in a former time—actually, a former millennium even—I made certain to test (and retest; and, of course, triple-check again, to verify) those waters for myself, too. But, that element was a part of *my own personal path*—a path which at some point or another had required me to look beneath every rock and down every alleyway to gain a handle of certainty as a *Messenger* of something greater—something that none of these other routes were reaching as a definite destination. If something like that really worked across the boards, its inclusion would be a part of this work; but there's no guarantees there. It may have been a part of my own journey, but it is found nowhere directly on *The Pathway* that Systemology represents. And this is just one example... But the point is: *Systemology* is not just a chronicle of *my* trip or some interactive diary to enforce following in *my* footsteps, which traced a tortuous journey; *Systemolo-*

gy is the chronicle of us all—and for that reason *Seekers* have discovered that it speaks to them directly."

As you may have surmised at this juncture, development of this "Mardukite" brand and its related works up through the "lower ('Master') grades"—and now at the threshold of the Wizard—is a significant body of work that no one, other than the present author, truly saw coming. Although hints might have been dropped in one or another introduction or preface, the truth is that only the present author knew where it was headed when initial preparations were laid out in the late 1990's. At the same time, the most accessible literary presentations began to emerge at the apex of the "New Age Magickal Revival" by Joshua Free—then concealing himself behind the pseudonym *'Merlyn Stone'*.

Aside from using pseudonyms (which began while attending high school and leading some of the earliest "coven"-styled precursors to the Mardukite movement; and with a dozen individuals carrying copies of *"The Sorcerer's Handbook"* and such around school), the guise of the occult, New Age mysticism and emphasis on practical magic, ritualism, &tc., permitted a certain freedom from the *Policies of Truth*; particularly while the work demonstrated over the last two decades all remained in formative stages. There is not enough space allotted to this single discourse for a proper relay of what all takes place behind-the-scenes or beneath-the-surface of the *Material World* at large—at least not enough in exclusion to other materials to ready a *Seeker* to effectively fight in the true *Invisible War* of our times.

The *Politics of Truth* is deserving and worthy of an entirely separate book dedicated to it—because the general public, even many of the New Age practitioners, believes that "we are all in this together"; that everyone proposing enlightenment is on the same page and that we are working together toward the same ends. But, for the most part, it is just one more "industry" among many that keeps the Grand Game going. And if you have been paying attention, then you will know how to participate and play it out and still remain *Self-Honest*.

UNDERSTANDING GSR-METERS & HOW TO READ THEM

> "When material [a mass or *'ridge'*] is restimulated by events or in session—if the material is too hard to experience or confront, it is repressed and there will not be an instantaneous response on the meter. The *ridge* will remain in restimulation but out of consciousness, until attention is directed to the item and it is confronted. This is a flight away from the material. If the client is able to view the material, some of the suppressed emotional charge is released, causing a *fall* in resistance. This happens instantly. However, mental defenses may kick-in and cause a backing off or resistance to the material, because its content may be hard to face. This stops the release of charge and the resistance may *rise*—still accessible but the client is fighting against it. A *rise*, then, relates to material that is being confronted, but is also fought against. If viewed directly, the contents may overwhelm the client, and the client moves away from it in fear, which causes high emotional arousal and *fall* in resistance, followed by a blocking-off of the material and subsequent *rise* in resistance and suppression of the experience."
> —Peter Shepherd, *GSR Meter Course*
> *Tools for Transformation, 2001*

In the late 1990's, the present author had the behavior of *Biofeedback Meters* demonstrated to them by an experienced individual. This introduction provided a great deal of certainty prior to reading, or being exposed to, oppositional literature and statements. Is there definitive proof that "heavy thoughts" are literally a "heavy mass" on an individual, complete with "electronic resistance"? Not necessarily. However, the activity seems to reflect that there is a relationship (a "positive coefficient" as you academicians would call it) concerning what *we* classify as *fragmentation*—and it may be that any opposition to this fact stems from a philosophic-semantic issue that does not concern us in the least so long as *we* can observe, record and communicate a reliable interconnected pattern of results (as we understand them) within *Systemology*.

> "The *Meter* was demonstrated to me while I was seated comfortably and holding the two *'cans'* (*electrodes*). So, he asks me to 'squeeze the cans'—and I did. A few seconds later, he repeated that—and I believe this happened three or four times; each time he made a small adjustment of the sensitivity. The final time he showed me that a deliberate squeeze caused the needle to move about two centimeters or about a third of the way on the *fall* or right-hand side of the dial-display. I thought, okay... He reaches over and gives my arm a little pinch and I watched the needle practically peg the pin on the *fall* side. A small adjustment of the Balancing-Arm and the needle was in the 'set' or 'balance' range again. Then he says, 'Now, go back to the moment I pinched you.' Sure enough, the needle swung over just as it had done before simply by directing attention to that moment. He said to go through the event, play it out so to speak, in my mind —and I did. He repeated for me to 'go back' and this time the needle swung, but not as severely. After resurfacing and confronting the event four or five times, the needle barely registered. I thought to myself: this is something I want to know more about..."

Even if our scientific semantics is not completely where it should be, this simple demonstration illustrates a lot of what is discussed in our preliminary Grades of Systemology. Does it always require this level of mathematical precision to determine success? Well, certainly not, or those previously using the *Tablets of Destiny*, *Crystal Clear* and *Metahum-*

man Destinations material would not have found any success. And we know for a fact that those who have utilized our work and properly participating with their presence to the procedures *have* found enough positive gain to keep them progressing and interested in pursuing this *Pathway.* What a *Biofeedback Meter* such as this allows for is a greater certainty, greater accuracy and a vast improvement in the amount of time it takes to "get something handled" and move forward with the work.

When working with a *GSR-Meter* for *systematic processing*, the most common term is "read"—such as when you hear someone say, "That *reads.*" More often than not it is indicating a decrease in resistance or "*fall.*" There are also rare instances where the *Meter*, or more accurately, the observed *needle*, doesn't read anything at all for anything no matter what you do. The term "stuck" is often applied and all this means is that the *Seeker* is not offering their presence to the session. There is a break in communication or reality for whatever reason. If such is truly the case, even the "pinch test" described above would not necessarily register anything. It is important to know whether or not a reaction is going to read, otherwise it gives an illusion that there is no "charge" on something that otherwise will be blown over—or *flown* over—when it should have been handled. Operating a session in this way, when the *Seeker* is not providing presence, will actually reduce a *Seeker's* participation even further because the session, methods and *Pilot* (ability) loses credibility—even at "subconscious" levels; even when the *Seeker* is the one causing, allowing or validating the break in reality or attention themselves.

So long as the sensitivity is kept constant—checked at the beginning with the "squeeze and release" tests described above—the *reads* on a *Meter* are able to be compared to other *reads.* For the "*falls*" you would be looking for the "largest" read or "*largest fall*" in relation to other reads. This is important when you are seeking to scout out a particular answer among variables. If you were to ask a *Seeker* which of their former jobs contributed the most fragmentation, there may be some "charge" on more than one answer; therefore you are looking for the biggest reaction or *read* when each is given.

We frequently use the term *resurfacing* to denote bringing something up from beneath-the-surface. The quicker the response from the *Meter*, the closer something is to the surface. If something doesn't read, a *Pilot* should avoid focusing further attention on it. Of course, this does not mean that the *channel* is clear or there is no energetic charge held on the terminal in question—but it is not accessible or presently within the *Seeker's* reach or tolerance level to confront at that given time. Not to mention, without a *read*, there is no guarantee a *Pilot* can determine full erasure of that *fragmentation* or an **End Point** on other types of processing. This is, of course, what we mean about continuing a particular process or area of work so long as it is producing change in Awareness, but not to overrun.

When using a *GSR-Meter* it is a little easier to determine when an End Point is reached. It is critical to fully eliminate "reactive charge" from anything that either does *resurface* or that can be made to *resurface* so long as it is *reading* on the Meter. If a *Pilot* doesn't treat a process through to finality, the "Universe" (society, &tc.) most certainly will keep running it and the *Seeker* will become increasingly withdrawn.

For the purpose of establishing a standard for recording a session, we have established a chart for our *Systemology* that applies to many models of *GSR-Meter* used for 'spiritual defragmentation'. On such models, the dial-display has a 90-degree range—a quarter of a circle—illustrated with a 9-centimeter arc of potential motion: *one centimeter* per *ten-degrees*. In most cases, the area given to read the *"falls"* constitutes half of the *Meter*. It is the differences between reactions in this zone that are of primary interest for the session and its records. Although not all practitioners will have the same interpretive classification for *reads*, using our chart offers the greatest stability or consistency in what we are looking for.

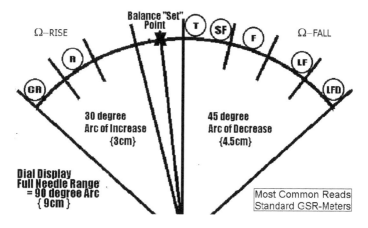

The Balance-Point or Set-Point provides a BASELINE reading and it reflects the basic state of the *Seeker* when at "rest" presently in the session, without being aroused or directly stimulated by inner thoughts or the environment, &tc. A *read* is then taken when the needle moves off of, or out of, the small 15-degree region given for this. Sometimes a TINY TICK is *read* within this region, but if all session activity remains that close to the Balance-Point, it may be that the sensitivity is too low. The answer to "Does it read?" can also be considered the answer to whatever yes/no question you pose as a PCL. Therefore a *read* typically means "yes."

The Physical Universe is solidified by compacted matter that philosophically are "lies." When an individual is confronting (facing up to) the truth about something, they are practically disintegrating it and hence you get a reduced mass and reduced resistance ("*fall*"). Therefore, it is possible to get an increase-decrease fluctuation during a single process. A PCL results in a FALL, meaning there is some level of energetic "charge" available for the *Seeker* to confront. But then they could find that while examining it, they suddenly feel "resistive" which literally adds "resistance" demonstrated by a RISE. However, if the *Seeker* overcomes this withdrawal and continues to confront it, you will continue to see a FALL (usually a "LARGE/LONG FALL"/"LF") until it finally and significantly "BALANCE DROPS" (requiring movement of the *Balancing-Arm* to keep it on the *Meter dial-display*). Since this is a LARGE/LONG FALL and a DROP it is often written "LFD" or LFBD. The basic *reads* as they appear marked on our chart are as follows:

(R) RISE (R)

Any movement of the needle on the left side of the "Set Point" (BA); no additional **differentiation** is made—unless it is a "Continuous Rise" (CR)—just the fact that the needle and resistance is *rising* (has *risen*). If it never did you would not get any "Balance-Arm action" at all in processing. An initial increase in resistance to a question means literally increased resistance *to* the question; it can *fall* once a *Seeker* permits themselves to confront it *As-It-Is.*

Since a *rise* generally indicates a *Seeker* does not want to confront what has been presented, it is best *not* to announce this *read* when it occurs. If pressed further in that direction the *Seeker* will break with reality and communication and potentially go "out of session."

(CR) CONTINUOUS RISE (CR)

A large enough *rise* to the left side of the meter that requires the Balance-Arm to be adjusted to keep the needle within range of the dial-display. A question that immediately "stops" a "rising needle" is a change in characteristics and should be considered the same as a *Fall.*

Sessions where the *reads* do not seem to be coming as expected may require monitoring such changes of characteristics rather than other *reads*. So, if the needle is continuously *rising* but a question stops its motion—or it has been doing nothing but then decides to dance a jig— this is the indicative pattern change.

(BA) or (BP)   BALANCE-ARM SET POINT   (BA) or (BP)

The reading taken when the armature fixes the needle on the set point (or at least in the balanced range). If *Low* BA/BP—is below "2.0" (5000 Ω)—exceptionally decreased resistance possibly hyper-vigilant or overwhelmed; If *High* BA/BP—above "4.5" (35,000 Ω)—increased resistance is possibly withdrawal, dissociation and/or detachment.

If the BA/BP is *High* at the start of the session, the *Seeker's* attention is already directed on some "mass" elsewhere. You can start to free up these attention units by two-way communication with the *Seeker* about "where" their attention is. "Do you have your attention on anything?" "Is there anything you would like to tell me?" "Since your last session, is there anything you would like to tell me about?"

Although "solo-metering" is not trained for this *Grade-IV pre-A.T.* level of work, when combining two electrodes with a coupler —making certain they do touch—to hold in one hand, the BA/BP will be higher than standard (by a factor of as much as "0.5" higher) reads. Therefore what might be "2.1" when each electrode is held in its own hand, would then potentially be around "2.6" when soloing with one hand.+

(X)   NO/NULL READ   (X)

As the name suggests, there is no read and the needle remains at rest at the "Set Point" (BA). "No charge" or an answer of "no" should be distinguishable from a "stuck needle" based on characteristics of meter reads throughout the session up to this point or from a proper session setup that guarantees the *Seeker* is participating or has presence in session.

(T)   TICK/TINY READ   (T)

A rapid *fall* of less than a few millimeters to the right of the "Set Point" (BA); as the name suggests, it barely counts as read. It may or may not even leave the "Balanced Range." If you get a small "trace read" from a question, trying varying the wording. If the same small "tick" or "tiny read" is all that occurs after three inquiries, move on.

(SF) SMALL/SHORT FALL (SF)

Up to one millimeter (or ½ an inch) *fall* to the right side of the "Set Point" (BA). Any amount of *fall* is still a *fall;* if you are still getting a *read* after several runs or exhausted question/answer, the *Seeker* still "hasn't told all" or else you are dealing with a "past life" or an area they do not "consciously know about."

If a decent *read* occurs when the *Seeker* hasn't said anything, inquire about it. "What was that there?" "What did you just think of there?" "Did you have a thought there?"

(F) FALL (F)

One to two millimeters (½ inch to one inch) *fall* to the right side of the "Set Point" (BA). Any length of *fall* is a standard *read* or "Yes" answer to your question; for some techniques the largest/longest read is the answer.

(LF) LARGE/LONG FALL (LF)

Two to six millimers (1 to 3 inches) *fall* to the right side of the "Set Point" (BA). Among several possible *reads*, the largest/longest *read* or *fall* is the answer.

(LFD/LFBD) LARGE/LONG FALL BALANCE DROP (LFD/LFBD)

A large enough *fall* to the right side of the meter that requires the Balance-Arm to be adjusted to keep the needle within range of the dial-display. A massive discharge of this caliber accompanies the *Seeker* having confronted (faced-up-to) or seeing (knowingly duplicating creation of) something *As-It-Is*, thereby duplicating and eradicating what and where something is by consciously placing one's own there—seeing it for what *It Is* on one's own volition.

148

GSR-METERS APPLIED TO SYSTEMATIC PROCESSING[*]

> "If the [Seeker] knew about the subconscious reactive contents of the mind, they wouldn't be subconscious or reactive. But the *GSR-Meter* responds to the reactive emotional charge. Hence, you don't follow up something unless it gives a read. You don't let the [Seeker's] analytical (cognitive) mind control the session or give it free reign to talk about anything it likes. It is a [Pilot's] responsibility to control the session. The [Pilot] has more control over the [Seeker's] case, since the [Seeker] is influenced by the case."
>
> —Peter Shepherd, <u>GSR Meter Course</u>
> *Tools for Transformation, 2001*

This entire unit of our book has provided a tremendous amount of basic fundamentals regarding history, purposes and usage of *GSR-Meters* for personal development when applied to *our systematic processing*. Mathison's own work "*Super-Visualization*" includes a sporadic "session script" that offers examples of what one might expect when applying *GSR-Meters* to standard methods similar to our own presentation in previous *Systemology* texts. Use of a *Meter* does not in itself solve the matter of getting the *Seeker* to participate *presence* in sessions, with attention fully on *processing*; there are no substitutes for skillfully *Piloting* a *Seeker*—it must be learned and practiced. This includes certainty of handling a *Meter* when applied to processing, which is best gained by experience.

Having the *Seeker* "squeeze the cans" (and then release) is a popular way of setting/adjusting the sensitivity before a session really begins. Once begun, it is best if it does not have to be readjusted. When you are rapidly comparing relative lengths of various *falls*, the sensitivity must remain constant. There are ways of

---

* Strongly based on Volney Mathison's "*Super-Visualization (formerly 'The Manual of Electropsychometry')*" revised 1956 edition.

testing this before a formal start of session. And then there are also instances (especially in *Ethics Processing* for *Personal Integrity*) when you really want to see if a question is getting a solid *read* or not. You can always raise the sensitivity for that particular PCL, but make sure to return it to where it was afterward.

If everything that you are asking or saying is getting large reads, you may need to turn the sensitivity down. A simple determinant of basic stress levels can be used at the beginning to check this. Simply as: "How are you going to feel about my asking you a lot of personal questions?" You aren't really concerned about the answer given so much as the read on the *Meter*. In fact, on an episode of the British comedy "*I.T. Crowd,*" a "stress expert" is demonstrating just how little it takes to experience stress using a similar type of *GSR-Meter*. All he says is "Alright, I am now going to ask you a very personal question." And the needle surges very strongly. He doesn't actually ask anything else; the demonstration (as described) speaks for itself. If there is a strong *read* in response to this, it is likely that the *Seeker* has experienced uncomfortable interrogation in the past, either from a family member or some other source. It is helpful if communication can be used between the *Pilot* and *Seeker* to quiet these *reads* before proceeding.

If a *Seeker's* attention is not directed precisely on the session and PCLs, there is no way to determine what the *reads* on a *Meter* actually pertain to. Having the *Seeker* acknowledge the *Pilot*—a reality on the fact that the *Pilot* is the *Pilot*—is quite critical for the *Pilot* being able to get (and keep) the *Seeker* in session. There is at least one key reason why this is sometimes difficult— and this can be checked with the *Meter* prior to a true session start. *Pilot* asks: "Do I remind you in some way of a person you have known whom you feared or disliked?" If there is no *read* on that, or if there is only a *tiny tick*, consider rephrasing the PCL slightly: "Is there anything about me that is similar to some person that bothered or injured you in the past?" If any of these types of questions indicates a "yes," then *defragment* the line using basic communication to illustrate differences as with the previous question on being asked questions. Resolving things like this is, of course, critical for success; but it also directly facilitates getting the Seeker to participate with *presence* in the session.

As a chiropractor, Mathison's initial interests for using an *Elctropsychometer* pertained to the physiological body long before concepts of *spiritual defragmentation* became **paramount**. Therefore, in his manual—prior to the *Test Questionnaire* (given hereafter)—he describes a progressive *'Deep Meditation' technique* that is otherwise very similar to *'Energetic Body Scanning'*. The *Pilot* would give the PCL: "Toes, left foot, relax."[‡] The *Seeker* would then silently deliver the PCL/message to the *genetic vehicle* and report back with "Okay" after having done so. The *Pilot* closes that communication cycle with an acknowledgment ("Thank You") and begins the next: "Now, ankle, left foot, relax." And onward in this fashion they continue, treating each portion of the body. If at any point the *Pilot* sees a "sharp needle surge" on the *Meter* in relation to a certain part of the body, nothing is said, but a notation is made. Once the list of all body areas is completed, the *Pilot* returns to those which were indicated and if the unrest still persists, additional attention is given to them with the command "Be at ease."

‡   Alternatively, "Let go" or "Let go of the tension" could be used for this PCL in place of "relax."

EXPLORATORY TECH. FOR SYSTEMATIC PROCESSING*
OPENING ASSESSMENT QUESTIONNAIRE EXAMPLE

> "A sharp prolonged meter surge on *'How do you feel about your name?'* indicates one of two things: the (*Seeker*) is using a false, an assumed, or an altered name—or—more commonly, the (*Seeker*) dislikes their name for some specific reason which they can readily clarify. A disliked name has some unpleasant or silly connotation or association. Sometimes a name is changed to forget a hated parent, a past mate, or the like. Meter surges on such situations are all significant and should be discussed until tension on them subsides. Laughter, yawns and sighs will cause major needle surges, owing to flash metabolic effects, and may, in general, be disregarded. Do not permit the (*Seeker*) to tap on the electrode with finger or thumb. Minor needle surges may merely indicate mental activity. Major surges indicate areas of pain or tension."
>
> —Volney Mathison, *Super-Visualization*
> *Manual of Electropsychometry, 1956*

We conclude the present unit of our book with the original *Test Questionnaire* that appears in Mathison's *Electropsychometry Manual* from 1956. Strong *reads* or "surges" (as he calls them) should be reduced with *processing-style* communication (as learned throughout our professional *Systemology* texts). As an "assessment," this is really meant to "open a case" and not necessarily "solve" every aspect of a *Seeker's* life. It allows a *Pilot* to get a general idea of where significant trouble-spots are. An attempt should be made, however, to reduce the "charge" on anything found to give major *reads* before continuing on.

1. How do you feel about your name?
2. What is your occupation? How do you feel about it?

---

* Strongly based on Volney Mathison's "*Super-Visualization (formerly 'The Manual of Electropsychometry')*" revised 1956 edition.

152

3. How do you feel about your mother? About your father?

4. What sort of person do you fear? Hate?

5. Mention, by way of example,* one of the worst things that has happened to you.

6. What do you think of a person that commits suicide?[†]

7. Have you ever been in a hospital?

8. Have you ever been injured in an accident?

9. Whom did you hate or fear most when you were a child?

10. Mention some things you are very anxious about or that you feel should not occur. Mention some things you would fight or struggle against to keep them from happening.

11. Who loves you?

12. Who used to love you, but no longer does?

13. Can you think of a time when you wished someone would love you?

14. Do you feel remorse, regret or blame over the way you have treated some person? Mother? Father? Wife? Husband? &tc.

15. If you were writing a novel and you had to depict some injurious thing happening to a baby or a child, what would have this thing be?

16. Have you ever been struck or severely beaten?

17. What do you think of a homosexual person?[√]

∞ *"By way of example."* We interpret this to mean a non-specific type.

† Mathison indicates here that "sharp needle action" may mean the (*Seeker*) is or has been a "suicide hazard." In a later remark, he states that a "heavy surge" indicates the (*Seeker*) has lost someone close to them that way, or—"and more commonly"—that the (*Seeker*) has either attempted or considered it themselves. He recommends that the cause of this needle reaction be uncovered and explored (via communication) until "discharged or reduced" before continuing on with the questionnaire.

√ This was written during a period of time when such was commonly and socially considered "deviant sexual behavior," just as "masturbation" was.

18. How do you think women feel about you?

19. How do you think men feel about you?

20. How do you think children feel about you?

21. Have you ever been through an unhappy love experience?

22. Do you love your wife/husband?‡

23. How do you think your wife/husband feels about you?

24. Have you ever been attacked or severely shocked sexually?*

25. Are you satisfied with your present sexual relations?

26. Have you ever had a bitter quarrel with a man? Woman? Mention actual incidents.

27. What do you think about the use of contraceptives? Abortions?

28. What do you think about illegitimate children?

29. What do you think of a woman who is frigid? Or a man who is impotent?

30. What do you think of a sexual sadist? Masochist?

31. Have you ever been jeered at, made fun of, or painfully rejected?

32. What things do you keep doing that you wish you didn't do?

33. What changes do you wish to make in yourself?

34. Mention three goals or ambitions that you have wished to achieve—and which you have achieved.

35. Mention three goals or ambitions that you have wished to achieve—and which you have not achieved.

---

‡ This is asked without the "mate" present. Mathison remarks that "surges on this may not indicate lack of love"—rather, they *do* but tension is attached, such as situations where the couple "fights too much" or they "fear losing" them.

* Mathison remarks later on that "if the (*Seeker*) registers tension on some of the sexual-area questions, it may not be advisable to explore causes or details unless the (*Pilot*) is certain they have the trust and confidence of the (*Seeker*)." Mathison is mainly concerned here about situations where the (*Pilot*) is male and the (*Seeker*) is female—or vice versa.

appendix

+ Toward a Strong Systemology Society +
+ Systemology & Personal Integrity +
+ Book of Law of the New World +
+ A Creed of Mardukite Zuism +
+ A Systemology Glossary +
+ Suggested Reading +

:: TOWARD A STRONG SYSTEMOLOGY SOCIETY ::
ORGANIZATIONAL ETHICS STANDARDS[‡]
WIZ-0 GENERAL INSTRUCTION

As stated in the original *Mardukite Zuism* introductory booklet:[*]

> "The greatest good contributes to the greatest continuation of optimum existence and survival for the greatest *Sphere* of inclusion."

This means by protecting and maintaining the integrity of a strong and healthy *organization—"Org,"* or *"Society"* as we often term it—we "best contribute to its continuation." And mostly all who have *"Self-Honestly"* participated in this *Pathway* will agree that our *Mardukite* and *Systemology* work is worthy of persistence.

It is each individual's responsibility to provide *Self-Honest* support to the *Organization* that has assisted them in realizing *Self-Honesty* (whether directly or by way of print-publications). This expectation appears within the very *"Creed"* of *Mardukite Zuism* (and *Systemology*):

> "We support the continuation of, and proper communication of, the true legacy of 'Human' history—and a fundamental ability of every 'Human' to realize that they are a 'Free Spirit' occupying a 'Free Zone' of Self-Determinism."

We can be certain that any 'group' (much like an 'individual') carries its own a calculable *"Beta-Awareness Score"* representative of its "general health"—and the *Mardukite Org* is no exception. Maintaining proper 'Utilitarian Ethics' in

---

[‡] A revised facsimile based on original supplemental handouts written by Joshua Free for the *Mardukite Academy of Systemology* during the *"Intro to the Wizard's Way: Ethics and Beyond"* R&D cycle, which was active July 2021 through January 2022 at *Mardukite Babylonia SLV Borsippa HQ.*

[*] Material reissued in (*appendices* of) other Systemology/Zuism titles.

functional operations, the *Organization* ensures we maintain "Order" and (by demonstration of the *Spheres*) protect the integrity of 'individual' Seekers themselves—along with their 'homes' and families. In total, this supports a healthier 'Humanity'.

In some regards, the *Mardukite Org* represents 'dangerous' work—but only when misunderstood; either out of sheer ignorance, or blatant misrepresentation. Many individuals mistake our *Organization* as idealizing a *"Cure"* or *"Help"*—yet our methods quite literally epitomize the true spirit of *"Self-Help."* We assist navigating a survey of the *Seeker's* own considerations. Breakthrough-insights and new realizations are still up to each individual to wholly actualize themselves. We are not substituting "religion" for "Truth"; no "pills" or "magic spells" replace necessity of *actual* processing (work). Otherwise, an individual would simply be even more the "effect" of some outside, other-determined or enforced idea, rather than "originating" their own Reality Agreements.

When it comes to executing clear judgment and evaluation, our greatest asset is increased *Actualized Awareness.* This is important for development and security of an *Organization*, for a healthy and peaceful *Home*, and for a happy *Individual.* It is equally important that we have "true knowledge" in which to evaluate from—and that our process of evaluation is free of *fragmentation.* This is particularly important when involved with other individuals or their placement into positions and roles. **Beta-Awareness Test** *(BAT)* scores may be of particular significance here (where it concerns our own organization).

Human lives are composed of facts—pieces of data. All of the available data an individual knows about someone else is brought together to form the composite image or overall opinion that is carried in future considerations and interactions. In the future, when our underground *Organization* grows and requires greater centralization, it may be necessary to keep files on everyone and everything that we encounter—both personally and as an *Organization*. In the meantime, most of this data-storage and evaluation is handled with personal memory. Our heightened *Awareness*, more often than not, contributes to "right judgment." Those situations where it does not: we are often "too close" or carry too much "emotion" in those instances to always see clearly. This is another one of those little-spoken-of shortcomings of the Human Condition.

When necessary, the use of "Private Investigators" is preferred to personal involvement of our members and ranks. As many of the basic facts should be organized ahead of time—but where it concerns time and resources, the most serious instances generally require a P.I. to be most effective. This should only be used for specific applications and not for general circumstances. One key instance that always demands further investigation is any individual that openly communicates and/or acts against the *Organization*. In this wise, it is critical to know as many facts as possible about someone that is intentionally setting themselves up as opposition. In any instance where legal action is not to be taken, then open posting and wide distribution of collected data is preferred to stashing it away.

Δ Δ Δ Δ Δ Δ

History demonstrates that one key revolutionary turning point is the most destructive on a wider scope, whether in an organization or for society (civilization) as a whole: *fragmented humans* in *large masses* with *crude weapons.* This is what has forced out the "gods" represented in all ancient mythologies. Certainly the "gods" had their own issues with each other, but what changed things the most from the *'way they were'* to the *'way they are'* now is exactly as just described. Usually this does not happen all at once or "come from nowhere" as it were—there are obviously small demonstrations, revolts and coups that all lead up to it.

At an "organization" level, it is the responsibility of *Organization Members* to safeguard themselves and the property (physical and intellectual) of the *Org* in order to ensure its continuation.

In the United States, the right to **protest** is protected under the First Amendment—and this applies to all sides. As carefully explained to the present author by those involved in such demonstrations, these rights apply the strongest in "traditional public forums" that include streets, sidewalks and parks. When it concerns private property, such as that of an organization, uphold of this right is discretionary to the owners of the property. For example, in a public park you may photograph anything "in plain view." However, if held on private property, it again is at the discretion of the property owners.

The idea that an individual organizing a protest requires a permit is a misconception. However, that being said, a "peaceful protest" is not allowed to block or inhibit the flow of traffic. If a march or demonstration is to do so, then a permit *is* required. When not "permitted" a law-enforcement officer does have the authority to have you move out of the way of automobile traffic. Another instance requiring a permit would be an assembly or rally that intends to use "sound amplification" of any kind—such as a P.A. System (and potentially a megaphone). This information is provided because we cannot definitively predict the future of our *Org*, nor how it will be viewed once its infrastructure and purpose publicly extends beyond the written word.

> Remember that as a *Systemologist*,
> you represent the full body
> of the *organization* and its *membership*
> in your everyday life.
> *Conduct yourself accordingly*.

Concerning law enforcement representatives: *respect them—or in the case of heavily fragmented one's, respect the position they represent.* Although they do become conditioned over time to "suspect everyone" and generally get to handle the "worst" of how humanity behaves, even this must first begin with fragmented individuals unable to control themselves properly. *Fragmentation* is spread like a disease. If all individuals were able to conduct their actions in line with the *Ethics* illustrated in this book, we would still employ peace officers, but their jobs would be much easier. Any individual put under intense stress and strain is at risk for trigger *reactive-responses*; so don't give them a hard time.

To ensure the highest caliber of behavior, safety and legality when conducting protests, one of the leading activist organizations on the planet, known as *Anonymous*, expresses five key points when training their members for demonstrations: 1) *Respect Police*; 2) *Never use violence*; 3) *Never threaten violence*; 4) *Do not throw anything*; and 5) *Do not be insulting.* If our Organization—and its membership—can execute the same tact in their behavior (and when encountering opposition) it will always be the *other side* that comes out looking criminal. We are not a criminal organization—and there are no laws governing against replacement of a standard-issue Human population with *Metahumans.* If given the means we could "upgrade" the entire planet to *Metahuman* status within a single generation—but, just do your *Self-Honest* best. That's all anyone can ask of you.

162

:: SYSTEMOLOGY OF PERSONAL INTEGRITY ::
TECH REPORT FOR SYSTEMOLOGY PILOTS[‡]
GRADE IV/V WIZARD-0/1 ROUTE-3E/0
RESPONSIBILITY & JUSTIFICATION

A *Self-Honest* and "Awakened" *Seeker* needs only to look out in the world around us to see just how far down a dwindling spiral the Human Condition has progressed. Yet, in looking out, it seems just as critical that we are looking "in"—as the world that is manifested "out there" is an agreement of participation by what is going on "in here" and there really is no distinction between the two when we get right down to it. We all strongly benefit from the fact that at its basic state, the *Alpha Spirit* is actually righteous and good—if not otherwise *amoral* down here when serving a higher Ethic— simply working to get along in the continuation of its own existence. Were this not the case, we would have no chance at rehabilitating presence and *Awareness* of the actual *Self* that is behind the helm and restoring to it the full control of how we experience the *beta-existence* that we each participate in maintaining as reality.

Although programmed purposes and implanted goals are treated more directly at higher level Wizard Grades (because they pertain to lives prior to this one), it is easy to see that this subject reoccurs sporadically within our *Systemology* texts (and Grades) all along the way. Even in "*Crystal Clear (Handbook for Seekers)*" we began to ask a *Seeker* if the goal and motivation for their behavior is actually their own —*Self-determined*—or does it come from another—*Other-determined*—source. Accumulated involvement in dangerous situations, states of confusion, unjust destruction and being

---
[‡] A revised facsimile based on original Tech Reports compiled by Joshua Free for the *Mardukite Academy of Systemology* during the completion of the "*Intro to The Wizard's Way: Metahuman Ethics and Beyond*" cycle of developmental work at *Mardukite Babylonia SLV Borsippa HQ* in January 2022; officially issued in February 2022.

at the effect end of faulty—or blatantly false—information, all lend to fragmented purposes that may very well be painted to appear "for our own good." Instead they are actually non-survival (or counter-survival) oriented, leading us away from routes to achieve "greater heights"—higher more ideal states of *Beingness*—including the "Universe" preceding this one.

As ancient Babylonian Star-Gate lore suggests—and even the better known Judaic Kabbalah based on it—our *Awareness as Self* has descended a great many "Spheres of Existence," each one a little more condensed and a little more solid, and *fragmentation* carried with us certainly reflects that—becoming more rigid and fixed each time. Again, some of this has been done *to* us, implanted by a class of beings seeking to seal away our access to their realm. But, once this is the case, we are quite effective in doing it to ourselves and each other. This very pattern is what constitutes our occupation of *Awareness* and POV to a "prison" or "penalty" Universe such as the one treated around us as *beta-existence*. But, of course, we have descended to a lower grade *beta-existence here* than what was once considered former, which is only slightly referenced within pre-Wizard Grades of Systemology as the "Magic Universe" or "Magic Kingdom."

Just as we certainly did not all-at-once "fall from grace" of our perfected *Alpha* state, so must we *ascend* on a gradient scale—each carefully mapped step guaranteeing certainty for occupying our *Beingness* or *Awareness* in higher universes. It is obvious then that it is into the "Magic Kingdom" that we next seek to open a "Gateway." We have moved in that direction since the beginning, carefully releasing our hold on—and the hold on us—as we progress through the gradients of Systemology. Material given in "*Imaginomicon*" (*Liber-3D*) builds up from premises first established in "*Crystal Clear (Handbook for Seekers)*" (*Liber-2B*), just as the present volume (*Liber-3E*) advances upon where we have successfully reached with

"*Metahuman Destinations*" (*Liber-Two*). All of which are, in turn, treating a fundamental development of ledges to reach upward from.

For a *Seeker* that is 'approaching' the Wizard Grades, there is no doubt that there are amazing and fantastical vistas yet to be explored within our work. This present "*Way of the Wizard*" volume is one of several checkpoints along the *Pathway*. But it is entirely critical for any lasting success in the higher ranks and levels of if of our *Systemology*. By reclaiming a true Ethic—by resolving the matters of *Hostile-Acts* and *Hold-Backs* that are determinable from *this* lifetime—the way forward is cleared much faster.

The *Pilot* must address any and all "*Problems*" that a *Seeker* has their 'present attention' (*Pressence*) on—focus on the "*elephant in the room*" (*factual/actual* or *imagined/realized*) before addressing other considerations. The subject of "Problems" is taken up in "*Metahuman Destinations*," but the truth is that the lower on the *Beta-Awareness Scale* an individual is, the more of their attention and sense of *Beingness* is wrapped up or entangled with problems—the more problems they perceive they have which are not solved. In fact, the lower a person is in *Awareness*, the more insistent they are that the problems have to be solved "right now." [If the GSR's *Balance Point* is high at the start of session, *do not* conduct '*standard processing*'; find out what the *Seeker's* attention is on and/or what "*Loss*" they are 'sad'/'upset' about. No other 'systematic' gains will occur while a *Seeker* is in this position.] In order to dissolve significance of emotional entanglement, the *Seeker* should be prompted to identify as many aspects of the event, time and place *As-It-Is*.

In the instance of Goals and Purposes, the problems are often hidden or buried from view—they are not "confronted" and when using GSR in processing, they cause the needles to "*rise*" significantly. Basically, the individual is increasing their resistance against whatever it is they don't want to face. We might say it indicates being overwhelmed. This is where we find the "breaks" in communication and/or reality. This is why our *Acension* is handled on a gradient scale—an individual must have reality on it—realization—before they can find themselves confronting the *actuality.*

Major *Self-determined* life-changes (not necessarily enforced) —or actions/movements—are generally preceded by a major confusion. These are moments when *Awareness* is reduced and therefore susceptible to programming, encoding and implanting. The same thing could be said for physical trauma, shock or unconsciousness. The effects on a *Seeker* can be reduced if the "imprinting incident" (*&tc.*) is resurfaced—but it must be at the point of origination, the very first moment or instance of the event. Otherwise the results will not be permanent. It is not unlike a chain, which is found in *systematic processing* to only reduce if the earlier incident or earlier beginning is found. Otherwise the imprinting and/or associative Mental Imagery can potentially become stronger. This is why after being processed a couple of times, the *Pilot* asks the *Seeker* if the intensity or imagery is getting stronger or thinner. If it does intensify, then you're not working with the "whole thing." Just as if the *fall* on the GSR continues, there *Seeker* still has more *Hold-Backs* -or- the incident is rooted in a "past life" and the *Seeker* has no reality on it.

A *Fragmented Purpose* is rigidly fixed in place in such a way that the *Seeker* didn't likely agree to it or may not even be 'aware' of it—thus it is not *Self-determined* and is certainly not resolved (or dissolved) "*As-It-Is*" in basic processing or managed in regular every-day life. Such a purpose may or may not be overtly displayed with *Hostile* or *destructive* intentions, but they are certainly present—even if, again, beneath the surface and outside the normal reach of a *Seeker.* When 'processing-out' a *Fragmented Purpose*, the *Seeker* must confront the nature of the actual intention they have and not simply a statement of action or what someone else intended. When it comes to *Ethics Processing* and personal integrity strengthening, we are concerned primarily with the "intention" that the *Seeker* had—and without attempts to justify it. When asked what they've done, too often a *Seeker* will set up their *Awareness* on the "defensive side" and immediately begin to give obvious facts, excuses and justification. These are not the type of answers we want to see accepted in Route-3E (*&tc*).

Fragmented Purposes reduce the appearance of an individual's integrity. They are not necessarily always "on" or dramatizing the programming—it may be triggered or stimulated into action by any number of things. However, when they are in this "*mode*," they often are perceived by others to be at least a little bit "crazy" if not fully insane depending on the intensity of the programmed purpose. It is a patterned tendency and not random, which means that there are indicators that can be watched for and this information leads to better 'processing-out' the whole thing. The *Pilot* is looking to find the underlying *Fragmented Purpose* that systematically leads to a behavioral-chain or pattern of *Hostile-Acts*. Whether or not the *Fragmented Purpose* is installed as part of between-lives implanting, at Grade-IV (and *pre-A.T. Wizard-0*) the focus remains on the present life. However, higher treatments of the same applied-philosophy would undoubtedly reveal more information from the *BackTrack*—and of course the *Pilot* is not permitted to invalidate whatever a *Seeker* says.

One of the main reasons why this type of *processing* is so significant is because of how much attention and energy is placed on personal restraint—the *Hold-Backs*. An individual is actually straining themselves to not do "the usual." A skilled *Pilot* [*Class-3E* or higher] that has worked into Grade-V is permitted to process a *Seeker* into the Abyss or chasm that separates this life from others—which we refer to as the *BackTrack* because it is the course already laid down behind us. When we say "purpose" we of course mean the *Alpha* qualities beyond only this existence, pertaining likely to "*Will-Intention*" (5.0) and/or "*Alpha Thought*" (6.0). As such, *Purpose Defrag* methods are not a replacement for standard

Ethics Processing. Application of *Justification Processing* may also be required for the full defragmentation effect.

Underlying the *Fragmented Purpose* is a *Hostile-Act* of "commission"—something they have *done*, as opposed to one of "omission" (something they didn't do or neglected) that the *Seeker* is likely to 'give up' much easier under questioning than something they've done. Like other forms of *Processing*, a *"Purpose Defrag"* is incredibly basic, requires specific expert handling and will not result in a *Seeker* sprouting wings and rising up to be an instantaneous deity. This is just one of many aspects to breaking through and past this juncture of the *Pathway* and into the *Actualizing-Ascension Tech* ("*A.T.*") of upper-level Systemology. As such, it can be overrun beyond its *End Point*, at which you risk losing the gains it provides.

> Unlike use of *Grade-III* materials, such as *"Crystal Clear"*—or even application of *"Metahuman Destinations"* and *"Imaginomicon"*—a *Pilot* must be specially skilled with practice and certified as "*Class-3E*" (or above) to operate this material in a session. Also: while this will not come without difficulty to some that have been following along the *Pathway*, the odds of complete success *without* using an appropriate type of *GSR-Meter* (which requires its own area of expertise as described in *Liber-3E*) are about 1000-to-1.

THE SYSTEMOLOGY OF JUSTIFICATION, MANIPULATION & RESPONSIBILITY[†]

As long as the *Pilot* handles *processing* fully and systematically, which may include necessary application of "*The Systemology of Justification and Responsibility*," it is possible to free up the *Seeker* enough to pursue the higher-level Wizard Grades. However, if the *Pilot* does not maintain proper control and steering of the session, allowing the *Seeker* to run

[†] Supplemental to the former document; officially issued March 2022.

all around the actual procedure, then they've both *had it* and are wasting processing time. This is not meant to sound overly harsh or rigid—but we are dealing with a key area here that is going to essentially make or break progress on the *Pathway*. It wasn't until intensive work on *Grade-V* began at the *Systemology Society* in 2021, that we realized "*The Way of the Wizard*" (*Liber-3E*) was critical—necessary as an inter-mediary transition.[*]

Another critical step to handling and elevating *Personal Integrity* is "*justification defragmentation*." If the matter is not obvious—assuming the *Seeker* has not focused on their own *justifications*, they can be obtained by asking for them. Whenever a *Hostile-Act* or *Hold-Out* is discovered, the *Pilot* simply asks if the *Seeker* has justified that behavior in any way. If using GSR, the matter should be asked about until there is no charge regarding the act. Although standard *Pilot* training in "3E" distinguishes a "read" on a *GSR-Meter* to mean "yes," it can also mean that there is still a charge on a line. So if after there are no immediate reads on a interrogative question, and you ask "Do you agree that this PCL is clear/defragmented?" and you get a read, then there is still a charge on the line.[‡]

You do a *Seeker* a great disservice by allowing vague answers and generalities to "fly" during *Personal Integrity Defragmentation*. A *Pilot* is also encouraged to have gotten their own *Hold-Outs* defraged (as part of their "*Class-3E*" certification) so that they are not likely to sidestep the same areas in others. Although we are concerned with actions, the 'things' that a *Seeker* has "heard" (from others) or "thought" (but

---

[*] All fundamentals should be run as a repetitive PCL until the *Seeker* appears to run out of answers. Any further answers hidden may be detected by GSR—asking the *Seeker* what '*that*' is that came to mind each time there is a read (however slight or tiny).

[‡] According to an anonymous professional therapeutic processor that this article is written in collaboration with, the *Pilot* should never say "that *still* reads" and should say instead that "there *is another* read here" or "I'm getting *another* read here." Otherwise you risk invalidating the *Seeker*.

not acted on) can also create "mental mass" and thus should be flattened with two-way communication, but not emphasized or targeted directly. Spending an entire session on such will not advance the *Seeker*; yet, parts of these actually relate to a *Seeker's* "justifications" and so they are (to that degree) important. However, *Hold-Outs* on actual *Hostile-Actions* are immensely more important. It is also critical to pinpoint the time-place of events to be certain a *Seeker* desensitizes the charge *As-It-Is.* If *GSR-Meter* reads aren't quieting down, ask for a similar occurrence that took place earlier in the past. You want to target the *first* time the *Seeker* acted in such a way—which is the *imprinting incident* on which all other mass/fragmentation is built upon.

At the inception of the Games Universes, *Alpha-Spirits* went to great lengths to trick and deceive each other with "*Illusion*" for the sake of fun and entertainment—similar in nature to the purpose of "special effects" in movies and formerly "stage magic." Eventually this became a means for entrapment and slavery. This is not always easy to detect because of illusive shields and veils that—at **WILL**—can conceal thoughts and intentions. In the old days of Systemology —circa 2008 through 2012—the key word was "distraction"; and by this we meant the misdirection of attention and *Awareness* that kept a *Seeker* from facing up to (confronting) the truth of Reality of *As-It-Is.* "Route-2" (*Analytical Recall*) and "Route-3C" (*Circuits*) methodology may be used to increase *Awareness* on these occurrences.

Those who are familiar with "*Systemology: The Original Thesis*" (the "Patterns and Cycles" section) understand that civilization on this planet socially operates to the tune of an 84-year cycle (congruent with the orbit of Uranus). It is not unrealistic to assume that we are entering into a period that is consistent with conditions similar to what led us into *World War II.* To prevent: How is this type of travesty safeguarded against (?), you may wonder. Well it requires "proofing up" or "strengthening" against succumbing to the type of confusion that will allow the patterned sequence to take place in the world... In the case of WWII, we find (at its inception) a major economic depression—which is, of course, a large-scale social "confusion" for society as a whole. This is not unlike conditions the world is streaming toward today, where we start seeing a division of the population forming two main classes: the truly needy and the truly greedy.

FALSEHOOD—FIGHTING (EXPANDED 3C, BASIC 3E)

Circuit-1 — Recall a time when you tricked another into fighting.

Circuit-2 — Recall a time when you were tricked into fighting.

Circuit-3 — Recall a time when another tricked others into fighting.

FALSEHOOD—DISTRACTION/ATTENTION (3C, BASIC 3E)

Circuit-1 — Recall a time when you intentionally distracted another.

Circuit-2 — Recall a time when another distracted you.

Circuit-3 — Recall a time when another distracted another.

FALSEHOOD—CONFUSION (EXPANDED 3C, BASIC 3E)

Circuit-1 — Recall a time when you confused another or others.

Circuit-2 — Recall a time when another/others confused you.

Circuit-3 — Recall a time when another confused another/others.

Cr.0/A.T. — Recall a confusion.
\ What concept was used to handle or reduce it?

The term "instigator" seldom appears in common conversation—but we know that there are those out there that encourage confusion, or at the very least have learned to take advantage of it. There are especially those that profit or benefit, even if only for personal entertainment, from *instigating* conflict between others—sometimes even to have an opponent eliminated for them. Well, this is what happens in the midst of a confusion that leads to something like *WWII*. In the state of confusion, an individual is left to grasp onto something *real*, some "stable data" that may or may not be analyzed for its truth before it is accepted. In the case of *WWII*, the Jewish population was targeted as the enemy or cause for the depression. Of course, this wasn't true—in spite of what some *Protocols of the Learned Elders of Zion* document might suggest.

There are several ways in which information may be mishandled, thereby becoming false information or false data. When operating in a confusion or points of low-*Awareness*, this data is often accepted without scrutiny. Many of the tactics further reduce *Awareness* and affect clarity of memory.

• "Passing the Buck" — Shifting the blame onto an individual, family, group or society (race, nation, &tc.), which is misdirecting *Awareness* from the true Source to a false one; this includes false accusations.

• "Remember When" — Shifting the dating/timing of an event from actual data to invented data, thereby obscuring the facts and sometimes diminishing significance by presenting events as longer ago then they actually are.

• "Shifting Significance" — Exaggerating or downplaying the significance or importance of some data; this includes intentions to belittle, shame or embarrass an individual.

FALSEHOOD—BLAME (EXPANDED 3C, BASIC 3E)

Circuit-1 — Recall a time when you shifted blame onto another.

Circuit-2 — Recall a time when another shifted blame onto you.

Circuit-3 — Recall a time when another shifted blame onto others.

FALSEHOOD—SHIFTING TIME (EXPANDED 3C, BASIC 3E)

Circuit-1 — Recall a time when you were misleading about the time some event occurred.

Circuit-2 — Recall a time when another misled you about the time some event occurred.

Circuit-3 — Recall a time when another misled another about the time some event occurred.

FALSEHOOD—SIGNIFICANCE (EXP. ROUTE-2, BASIC 3E)

Circuit-1 — Recall a time when you exaggerated the importance of something.
\ Recall a time when you downplayed the importance of something.

Circuit-2 — Recall a time when another exaggerated the importance of something to you.
\ Recall a time when another downplayed the importance of something to you.

FALSEHOOD—EMBARRASSMENT (EXP. 3C, BASIC 3E)[‡]

Circuit-1 — Recall a time when you acted to make another feel embarrassed.

Circuit-2 — Recall a time when another acted to make you feel embarrassed.

Circuit-3 — Recall a time when another acted to make another feel embarrassed.

Cr.0/A.T. — Recall a time when you made yourself feel embarrassed.

FALSEHOOD—MANIPULATION 1 (RTE 3C/3E, PRE-A.T.)

::A:: — Spot a time when you were told someone or something was "bad."

[‡] "*Falsehood—Stupidity Exp. Route-3C (Basic 3E)*" is run identically, but replacing "embarrassed" with "stupid."

::B:: — Identify the person that told you.

::C:: — Did that person have "personal interests" **invested**? How did they?

FALSEHOOD—MANIPULATION 2 (PRE-A.T.)

::A:: — Spot a time when you were told something that you found out to be true.

::B:: — Spot a time when you were told something that you found out to be false.

FALSEHOOD—MANIPULATION 3 (ADV. 3C, Route-3E)*

Circuit-1 — How have you manipulated another?

Circuit-2 — How has another manipulated you?

Circuit-3 — How has another manipulated others?

When using the *GSR-Meter*, a *Pilot* learns to recognize the significance of an immediate reaction of the needle or '*instant read*'. Even when the *Seeker* does not have an immediate answer, because they are now searching their databases for it, the immediate response of a needle should be used as the indicator. Assuming the *Seeker* does take a moment to '*think*' about it, it is likely that when they hit upon it, the *Pilot* will see the same quality of needle reaction on the *Meter*. With these kinds of processes, it is *then* that a *Pilot* should indicate a '*read*' to the *Seeker*, by saying "*there*" or "*that*" or "*what is* that(?)" (of which a *Seeker* would know from previous experience or education that they are being asked *What-Is-It* they are looking at; and the *Pilot* is to acknowledge the *As-It-Is* answer received).√

As expressed throughout Grade-III and Grade-IV work, "*Willingness to be Responsible*" has nothing to do with blame

---

* "*Falsehood—Manipulation 4, Advanced Route-3C (Route-3E)*" is run identically, but replacing "manipulated" with "misled."

√ An addition review (read through) of "*Metahuman Destinations*" (*Liber-Two*) may be necessary after completing *Liber-3E* in order to achieve effective *Pilot*-training to the extent that we can.

and guilt; it has everything to do with *True Power*—the ability to be *at cause* over things. "Justification" is a common occurrence when handling "Route-3E" because when an individual acts in a manner that is later considered "wrong," there is a natural encoded tendency to "lessen the importance/significance" or else "justify" the actions. This not only strengthens the imprinting of the *"Harmful-Act"* but also requires that the individual maintain certain false beliefs in order to support these "justifications." Maintaining any falsehoods is a conflict with *Self-Honesty* and perpetuates distortions in '*thinking*' and the way in which one views and interacts with the '*world*'. It is high-time that you are able to confront (*face up to*) actions without feelings of regret, blame or the urge to justify them; without which it is impossible to shed skin of the Human Condition and rise above the gravity of this *beta-Existence.*

JUSTIFICATION—HOSTILE-ACTS DEFRAG. (EXP. 3E, A.T.)

Circuit-1 — What have you done to another?
\ How did you justify that?

Circuit-2 — What has another done to you?
\ How did they justify that?

Circuit-3 — What has another done to others?
\ How did they justify that?

Cr.0/A.T. — What have you done to yourself?
\ How did you justify that?

JUSTIFICATION—EXCUSES (EXPANDED ROUTE-2, 3E)

Circuit-1 — What do you use as an excuse?
\ How could you survive without excuses?

Circuit-2 — What do others use an excuse?
\ How could they survive without excuses?

The final key for accessing *The Wizard's Way*—and the transition from Grade-IV to Grade-V and the upper-level Wizard Grades—is to **process-out** what facets we carry regarding "Domination" of others for our material survival; the material survival of these "bodies" anyways. We have been in the habit of attacking and competing with one another for far too long, under an illusion that there can only be one "winner" or that "more for you equals less for me." The systems are designed for this, but it is not truth. Not really. PCLs for this may begin with spotting and analyzing what you have done to "dominate" "stop actions" and "inhibit" others. All of these contribute to our sense of personal "superiority."

Superiority and Domination games are implanted to "keep the masses from uprising" against those that are actually in a position of superiority in calling the shots of the *Game* and the implants themselves. Keep them fighting amongst each other and they will never "remember who the enemy is." But these are *Games* of the lowest order; they are not for our greater good or for the greater survival of the whole. They keep us trapped on a dwindling spiral that will ultimately doom us all if we allow it. If you examine your *kabbalistic* models you will see just how far things have progressed—or rather digressed and regressed—from the Source. Where do you think things will go from here?

Although future "Wizard Grade" materials will expand upon the next steps on the Pathway toward our Ascension—treating the *BackTrack* of our spiritual existence—the present author closes this volume with a quote from the late defragmentation-philosopher *Ken Ogger:*—

> "Each of us has something by which we prove that we are superior to others. It will be some basic characteristic that we have worked on to the exclusion of other things, and so you will be good at it. It will be something like being *holy* or *good* or *strong* or *intelligent* or some similar thing by which you make yourself better than others. Even the enlightened beings who have managed to pull out of this game of domi-

nation will have this item. The difference is that they choose not to use it against others. And please note that this is a self-destructive game. You're best characteristic, which you use against others if you choose to play this game, will eventually deteriorate because of the harm that you are doing with it. And so eventually you must abandon it and shift over to something which is not so badly deteriorated. As a result, this item will only stretch back for a limited number of lifetimes. If you go back early enough, you will find some other thing which you once used and have since abandoned."

In the Magic Universe, the name of the *Game* was "*To Enjoy*"—and down here it is "*To Survive.*" Once we descend to an even lower level of "*To Exist,*" the gravity of the next Universe down will be inescapable. Imagine your consciousness being trapped within a rock or granule of sand for all eternity. Sure you'll remain an eternal being, but what chance of movement upward will remain then?

This is the reality that is facing us today.

And we are approaching the end of this cycle quite quickly.

:: BOOK OF THE LAW OF THE NEW WORLD ::
SYSTEMOLOGY PILOT TECH REPORT[‡]
GRADE-V WIZARD-1 CLASS-3E
A METAHUMAN ETHIC
2022 VERSION 1.1

The "Mardukite" Organization—and its movement—was launched in 2008, exactly *14 years* ahead of the coming dawn of a *brave* "New World" for Metahumans in 2022. This development over a decade ago was intentionally and purposely directed by certain Anunnaki factions, particularly those in support of "Marduk" and the vision and call of ancient Babylon; and in our case, a *"New Babylon."* The *Armageddon Clock* begins ticking strongly in 2022, after *14 years* of being warned and coddled. And while this latest volume—*Liber-3E* —is set to be released in the middle of that year, those few who are the *Chosen Ones*, from the *many called*, will have already heard the trumpet-cries for *Self-Honesty* and personally beheld the *vision and the voice* for several years leading up to 2022. If you have been waiting for a cataclysm, for a 'second coming', for an obvious momentous occasion in which to begin changing your life, you're too late. For the rest of us, there is *The Pathway*.

"Book of the Law of the New World" was a codename for *"Projekt Ethics"*—or else "Liber-3E" during its original development from mid-2021 through early-2022. Basic principles of "The Law" (as a written code illustrated here) are based on a combination of *A New Metahuman Ethic*, the guidelines set down for *Utilitarian Systemology*, and information gathered by other spiritual and metaphysical leaders that have had

---

[‡] A revised facsimile based on original an Tech Report compiled by Joshua Free for the *Mardukite Academy of Systemology* during the completion of the *"Intro to The Wizard's Way: Metahuman Ethics and Beyond"* cycle of developmental work at *Mardukite Babylonia SLV Borsippa HQ* in January 2022; officially issued as a supplement to former documents in March 2022.

some type of contact with the Anunnaki, during the past several decades, in regards to the *"New World."*

*** MINOR INFRACTIONS ***

Those individuals conducting *"minor"* acts of 'counter-survival' are subject to critical review of *Ethics* and implanted *False Purposes.* They are likely salvageable if they are able and willing to defragment themselves *and* change their order of conduct in the immediate future.

• Those who produce and propagate (via distribution, marketing, &tc.) material goods and/or ideas that are harmful to individuals and/or the ecological environment of planet Earth.

• Those who are oppositional to positive social reformation of civic policies that better equalize the survival and betterment to the highest *Sphere of Existence*, meaning both individuals *and* the ecological environment on planet Earth—and elsewhere in the **cosmos** (since the *False Purposes* of humanity appear to seek a reach onto other planets, &tc).

• Those who are not *Beta-Defragmented* and perhaps even suppress others from achieving such—including those operating under implanted *False Purposes.*

*** INTERMEDIATE VIOLATIONS ***

Those individuals who are following implanted *False Purposes* that lead to an '***Intermediate***' degree of *Fragmentation* are on the cusp of being salvageable; though it entirely depends on the individual themselves and how tightly they seek to cling to their materialistic programming. They will require a greater degree of *processing* in order to let go of their superiority and greed—which has given the gravity of this existence a greater hold on them, due to material *and* mental masses that they cling to. Quite simply, a *Pilot's* work is 'cut out for' them; resources *may* be better applied to those operating under '*minor infractions*' such as those who are simply ignorant of how to attain *Beta-Defragmentation*, and that "*help*" is available.

• Those "*Irresponsible Parents*" that have enforced physical punishment on their children or promoted that their children have values that would otherwise be deemed infractions of the *New World*.

• Those who kill, particularly animals—and including hunters believing their justification that it's "for food."

• Those who own and operate "*factory farms*" where animals live out "*miserable lives*"—even if they are not blatantly "*tortured.*"

• Those who eat meat.

*** <u>MAJOR CRIMES</u> ***

Those individuals guilty of "*major*" crimes are generally not worth the time and attention of a *Pilot*, whose efforts could be better served for treating those that are more likely to achieve *Beta-Defragmentation* and are thus more salvageable. Certainly an individual could have a 'change-of-heart' during their lifetime, but if they are still committing "*major*" crimes at the inception of the "New World," they are more than likely expendable members of the population—suppressive persons that are treated as "Fair Game" by up-and-coming Metahumans (provided their treatment does not incite a "*good*" person to commit violations). NOTE: Leave their handling to the Anunnaki Elite and pursue your own *Pathway to Self-Honesty.* Fight them peacefully using social reform until the point in which they are deemed unnecessary by those powers that are here (or coming here) to 'clean up the mess'.

• Those who are violent and physically abusive to any lifeform.

• Those who use their careers, "*religious fanaticism,*" elected offices—or any form of justification—to support torture, murder, rape, enslavement and "forced prostitution" of any lifeform, including animals, or the destruction of the ecological environment on planet Earth.

• Those who participate in any form of animal abuse, including abandon, neglect, indefinite chaining, physical punishment, blatant "dog-fight" type activities, *"legal mutilation" (removal of claws, vocal cords, &tc.)*, or operation of "puppy mill" type activities.

• Those who have *"sold out for power or greed"*—and/or participate in any agenda set forth by the *Zeta Reticuli (Grays),* which are technically enemies of the Anunnaki "New World" Agenda.

:: THE CREED OF MARDUKITE ZUISM ::
PRINCIPLES OF BELIEF

1.) We believe in an Absolute Being, which is Infinite —(the ABZU)—the All-as-One encompassing Source of all Being, Knowing and Awareness to all Alpha/Spiritual (AN) and Beta/Physical (KI) states of existence.

2.) We believe in a spiritual energy of all Life and Awareness (ZU) in the physical universe that is an effect of a spiritual cause; a Spirit that is cause. This Spirit—in its Alpha state—is the True Self "I-AM" Individual Identity that many have called the "soul."

3.) We believe that the Human Condition is a genetic vehicle used by a spiritual source (AN) to experience the Finite as physical existence (KI)—that we are Awareness (ZU) projected onto a genetic vehicle—and that while the vehicle/body may perish to physical **entropy**, the "Alpha Spirit" remains immortal and Self-directed to the extent of its own Actualized Awareness.

4.) We believe that the highest form of worship and spirituality is the actualization and advancement of our "Self" as Spirit in Self-Honesty—and that Self-Honesty is the I-AM Alpha state of Being and Knowing, which is realizable in this lifetime.

5.) We believe that the purpose of all existence is: to exist—and that the **Prime Directive** of all spiritual Life is: continued existence of spiritual Life and co-creation of habitable Reality. "Good" and "Moral" actions are evaluated to the extent of this end.

6A.) We believe that no Life exists in exclusion to all other Life—and that the conditions of a habitable

Reality extending from Self include: Home; Community; All Humanity; All Life on Earth; All Life in the Universe; All Spiritual Life; and the Infinite.

6B.) We believe in a continued evolution of Alpha Spirit awareness developed beyond one physical life, and that a Spirit experiences many.

7A.) We believe Mardukite Zuism is: a 21st Century AD synthesis of the 21st Century BC wisdom collected on cuneiform tablets and experienced in ancient Mesopotamia, esp. Babylon.

7B.) This cuneiform library includes details concerning: beings called the Anunnaki; ordering of the Cosmos; creation of Humanity; and an entire legacy of systematized traditions.

8.) We believe in the continuation of, and proper communication of, the legacy of true Human history —and the ability of every Human to realize that they are a Free Spirit in a Free Zone of Self-Determinism: No "evils" can affect intentions if an individual is holistically Self-Actualized in Self-Honesty.

:: SYSTEMOLOGY GLOSSARY* ::

—A—

A-for-A (one-to-one) : an expression meaning that what we say, write, represent, think or symbolize is a direct and perfect reflection or duplication of the actual aspect or thing—that "A" is for, means and is equivalent to "A" and not "a" or "q" or "!"; in the relay of communication, the message or particle is sent and perfectly duplicate in form and meaning when received.

acknowledgment : a response-communication establishing that an immediately former communication was properly received, duplicated and understood; the formal acceptance and/or recognition of a communication or presence.

actualization : to make actual, not just potential; to bring into full solid Reality; to realize fully in *Awareness* as a "thing."

affinity : the apparent and energetic *relationship* between substances or bodies; the degree of *attraction* or repulsion between things based on natural forces; the *similitude* of frequencies or waveforms; the degree of *interconnection* between systems.

agreement (reality) : unanimity of opinion of what is "thought" to be known; an accepted arrangement of how things are; things we consider as "real" or as an "is" of "reality"; a consensus of what is real as made by standard-issue (common) participants; what an individual contributes to or accepts as "real"; in *NexGen Systemology*, a synonym for "*reality.*"

alpha : the first, primary, basic, superior or beginning of some form; in *NexGen Systemology*, referring to the state

---

* Excerpted from *NexGen Systemology Glossary v.4.4*; only those words which actually appear in this present volume are included.

of existence operating on spiritual archetypes and postulates, will and intention "exterior" to the low-level condensation and solidarity of energy and matter as the 'physical universe'.

alpha control center (ACC) : the highest relay point of *Beingness* for an individuated *Alpha-Spirit*, *Self* or "I-AM"; in *NexGen Systemology*—a point of spiritual separation of ZU at (7.0) from the *Infinity of Nothingness* (8.0); the truest actualization of *Identity*; the highest *Self-directed* relay of *Alpha-Self* as an *Identity-Continuum*, operating in an *alpha-existence* (or "Spiritual Universe"–AN) to *determine* "Alpha Thought" (6.0) and WILL-*Intention* (5.0) *exterior* to the "Physical Universe"–(KI); the "wave-peak" of "I" emerging as individuated consciousness from *Infinity*.

alpha-spirit : a "spiritual" *Life*-form; the "true" *Self* or I-AM; the *individual*; the spiritual (*alpha*) *Self* that is animating the (*beta*) physical body or "*genetic vehicle*" using a continuous *Lifeline* of spiritual ("*ZU*") energy; an individual spiritual (*alpha*) entity possessing no physical mass or measurable waveform (motion) in the Physical Universe as itself, so it animates the (*beta*) physical body or "*genetic vehicle*" as a catalyst to experience *Self*-determined causality in effect within the *Physical Universe*; a singular unit or point of *Spiritual Awareness* that is *Aware* that it is *Aware.*

alpha thought : the highest spiritual *Self-determination* over creation and existence exercised by an Alpha-Spirit; the Alpha range of pure *Creative Ability* based on direct postulates and considerations of *Beingness*; spiritual qualities comparable to "thought" but originating in Alpha-existence (at "6.0") independently superior to a *beta-anchored* Mind-System, although an Alpha-Spirit may use Will ("5.0") to carry the intentions of a postulate or consideration ("6.0") to the Master Control Center ("4.0").

AN : an ancient "Sumerian" cuneiform sign for Heaven or "God"; in *Mardukite Zuism and Systemology* designating the *'spiritual zone'* (or *'Alpha Existence'*); the *Spiritual Universe*—comprised of spiritual matter and spiritual energy; a direction of motion toward spiritual *Infinity*, away from or superior to the physical (*'KI'*); the spiritual condition of existence providing for our primary *Alpha* state as an individual *Identity* or *I-AM-Self* which interacts and experiences *Awareness* of a *beta* state in the *Physical Universe* (*'KI'*) as *Life*.

Ancient Mystery School : the original arcane source of all esoteric knowledge on Earth, concentrated between the Middle East and modern-day Turkey and Transylvania c. 6000 B.C. and then dispersing south (Mesopotamia), west (Europe) and east (Asia) from that location.

apparent : visibly exposed to sight; evident rather than actual, as presumed by Observation; readily perceived, especially by the senses.

a-priori : from "cause" to "effect"; from a general application to a particular instance; existing in the mind prior to, and independent of experience or observation; validity based on consideration and deduction rather than experience.

archetype : a "first form" or ideal conceptual model of some aspect; the ultimate prototype of a form on which all other conceptions are based.

ascension : actualized *Awareness* elevated to the point of true "spiritual existence" exterior to *beta existence*. An "Ascended Master" is one who has returned to an incarnation on Earth as an inherently *Enlightened One*, demonstrable in their actions—they have the ability to *Self-direct* the "Spirit" as *Self*, just as we are treating the "Mind" and "Body" at this current grade of instruction; previously treated in *Moroii ad Vitam* as a state of Beingness after *First Death*, experienced by an *etheric body*, which is able to maintain consciousness as a personal identity continuum with the same *Self-directed* control and communication of Will-Intention that is exercised, actualized and developed deliberately during one's present incarnation.

assessment scale : an official assignment of graded/gradient numeric values.

associative knowledge : significance or meaning of a facet or aspect assigned to (or considered to have) a direct relationship with another facet; to connect or relate ideas or facets of existence with one another; a reactive-response image, emotion or conception that is suggested by (or directly accompanies) something other than itself; in traditional systems logic, an equivalency of significance or meaning between facets or sets that are grouped together, such as in *(a + b) + c = a + (b + c)*; in NexGen Systemology, erroneous associative knowledge is assignment of the same value to all facets or parts considered as related (even when they are not actually so), such as in *a = a, b = a, c = a* and so forth without distinction.

attenergy : *NexGen Systemological NewSpeak* for "attention energies"; the flow of consciousness "energy" that is directed as "attention"; semantic recognition of an axiom from the *Arcane Tablets* that states: "energy flows where attention goes."

attention : active use of *Awareness* toward a specific aspect or thing; the act of "attending" with the presence of *Self*; a direction of focus or concentration of *Awareness* along a particular channel or conduit or toward a particular terminal node or communication termination point; the Self-directed concentration of personal energy as a combination of observation, thought-waves and consideration; focused application of *Self-Directed Awareness*.

authoritarian : knowledge as truth, boundaries and freedoms dictated to an individual by a perceived, regulated or enforced "authority."

awareness : the highest sense of-and-as Self in knowing and being as I-AM (the *Alpha-Spirit*); the extent of beingness directed as a POV experienced by Self as knowingness.

axiom : a fundamental truism of a knowledge system, esp. *logic*; all *maxims* are also *axioms*; knowledge statements that require no proof because their truth is self-evident; an established law or systematic principle used as a *premise* on which to base greater conclusions of truth.

—B—

Babylonian : the ancient Mesopotamian civilization that evolved from *Sumer*; inception point for systematization of civic society and religion.

Back-Scan : to apply Awareness, *Zu-Vision* or "Alpha-Sight" (*exterior* to the *Human Condition*) and *resurface* impressions for recreating *Mental Imagery* of the *Backtrack* within one's own Personal Universe and treat with Wizard-Level (*Grade-V+*) methodology.

Backtrack : to retrace one's steps or go back to an early point in a sequence; an applied spiritual philosophy within *Metahuman Systemology* "*Wizard Grades*" regarding continuous existence of an individual's "*Spiritual Timeline*" through all lifetime-incarnations; the course that is already laid behind us; a methodology of systematic processing methods developed to assist in revealing "hidden" *Mental Images* and *Imprints* from one's past and reclaim attention-energies "left behind" with them by increasing ability to manage and control personal energy mechanisms fixed to their continuous automated creation.

band : a division or group; in *NexGen Systemology*, a division or set of frequencies on the ZU-line that are tuned closely together and referred to as a group.

BAT (Beta-Awareness Test) : a method of *psychometric evaluation* developed for *Mardukite Systemology* to determine a "basic" or "average" state of personal *beta-Awareness*; first developed for the text "*Crystal Clear.*"

beta (awareness) : all consciousness activity ("*Awareness*") in the "Physical Universe" (KI) or else *beta-*

existence; *Awareness* within the range of the *genetic-body*, including material thoughts, emotional responses and physical motors; personal *Awareness* of physical energy and physical matter moving through physical space and experienced as "time"; the *Awareness* held by *Self* that is restricted to a physical organic *Lifeform* or "*genetic vehicle*" in which it experiences causality in the *Physical Universe*.

beta (existence) : all manifestation in the "Physical Universe" (KI); the "Physical" state of existence consisting of vibrations of physical energy and physical matter moving through physical space and experienced as "time"; the conditions of *Awareness* for the *Alpha-spirit* (*Self*) as a physical organic *Lifeform* or "*genetic vehicle*" in which it experiences causality in the *Physical Universe*.

beta-defragmentation : toward a state of *Self-Honesty* in regards to handling experience of the "Physical Universe" (*beta-existence*); an applied spiritual philosophy (or technology) of Self-Actualization originally described in the text "*Crystal Clear*" (*Liber-2B*), building upon theories from "*Systemology: The Original Thesis*."

biological unconsciousness : the organism independent of the sentient *Awareness* of the *Self* to direct it; states induced by severe injury and anesthesia.

biomagnetic/biofeedback : a measurable effect, such as a change in electrical resistance, that is produced by thoughts, emotions and physical behaviors which generate specific 'neurotransmitters' and biochemical reactions in the brain, body and across the skin surface.

—C—

capable : the actual capacity for potential ability.

catalyst : something that causes action between two systems or aspects, but which itself is unaffected as a variable of this energy communication; a medium or intermediary channel.

channel : a specific stream, course, current, direction or route; to form or cut a groove or ridge or otherwise guide along a specific course; a direct path; an artificial aqueduct created to connect two water bodies or water or make travel possible.

charge : to fill or furnish with a quality; to supply with energy; to lay a command upon; in *NexGen Systemology* —to imbue with intention; to overspread with emotion; application of *Self-directed (WILL)* "intention" toward an emotional manifestation in beta-existence; personal energy stores and significances entwined as fragmentation in mental images, reactive-response encoding and intellectual (and/or) programmed beliefs; in traditional mysticism, to intentionally fix an energetic resonance to meet some degree, or to bring a specific concentration of energy that is transferred to a focal point, such as an object or space.

circuit : a circular path or loop; a closed-path within a system that allows a flow; a pattern or action or wave movement that follows a specific route or potential path only; in *NexGen Systemology*, "*communication processing*" pertaining to a specific flow of energy or information along a channel; *see* also "*feedback loop.*"

Circuit-1 : in *Grade-IV* "communication processing" (introduced in *Metahuman Destinations* as *Route-3*), the flow of energy and information connected to outflow, what *Self* has expressed, projected outwardly or done.

Circuit-2 : in *Grade-IV* "communication processing" (introduced in *Metahuman Destinations* as *Route-3*), the flow of energy and information connected to inflow, what "others" have done to *Self,* what it has received inwardly or had *happen to.*

Circuit-3 : in *Grade-IV* "communication processing" (introduced in *Metahuman Destinations* as *Route-3*), the flow of energy and information connected to cross-flows, what *Self* has witnessed of others (or another) projecting or doing toward others (or another).

Circuit-0 : a more advanced concept introduced to *Grade-IV* "communication processing" (as listed on SOP-2C in *Metahuman Destinations* for "*Pre-A.T*" or "*Route-0*" applications), which targets *'postulates'* and *'considerations'* generated and stored by *Self* for *Self* and the direction, energy or flows representing what *Self* "does" for and/or to *Self*. This circuit is treated further in *Wizard Level* work,

code (ethics) : an outline of *ethical* standards regarding social participation and acceptable behavior; not generally enforced as *law* itself, but a standard that reasonable individuals are actualized (or civil) enough to *Self-Determine* (by choice) their own following (or adherence) if it is *right* and *good*; shared reality agreements that promote optimum conditions of continued existence ("SURVIVAL" in *Beta-existence*; "CREATION" in *Alpha*) for the highest affected "Sphere of Existence" (on the *Standard Model*).

codification : process of collecting, analyzing and then arranging knowledge in a standardized and more accessible systematic form, often by subject, theme or some other designation.

collapsing a wave : also, "*wave-function collapse*"; in *Quantum Physics*, the concept that an Observer is "collapsing" the wave-function to something "definite" by measuring it; defining or calculating a wave-function or interaction of potential interactions by an Observation; in *NexGen Systemology*, when a wave of potentiality or possibility because a finite fixed form; Consciousness or *Awareness* "collapses" a wave-function of energy-matter as a necessary "third" Principle of Apparent Manifestation (first described in "*Tablets of Destiny*"); potentiality as a wave is collapsed into an apparent "*is*", the energy of which is freed up in systematic processing by "*flattening*" a "collapsed" wave back into its state of potentiality.

command : in *Metahuman Systemology*, responsibility and ability of Self (I-AM) as operating from its ideal "exterior" *Point-of-View* as Alpha Spirit; to direct communication for control of the *genetic vehicle* and Mind-Body connection that is perfectly duplicated from a source-point to a receipt-point along the ZU-line.

command line : see "*processing command line*" (PCL).

common knowledge (game theory) : facts that all "players" know, and they know that all other "players" also know—such as the very structure of the "game" being played.

communication : successful transmission of information, data, energy (&tc.) along a message line, with a reception of feedback; an energetic flow of intention to cause an effect (or duplication) at a distance; the personal energy moved or acted upon by will or else 'selective directed attention'; the 'messenger action' used to transmit and receive energy across a medium; also relay of energy, a message or signal—or even locating a personal POV (viewpoint) for the Self—along the *ZU-line*.

communication (circuit) processing : a methodology of Grade-IV Metahuman Systemology that emphasizes analysis of all Mind-System energy flows (information) transmitted and stored along circuits of a channel toward some terminal, thing or concept, particularly: what Self has out-flowed, what Self has in-flowed, and the cross-flows that Self has observed; also "*Route-3*"

compulsion : a failure to be responsible for the dynamics of control—starting, stopping or altering—on a particular channel of communication and/or regarding a particular terminal in existence; an energetic flow with the appearance of being 'stuck' on the action it is already doing or by the control of some automatic mechanism.

computing device : a calculator or modern computer; a mechanism that performs specific functions, particularly input, output and storage of data/information.

concept : a high-frequency thought-wave representing an "idea" which persists because it is not restricted to a unique space-time; an abstract or tangible "idea" formed in the "Mind" or *imagined* as a means of understanding, usually including associated "Mental Images"; a seemingly timeless collective thought-theme (or subject) that entangles together facets of many events or incidents, not just a single significant one.

conceptual processing : a Wizard-Level methodology introduced intermittently throughout materials of Metahuman Systemology that emphasizes fully "getting the sense of" (or "contacting the idea of") a particular condition as prompted by a PCL and on one's own determination; a systematic practice-drill regarding considerations and postulates (Alpha Thought) regarding various reality agreements; a *Route-0* variant employing *Creativeness* and *Imagination* for systematic processing; also *Route-0E* when used for *Ethics Processing.*

condense (condensation) : the transition of vapor to liquid; denoting a change in state to a more substantial or solid condition; leading to a more compact or solid form.

condition : an apparent or existing state; circumstances, situations and variable dynamics affecting the order and function of a system; a series of interconnected requirements, barriers and allowances that must be met; in "contemporary language," bringing a thing toward a specific, desired or intentional new state (such as in "conditioning"), though to minimize confusion about the word "condition" in our literature, *NexGen Systemology* treats "contemporary conditioning" concepts as imprinting, encoding and programming.

conflict : the opposition of two forces of similar magnitude along the same channel or competing for the same terminal; the inability to duplicate another POV; a thought, intention or communication that is met with an opposing counter-thought or counter-intention that generates an energetic cluster.

confront : to come around in front of; to be in the presence of; to stand in front of, or in the face of; to meet "face-to-face" or "face-up-to"; additionally, in *NexGen Systemology*, to fully tolerate or acceptably withstand an encounter with a particular manifestation or encounter.

consciousness : the energetic flow of *Awareness*; the Principle System of *Awareness* that is spiritual in nature, which demonstrates potential interaction with all degrees of the Physical Universe; the *Beingness* component of our existence in *Spirit*; the Principle System of *Awareness* as *Spirit* that directs action in the Mind-System.

consideration : careful analytical reflection of all aspects; deliberation; determining the significance of a "thing" in relation to similarity or dissimilarity to other "things"; evaluation of facts and importance of certain facts; thorough examination of all aspects related to, or important for, making a decision; the analysis of consequences and estimation of significance when making decisions; in *NexGen Systemology*, the postulate or Alpha-Thought that defines the state of beingness for what something "*is.*"

continuity : being a continuous whole; a complete whole or "total round of"; the balance of the equation ["–120" + "120" = "0" *&tc.*]; an apparent unbroken interconnected coherent whole; also, as applied to Universes in *NexGen Systemology*, the lowest base consideration of space-time or commonly shared level of energy-matter apparent in an existence, or else the lowest degree of solidity or condensation whereby all mass that exists is identifiable or communicable with all other mass that exists; represented as "0" on the *Standard Model* for the Physical Universe (*beta-existence*), a level of existence that is below Human emotion, comparable to the solidity of "rocks" and "walls" and "inert bodies."

control (systems) : Communication relayed from an operative center or organizational cluster, which incites new activity elsewhere in a system (or along the *ZU-line*).

correlate : a relationship between two or more aspects, parts or systems.

Cosmic Law : the "Law" of Nature (or the Physical

Universe); the "Law" governing cosmic ordering; often called "Natural Law" in sciences and philosophies that attempt to codify or systematize it.

Cosmos : archaic term for the "Physical Universe"; semantically implies chaos brought into order; in *NexGen Systemology*, can also include considerations of "Universes" experienced previously as a *beta-existence*.

counter-productive (counter-survival) : contrary to the greater or original purpose or intention; in *NexGen Systemology*, anything which brings *Life* away from its sustainable goal or position of *Infinite Existence*.

creative ability test : see "*CAT.*"

creativeness processing : a *systematic processing* methodology introduced in *Grade-IV Metahuman Systemology* (*Wizard Level-0*) that emphasizes personal use of "*Imagination,*" or else "creative ability" of Self and freeing considerations of the Alpha-Spirit to *Be* or *Create* anything within its Personal Universe, independent of reality agreements with beta-existence; also "*Route-0.*"

Crossing the Abyss : to enter the spiritual or metaphysical unknown in "Self-annihilation" to purify the Self and "return to the Source."

Crystal Clear : the second professional publication of Mardukite Systemology, released publicly in December 2019; the second professional text in Grade-III Mardukite Systemology, released as "*Liber-2B*" and reissued in the Grade-III Master Edition "*Systemology Handbook*"; contains fundamental theory of "*Beta-Defragmentation*" and "*Route-2*" systematic processing methodology.

cuneiform : the oldest extant writing system at the inception of modern civilization in Mesopotamia; a system of wedge-shaped script inscribed on clay tablets with a reed pen, allowing advancements in record keeping and communication no longer restricted to more literal graphic representations or pictures.

cuneiform signs : the cuneiform script, as used in ancient

Mesopotamia, is not represented in a linear alphabet of "letters," but by a systematic use of basic word "signs" that are combined to form more complex word "signs"— each sign represented a "sound" more than it did a letter, such as "ab," "ad", "ba", "da" *&tc*.

—D—

data-set : the total accumulation of knowledge used to base Reality.

defragmentation : the *reparation* of wholeness; collecting all dispersed parts to reform an original whole; a process of removing "*fragmentation*" in data or knowledge to provide a clear understanding; applying techniques and processes that promote a *holistic* interconnected *alpha* state, favoring observational *Awareness* of continuity in all spiritual and physical systems; in *NexGen Systemology*, a "*Seeker*" achieving an actualized state of basic "*Self-Honest Awareness*" is said to be *beta-defragmented*, whereas *Alpha-defragmentation* is the rehabilitation of the *creative ability*, managing the *Spiritual Timeline* and the POV of *Self* as Alpha-Spirit (I-AM); see also "*Beta-defragmentation*."

degree : a physical or conceptual *unit* (or point) defining the variation present relative to a *scale* above and below it; any stage or extent to which something *is* in relation to other possible positions within a *set* of "*parameters*"; a point within a specific range or spectrum; in *NexGen Systemology*, a *Seeker's* potential energy variations or fluctuations in thought, emotional reaction and physical perception are all treated as "*degrees*."

dichotomy : a division into two parts, types or kinds.

differential : the quantitative value difference between two forces, motions, pressures or degrees.

differentiation : an apparent difference between aspects or concepts.

displace : to compel to leave; to move or replace something with something else in its place or space.

dogma : religious doctrines or opinion-based beliefs (data-set) treated socially as fact, especially regarding "divinity" or "God" (the common "Human" interpretation of the "domain" of Infinity) represented by the "Eighth Sphere" on our original Standard Model of Systemology; religiously defined values, taboos and ethical standards emphasized by cultural/religious socialization and mythographic beliefs (even above any observable causal effects, logical sequences or verifiable proofs).

dramatization / dramatize : a vivid display or performance as if rehearsed for a "play" (on stage); a *'circuit'* recording *'imprinted'* in the past and, once restimulated by a facet of the environment, the individual "replays" it as through reacting to it in the present (and identifying that reality as present reality); acts, actions and observable behaviors that demonstrate identification with a particular character type, "phase" or personality program; a motivated sequence-chain, implant series or imprinted cycle of actions—usually irrational or counter-survival—repeated by an individual as it had previously happened to them; a reoccurring or reactively triggered out-flow, communication or action that indicates an individual "occupying" a particular *'Point-of-View'* (*POV*)—typically fixed to a specific (past) identification (identity) that is space-time locatable (meaning a point where significant *Attenergy*— enough to compulsively create and maintain a POV—is "stuck" or "hung up" on the *BackTrack*).

dynamic (systems) : a principle or fixed system which demonstrates its *'variations'* in activity (or output) only in constant relation to variables or fluctuation of interrelated systems; a standard principle, function, process or system that exhibits *'variations'* and change simultaneously with all connected systems; each '*Sphere of Existence'* is a dynamic system, systematically affecting (supporting) and affected (supported) by other *'Spheres'* (which are also dynamic systems).

—**E**—

echelon : a level or rung on a ladder; a rank or level of command.

EDA : "electro-dermal activity"; see also *GSR-Meter.*

electro-psychometer ("E-meter") : see *GSR-Meter.*

emotional encoding : the readable substance/material (data) of *'imprints'*; associations of sensory experience with an *imprint*; perceptions of our environment that receive an *emotional charge*, which form or reinforce facets of an *imprint*; perceptions recorded and stored as an *imprint* within the "emotional range" of energetic manifestation; the formation of an energetic store or charge on a channel that fixes emotional responses as a mechanistic automation, which is carried on in an individual's *Spiritual Timeline* (or personal continuum of existence).

encompassing : to form a circle around, surround or envelop around.

end point : the moment when the goal of a process has been achieved and to continue on with it will be detrimental to the gains; the finality of a process when the *Seeker* has achieved their optimum state from the current cycle (whether or not they run through it again at a later date with a different level of *Awareness* or knowledge base doesn't change the fact that it has flattened the standing wave

energetic exchange : communicated transmission of energetically encoded "information" between fields, forces or source-points that share some degree of interconnectivity; the event of "waves" acting upon each other like a force, flowing in regard to their proximity, range, frequency and amplitude.

enforcement : the act of compelling or putting (effort) into force; to compel or impose obedience by force; to impress strongly with applications of stress to demand agreement or validation; the lowest-level of direct control by physical effort or threat of punishment; a low-level method of control in the absence of true communication.

engineering : the *Self-directed* actions and efforts to utilize knowledge (observed causality/science), maths (calculations/quantification) and logic (axioms/formulas) to understand, design or manifest a solid structure, machine, mechanism, engine or system; as *"Reality Engineering"* in *NexGen Systemology*—intentional *Self-directed* adjustment of existing Reality conditions; the application of total *Self-determinism* in *Self-Honesty* to change apparent Reality using fundamentals of *Systemology* and *Cosmic Law.*

entanglement : tangled together; intertwined and enmeshed systems; in *NexGen Systemology*, a reference to the interrelation of all particles as waves at a higher point of connectivity than is apparent, since wave-functions only "collapse" when someone is *Observing*, or doing the measuring, evaluating, &tc.

entropy : the reduction of organized physical systems back into chaos-continuity when their integrity is measured against space over time; reduction toward a zero-point.

epicenter : the point from which shock-waves travel.

epistemology : a school of philosophy focused on the truth of knowledge and knowledge of truth; theories regarding validity and truth inherent in any structure of knowledge and reason; the original "school of philosophy" from which all other "disciplines" were derived; the study of knowing how to know knowledge, reason and truth.

erroneous : inaccurate; incorrect; containing error.

esoteric : hidden; secret; knowledge understood by a select few.

ethics : an intellectual philosophy concerning *rightness* and *wrongness* based on "logic" and "reason" (rationale) combined with observable consequences and tendencies of action or conduct; formal name for a "moral philo-sophy" (study of moral choices); in ancient times, originally treated *one-to-one* with "Cosmic Law" regard-ing *causation*, *order* and *sequence*; an objective (Universal) philosophy of *rightness* and *wrongness*, treated separate from culture-specific (subjective/relative) considerations, such as *morals* and *dogma*; in *NexGen Systemology* (*Grade-IV Metahuman Systemology*), a dy-namic philosophy (applying "logic-and-reason") to understand the nature of "reality agreements" concerning *rightness* and *wrongness*, then treating the most optimum conditions of continued existence ("SURVIVAL" in *Beta-existence*; "CREATION" in *Alpha*) for the highest affected "Sphere of Existence" (on the *Standard Model*).

ethics processing : a *systematic processing* methodology introduced for bridging *Grade-IV Metahuman Systemo-logy* (*Wizard Level-0*) with *Grade-V Spiritual Systemology* (*Wizard Level-1*) that emphasizes personal realization of "*Ethics*" and increased ability and respons-ibility to confront the "rightness" and "wrongness" of past actions (on the Backtrack), including defragmenta-tion of "*Harmful Acts*" (as *Imprinting Incidents*) and any corresponding "*Hold-Backs*" and "*Hold-Outs*" (which re-duce *Actualized Awareness* and prompt an individual to *withdraw* their *reach*); also "*Route-3E.*"

evaluate : to determine, assign or fix a set value, amount or meaning.

existence : the *state* or fact of *apparent manifestation*; the resulting combination of the Principles of Manifestation: consciousness, motion and substance; continued *survival*; that which independently exists; the *'Prime Directive'* and sole purpose of all manifestation or Reality; the highest common intended motivation driving any "*Thing*" or *Life*.

existential : pertaining to existence, or some aspect or condition of existence.

experiential data : accumulated reference points we store as memory concerning our "experience" with Reality.

extant : in existence; existing.

exterior : outside of; on the outside; in *NexGen Systemology*, we mean specifically the POV of *Self* that is *'outside of'* the *Human Condition,* free of the physical and mental trappings of the Physical Universe; a metahuman range of consideration; see also '*Zu-Vision*'.

external : a force coming from outside; information received from outside sources; in *NexGen Systemology*, the objective *'Physical Universe'* existence, or *beta-existence*, that the Physical Body or *genetic vehicle* is essentially *anchored* to for its considerations of locational space-time as a dimension or POV.

—F—

facets : an aspect, an apparent phase; one of many faces of something; a cut surface on a gem or crystal; in *NexGen Systemology*—a single perception or aspect of a memory or "*Imprint*"; any one of many ways in which a memory is recorded; perceptions associated with a painful emotional (sensation) experience and "*imprinted*" onto a metaphoric lens through which to view future similar experiences; other secondary terminals that are associated with a particular terminal, painful event or experience of loss, and which may exhibit the same encoded significance as the activating event.

faculties : abilities of the mind (individual) inherent or developed.

fallacy : a deceptive, misleading, erroneous and/or false beliefs; unsound logic; persuasions, invalidation or enforcement of Reality agreements based on authority, sympathy, bandwagon/mob mentality, vanity, ambiguity, suppression of information, and/or presentation of false dichotomies.

feedback loop : a complete and continuous circuit flow of energy or information directed as an output from a source to a target which is altered and return back to the source as an input; in *General Systemology*—the continuous process where outputs of a system are routed back as inputs to complete a circuit or loop, which may be closed or connected to other systems/circuits; in *NexGen Systemology*—the continuous process where directed *Life* energy and *Awareness* is sent back to *Self* as experience, understanding and memory to complete an energetic circuit as a loop.

flattening a wave : see "*process-out*" for definition; also see "*collapsing a wave.*"

flow : movement across (or through) a channel (or conduit); a direction of active energetic motion typically distinguished as either an *in-flow, out-flow* or *cross-flow.*

forgive(ness) : to let go of resentment (against an offender, source of *Harmful-Act*) or give up emotional (energetic) turbulence connected to inclinations to punish; a legal pardon; to intentionally "overlook" (as opposed to "forget") the repayment of a debt or sense of something owed.

fragmentation : breaking into parts and scattering the pieces; the *fractioning* of wholeness or the *fracture* of a holistic interconnected *alpha* state, favoring observational *Awareness* of perceived connectivity between parts; *discontinuity*; separation of a totality into parts; in *NexGen Systemology*, a person outside a state of *Self-Honesty* is said to be *fragmented.*

—G—

game : a strategic situation where a "player's" power of choice is employed or affected; a parameter or condition defined by purposes, freedoms and barriers (rules).

game theory : a mathematical theory of logic pertaining to strategies of maximizing gains and minimizing loses within prescribed boundaries and freedoms; a field of knowledge widely applied to human problem solving and decision-making; the application of true knowledge and logic to deduce the correct course of action given all variables and interplay of dynamic systems; logical study of decision making where "players" make choices that affect (the interests) of other "players"; an intellectual study of conflict and cooperation.

general systemology ("systematology") : a methodology of analysis and evaluation regarding the systems—their design and function; organizing systems of interrelated information-processing in order to perform a given function or pattern of functions.

genetic memory : the evolutionary, cellular and genetic (DNA) "memory" encoded into a *genetic vehicle* or *living organism* during its progression and duplication (reproduction) over millions (or billions) of years on Earth; in *NexGen Systemology*—the past-life Earth-memory carried in the genetic makeup of an organism (*genetic vehicle*) that is *independent of any* actual "spiritual memory" maintained by the *Alpha Spirit* themselves, from its own previous lifetimes on Earth and elsewhere using other *genetic vehicles* with no direct evolutionary connection to the current physical form in use.

genetic-vehicle : a physical *Life*-form; the physical (*beta*) body that is animated/controlled by the (*Alpha*) *Spirit* using a continuous *Lifeline* (ZU); a physical (*beta*) organic receptacle and catalyst for the (*Alpha*) *Self* to operate "causes" and experience "effects" within the *Physical Universe*.

gradient : a degree of partitioned ascent or descent along some scale, elevation or incline; "higher" and "lower" values in relation to one another.

GSR-Meters ("galvanic skin response"–"electropsychometer") : a *biofeedback* device used for measuring electrical resistance (in "Ohms") of the skin surface; one of many parts used in a polygraph system; a highly sensitive "Ohm-meter" with variable range, set points and amplification used to monitor electrical fluctuations of the skin surface.

harmful-act : a counter-survival mode of behavior or action (esp. that causes harm to one of more *Spheres of Existence*)—or—an overtly aggressive (hostile and/or destructive) action against an individual or any other *Sphere of Existence*; in *Utilitarian Systemology*—a shortsighted (serves fewest/lowest *Spheres of Existence*) intentional overtly harmful action to resolve a perceived problem; a revision of the rule for standard *Utilitarianism* for Systemology to distinguish actions which provide the least benefit to the least number of *Spheres of Existence*, or else the greatest harm to the greatest number of *Spheres of Existence*; in *moral philosophy*—an action which can be experienced by few and/or which one would not be willing to experience for themselves (*theft, slander, rape, &tc*); an iniquity or iniquitous act.

help : to assist survival of; aid continuing optimum success.

heralded : proclaimed ahead of or prior to; officially announced.

hold-back : withheld communications (esp. actions) such as "*Hold-Outs*"; intentional (or automatic) withdrawal (as opposed to reach); Self-restraint (which may eventually be enforced or automated); not reaching, acting or expressing, when one should be; an ability that is now restrained (on automatic) due to inability to withhold it on Self-determinism alone.

hold-outs : in photography, the numerous snapshots/pictures withheld from the final display or professional presentation of the event; withheld communications; in Utilitarian Systemology—energetic withdrawal and communication breaks with a "*terminal*" and its *Sphere of Existence* as a result of a "*Harmful-Act*"; unspoken or undiscovered (hidden, covert) actions that an individual withholds communications of, fearing punishment or endangerment of *Self-preservation* (*First Sphere*); the act of hiding (or keeping hidden) the truth of a "*Harmful-Act*"; a refusal to communicate with a *Pilot*; also "*Hold-Back.*"

holistic : the examination of interconnected systems as encompassing something greater than the *sum* of their "parts."

Homo Novus : literally, the "new man"; the "newly elevated man" or "known man" in ancient Rome; the man who "knows (only) through himself"; in NexGen Systemology—the next spiritual and intellectual evolution of *homo sapiens* (the "modern Human Condition"), which is signified by a demonstration of higher faculties of *Self-Actualization* and clear *Awareness*.

hostile-motivation : an *imprint* of a counter-survival action (or "*Harmful-Act*") committed by another against Self, stored as data to justify future actions (retaliation, *&tc.*); any *Sphere of Existence* (though usually an individual) receiving the effect of a "*Harmful-Act*"; an *imprint* used to rationalize "motivation" or "justification" for committing a "*Harmful-Act*"; in systematic *games theory*—the *modus operandi* concerning "payback," "revenge" and "tit-for-tat."

hot button : something that triggers or incites an intense emotional reaction instantaneously; in *NexGen Systemology*—a slang term denoting a highly reactive *channel*, heavily *charged* with a long chain of cumulative *emotional imprinting*, typically (but not necessarily) connected to a significant or "primary" *implant*; a non-technical label, first applied during *Grade-IV Professional Piloting "Flight School"* research sessions of Spring-Summer 2020, to indicate specific circuits, channels or terminals that cause a *Seeker* to immediately react with intense emotional responses, whether in general, directed to the *Pilot*, or even at effectiveness of processing.

Human Condition : a standard default state of Human experience that is generally accepted to be the extent of its potential identity (*beingness*)—currently treated as *Homo Sapiens Sapiens,* but which is scheduled for replacement by *Homo Novus*.

humanistic psychology : a field of academic psychology approaching a holistic emphasis on *Self-Actualization* as an individual's most basic motivation; early key figures from the 20th century include: Carl Rogers, Abraham Maslow, L. Ron Hubbard, William Walker Atkinson, Deepak Chopra and Timothy Leary (to name a few).

hypothetical : operating under the assumption a certain aspect actual "is."

—I—

identification : the association of *identity* to a thing; a label or fixed data-set associated to what a thing is; association "equals" a thing, the "equals" being key; an equality of all things in a group, for example, an "apple" identified with all other "apples"; the reduction of "I-AM"-*Self* from a *Spiritual Beingness* to an "identity" of some form.

identity : the collection of energy and matter—including memory—across a "*Spiritual Timeline*" that we consider as "I" of *Self*, but the "I" is an individual and not an identification with anything other than *Self* as *Alpha-Spirit*.

identity-system : the application of the *ZU-line* as "I"— the continuous expression of *Self* as *Awareness* across a "*Spiritual Timeline*"; see "*identity*."

imagination : the ability to create *mental imagery* in one's Personal Universe at will and change or alter it as desired; the ability to create, change and dissolve mental images on command or as an act of will; to create a mental image or have associated imagery displayed (or "conjured") in the mind that may or may not be treated as real (or memory recall) and may or may not accurately duplicate objective reality; to employ *Creative Abilities* of the Spirit that are independent of reality agreements with beta-existence.

Imaginomicon : the fourth professional publication of

Mardukite Systemology, released publicly in mid- 2021; the second professional text in Grade-IV Metahuman Systemology, released as "*Liber-3D*"; contains fundamental theory of "*Spiritual Ability*" and "*Route-0*" systematic processing methodology.

imperative : a high-level authoritarian command; a command triggering urgency and necessity of a certain goal or directive; see also "*Spheres of Existence*" and "*Prime Directive.*"

implant : to graft or surgically insert; to establish firmly by setting into; to instill or install a direct command or consideration in consciousness (Mind-System, &tc.); a mechanical device inserted beneath the surface/skin; in *Metahuman Systemology*, an "energetic mechanism" (linked to an Alpha-Spirit) composing a circuit-network and systematic array of energetic receptors underlying and filter-screening communication channels between the Mind-System and *Self*; an energetic construct installed upon entry of a Universe; similar to a platen or matrix or circuit-board, where each part records a specific type or quality of *emotionally encoded imprints* and other "heavily charged" *Mental Images* that are "impressed" by future encounters; a basic platform on which certain *imprints* and *Mental Images* are encoded (keyed-in) and stored (often beneath the surface of "knowing" or *Awareness* for that individual, although an implanted "command" toward certain inclinations or behavioral tendencies may be visibly observable.

imprint : to strongly impress, stamp, mark (or outline) onto a softer 'impressible' substance; to mark with pressure onto a surface; in *NexGen Systemology*, the term is used to indicate permanent Reality impressions marked by frequencies, energies or interactions experienced during periods of emotional distress, pain, unconsciousness, loss, enforcement, or something antagonistic to physical (personal) survival, all of which are are stored with other reactive response-mechanisms at lower-levels of *Awareness* as opposed to the active memory database and proactive processing center of the Mind; an experiential "memory-set" that may later resurface—be triggered or stimulated artificially—as Reality, of which similar responses will be engaged automatically; holographic-like imagery "stamped" onto consciousness as composed of energetic *facets* tied to the "snap-shot" of an experience.

imprinting incident : the first or original event instance communicated and *emotionally encoded* onto an individual's "*Spiritual Timeline*" (recorded memory from all lifetimes), which formed a permanent impression that is later used to mechanistically treat future contact on that channel; the first or original occurrence of some particular *facet* or mental image related to a certain type of *encoded response*, such as pain and discomfort, losses and victimization, and even the acts that we have taken against others along the Spiritual Timeline of our existence that caused them to also be *Imprinted*.

inadvertent : an unintended (knowingly) result caused by low-Awareness actions; applying effort (enacting change) outside Self-Honesty, leading to negligent oversights with harmful outcomes.

incarnation : a present, living or concrete form of some thing, idea or beingness; an individual lifetime or life-cycle from birth/creation to death/destruction independent of other lifetimes or cycles.

inception : the beginning, start, origin or outset.

incite : to urge on or cause; instigate; prove or stimulate into action.

individual : a person, lifeform, human entity or creature; a *Seeker* or potential *Seeker* is often referred to as an "individual" within Mardukite Zuism and Systemology materials.

infinite existence : "immortality."

inhibited : withheld, held-back, discouraged or repressed from some state.

iniquities : wickedness or wicked acts ("sinful" in

religious use); literal etymology, "that which is not equal"; synonymous with *Harmful-Acts.*

insistence : repeated use of a communicated energy into a form that demands acknowledgment, is more difficult to avoid or ignore.

intention : the directed application of Will; to intend (have "in Mind") or signify (give "significance" to) for or toward a particular purpose; in *NexGen Systemology* (from the *Standard Model*)—the spiritual activity at WILL (5.0) directed by an *Alpha Spirit* (7.0); the application of WILL as "Cause" from a higher order of Alpha Thought and consideration (6.0), which then may continue to relay communications as an "effect" in the universe.

intermediate : a distinct point between two points; actions between two points.

internal : a force coming from inside; information received from inside sources; in *NexGen Systemology*, the objective *'Physical Universe'* experience of *beta-existence* that is associated with the Physical Body or *genetic vehicle* and its POV regarding sensation and perception; from inside the body; within the body.

invalidate : decrease the level or degree or *agreement* as Reality.

invest : spend on; give or devote something in exchange for a beneficial result; to endow with.

—J—

justice : observable social actions (or consequential reaction) and predetermined civic (legal) processes employed in a society or group to uphold or enforce their reality agreements concerning "*law*"; a civic authority and administrative body responsible for carrying out practical/physical responses and penalties; the words, "*just*," "*justice*" and "*justification*," all stem from the Lat in "*jus*" (meaning "*morally right,*" "*law, in accordance with*" and "*lawful*") or "*iustus*" (expressing what is "true," "proper," "up-right" and "justified").

—K—

knowledge : clear personal processing of informed understanding; information (data) that is actualized as effectively workable understanding; a demonstrable understanding on which we may 'set' our *Awareness*—or literally a "know-ledge."

KI : an ancient cuneiform sign designating the '*physical zone*'; the *Physical Universe*—comprised of physical matter and physical energy in action across space and observed as time; a direction of motion toward material *Continuity*, away from or subordinate to the Spiritual ('*AN*'); the physical condition of existence providing for our *beta* state of *Awareness* experienced (and interacted with) as an individual *Lifeform* from our primary Alpha state of Identity or *I-AM-Self* in the *Spiritual Universe* ('*AN*').

—L—

law : a formal codified outline (or list) of *ethical* standards regarding social participation and acceptable behavior, like a "*code,*" except that it *is* enforced by civic consequences (or even "*Cosmic Law*") when not adhered to, usually with punishment coming either by the group (exclusively) or by involvement with an "outside party" or societal (legal) authority; a predictable sequence of naturally occurring events that will consistently repeat under the right conditions (such as "*Cosmic Law*" or "*Natural Law*").

learned : highly educated; possessing significant knowledge.

210

level : a physical or conceptual *tier* (or plane) relative to a *scale* above and below it; a significant *gradient* observable as a *foundation* (or surface) built upon and subsequent to other levels of a totality or whole; a *set* of "*parameters*" with respect to other such *sets* along a *continuum*; in *NexGen Systemology*, a *Seeker's* understanding, *Awareness* as *Self* and the formal grades of material/instruction are all treated as "*levels*."

Liber-One : First published in October 2019 as "*The Tablets of Destiny: Using Ancient Wisdom to Unlock Human Potential*" by Joshua Free; republished in the complete *Grade-III* anthology, "*The Systemology Handbook.*"

Liber-Two : First published in October 2020 as "*Metahuman Destinations: Piloting the Course to Homo Novus*" by Joshua Free; an anthology of the *Grade-IV* "Professional Piloting Course," containing revised materials from *Liber-2C*, *Liber-2D* and (most of) *Liber-3C.*

Liber-Three : see "*Liber-3E.*"

Liber-2B : First published in December 2019 as "*Crystal Clear: The Self-Actualization Manual & Guide to Total Awareness*" by Joshua Free; republished in the complete *Grade-III* anthology, "*The Systemology Handbook.*"

Liber-2C : First published in April 2020 as "*Communication and Control of Energy & Power: The Magic of Will & Intention (Volume One)*" by Joshua Free; revision republished as an integral part of the *Grade-IV* "Professional Piloting Course," in October 2020 within "*Metahuman Destinations*" (*Liber-Two*).

Liber-2D : First published in June 2020 as "*Command of the Mind-Body Connection: The Magic of Will & Intention" (Volume Two)*" by Joshua Free; revision republished as an integral part of the *Grade-IV* "Professional Piloting Course," in October 2020 within "*Metahuman Destinations*" (*Liber-Two*).

Liber-3C : First published in July 2020 as "*Now You Know: The Truth About Universes & How You Got Stuck* *in One*" by Joshua Free; a discourse in the *Grade-IV* Metahuman Systemology series; a revision of one part republished in October 2020 within the "*Professional Piloting Course*" manual, "*Metahuman Destinations*" (*Liber-Two*), a revision of the remaining part republished in June 2021 within the "*Imaginomicon*" (*Liber-3D*).

Liber-3D : First published in June 2021 as "*Imaginomicon: The Gateway to Higher Universes (A Grimoire for the Human Spirit)*" by Joshua Free; a manual completing the *Grade-IV* (Metahuman Systemology) professional series with a treatment of "Wizard Level-0."

Liber-3E (Liber-Three) : First published in 00000 as "*The Way of the Wizard: Utilitarian Systemology (A New Metahuman Ethic)*" by Joshua Free; a professional manual bridging *Grade-IV* (Metahuman Systemology, *Wizard Level-0*) with *Grade-V* (Spiritual Systemology, *Wizard Level-1*).

logic : philosophical science of correct *reasoning*.

—M—

malefactor : a person that knowingly commits *Harmful-Acts*; a source of frequent turbulence and destruction on a system.

manifestation : something brought into existence.

Marduk : founder of Babylonia; patron Anunnaki "god" of Babylon.

Mardukite Zuism : a Mesopotamian-themed (Babylonian-oriented) religious philosophy and tradition applying the spiritual technology based on *Arcane Tablets* in combination with "Tech" from *NexGen Systemology*; first developed in the New Age underground by Joshua Free in 2008 and realized publicly in 2009 with the formal establishment of the *Mardukite Chamberlains.* The text "*Tablets of Destiny*" is a cross-over from Mardukite Zuism (and Mesopotamian Neopaganism) toward higher spiritual applications of Systemology.

Master-Control-Center (MCC) : a perfect computing device to the extent of the information received from "lower levels" of sensory experience/perception; the pro-active communication system of the "*Mind*"; a relay point of active *Awareness* along the Identity's *ZU-line*, which is responsible for maintaining basic *Self-Honest Clarity* of *Knowingness* as a *seat of consciousness* between the *Alpha-Spirit* and the secondary "*Reactive Control Center*" of a *Lifeform* in *beta existence*; the Mind-center for an *Alpha-Spirit* to actualize cause in the *beta existence*; the analytical *Self-Determined* Mind-center of an *Alpha-Spirit used* to project *Will* toward the genetic body; the point of contact between *Spiritual Systems* and the *beta existence*; presumably the "*Third Eye*" of a being connected directly to the *I-AM-Self*, which is responsible for *determining* Reality at any time; in *NexGen Systemology*, this is plotted at (4.0) on the continuity model of the *ZU-line*.

"Master Grades" : literary materials by Joshua Free (written between 1995 and 2019) revised and compiled for the "Mardukite Academy of Systemology" instructional grades—"Route of Magick & Mysticism" (*Grade I, Part A*), "Route of Druidism & Dragon Legacy" (*Grade I, Part D*), "Route of Mesopotamian Mysteries" (Grade II) and "Route of Mardukite Systemology" or "Pathway to Self-Honesty" (*Grade III*).

maxim : the greatest or highest *premise* of a paradigm or particular literary *treatment*; a concise rule for conducting action or treating some subject; the most relevant "proverbial adage" applicable.

MCC : see "*Master-Control-Center.*"

mental image : a subjectively experienced "picture" created and imagined into being by the Alpha-Spirit (or at lower levels, one of its automated mechanisms) that includes all perceptible *facets* of totally immersive scene, which may be forms originated by an individual, or a "facsimile-copy" ("snap-shot") of something seen or encountered; a duplication of wave-forms in one's Personal Universe as a "picture" that mirror an "external" Universe experience, such as an *Imprint.*

Mesopotamia : land between Tigris and Euphrates River; modern-day Iraq; the primary setting for ancient *Sumerian* and *Babylonian* traditions thousands of years ago, including activities and records of the *Anunnaki.*

metahumanism : an applied philosophy of *transhumanism* with an emphasis on "spiritual technologies" as opposed to "external" ones; a new state or evolution of the *Human Condition* achievable on planet Earth, rooted in *Self-Honesty,* whereby individuals are operating *exterior* to considerations that are fixed exclusively to the *genetic vehicle* (Human Body) and independent of the *emotional encoding* and *associative programming* typical of the present standard-issue *Human Condition.*

Metahuman Destinations : the third professional publication of Mardukite Systemology, released publicly in October 2020; the first professional text in Grade-IV Metahuman Systemology, released as "*Liber-Two*" and containing materials from *Liber-2C, Liber-2D* and *Liber-3C*; contains fundamental theory of "*Professional Piloting*" and "*Route-3*" systematic processing methodology.

meter : a device used to measure; see *GSR-Meter.*

methodology : a complete system of applications, methods, principles and rules to compose a *'systematic'* paradigm as a "whole"—esp. a field of philosophy or science.

missed hold-out : an individual's *Hold-Out* that someone else nearly found out about, or which leaves the individual wondering if they did actually find out; undisclosed event when someone else's behavior or speech restimulates emotional-response-reactions ("worry" *&tc.*) about potential discovery of a withheld *Harmful-Act* or *Hold-Out*; in *systematic processing*, a Seeker's "held-out" (hidden) data that they expect to be discovered during a *session*, but which is *missed* by the Pilot.

morals : widely held culturally conditioned (socially learned) ethical standards of conduct used to "judge" *rightness* from *wrongness* of an individual's character, personality or actions (which may or may not be intellectually and emotionally influenced by "local" religious customs, taboos and *dogma*; basic social reality agreements determining "proper conduct" and "right actions" (behavior) based on civic *laws*, social *codes* and religious *doctrines* of a particular society or group and its own cultural experiences of *Reality*.

—N—

NexGen Systemology : a modern tradition of applied religious philosophy and spiritual technology based on *Arcane Tablets* in combination with "*general systemology*" and "*games theory*" developed in the New Age underground by Joshua Free in 2011 as an advanced futurist extension of the "*Mardukite Chamberlains*"; also referred to as "*Mardukite Systemology*," "*Metahuman Systemology*" and "*Spiritual Systemology*."

—O—

objective : concerning the "external world" and attempts to observe Reality independent of personal "subjective" factors.

one-to-one : see "*A-for-A*."

optimum : the most favorable or ideal conditions for the best result; the greatest degree of result under specific conditions.

organic : as related to a physically living organism or carbon-based life form; energy-matter condensed into form as a focus or POV of Spiritual Life Energy (*ZU*) as it pertains to beta-existence of *this* Physical Universe (*KI*).

—P—

paradigm : an all-encompassing *standard* by which to view the world and *communicate* Reality; a standard model of reality-systems used by the Mind to filter, organize and interpret experience of Reality.

parameters : a defined range of possible variables within a model, spectrum or continuum; the extent of communicable reach capable within a system or across a distance; the defined or imposed limitations placed on a system or the functions within a system; the extent to which a Life or "thing" can *be*, *do* or *know* along any channel within the confines of a specific system or spectrum of existence.

paramount : the most important; of utmost importance; "above all else."

participation : being part of the action; affecting the result.

patter : fast-talk; a manner of quickly delivered speech/words, esp. used to persuade or sell something.

patterns (probability patterns) : observation of cycles and tendencies to predict a causal relationship or determine the actual condition or flow of dynamic energy using a holistic systemology to understand Life, Reality and Existence as opposed to isolating or excluding perceived parts as being mutually separate from other perceived parts.

PCL : see *"processing command line."*

perception : internalized processing of data received by the *senses*; to become *Aware of* via the senses.

personality (program) : the total composite picture an individual "identifies" themselves with; the accumulated sum of material and mental mass by which an individual experiences as their timeline; a "beta-personality" is mainly attached to the identity of a particular physical body and the total sum of its own genetic memory in combination with the data stores and pictures maintained by the Alpha Spirit; a "true personality" is the Alpha Spirit as Self completely defragmented of all erroneous limitations and barriers to consideration, belief, manifestation and intention.

phase (identification) : in *NexGen Systemology,* a pattern of personality or identity that is assumed as the POV from *Self*; personal identification with artificial "personality packages"; an individual assuming or taking characteristics of another individual (often unknowingly as a response-mechanisms); also "*phase alignment.*"

phase alignment or "*in phase*" : to be in synch or mutually synchronized, in step or aligned properly with something else in order to increase the total strength value; in *NexGen Systemology*, alignment or adjustment of *Awareness* with a particular identity, space or time; perfect *defragmentation* would mean being "in phase" as *Self* fully conscious and Aware as an Alpha-Spirit *in* present *space* and *time*, free of synthetic personalities.

physics : regarding data obtained by a material science of observable motions, forces and bodies, including their apparent interaction, in the Physical Universe (specific to this *beta-existence*).

physiology : a material science of observable biological functions and mechanics of living organisms, including codification and study of identifiable parts and apparent systematic processes (specific to agreed upon makeup of the *genetic vehicle* for this *beta-existence*).

pilot : a professional steersman responsible for healthy functional operation of a ship toward a specific destination; in *NexGen Systemology*, an intensive trained individual qualified to specially apply *Systemology Processing* to assist other *Seekers* on the *Pathway.*

ping : a short, high pitched ring, chime or noise that alerts to the presence of something; in computer systems, a query sent on a network or line to another terminal in order to determine if there is a connection to it; in *NexGen Systemology*, the sudden somatic twinge or pain or discomfort that is felt as a sensation in the body when a particular terminal (lifeform, object, concept) is 'brought to mind' or contacted on a personal communication channel-circuit; the accompanying sensations and mental images that are experienced as an automatic-response to the presence of some channel or terminal.

player (game theory) : an individual that is making decisions in a game and/or is affected by decisions others are making in the game, especially if those other-determined decisions now affect the possible choices.

point-of-view (POV) : a point to view from; an opinion or attitude as expressed from a specific identity-phase; a specific standpoint or vantage-point; a definitive manner of consideration specific to an individual phase or identity; a place or position affording a specific view or vantage; circumstances and programming of an individual that is conducive to a particular response, consideration or belief-set (paradigm); a position (consideration) or place (location) that provides a specific view or perspective (subjective) on experience (of the objective).

postulate : to put forward as truth; to suggest or assume an existence *to be*; to provide a basis of reasoning and belief; a basic theory accepted as fact; in *NexGen Systemology*, "Alpha-Thought"—the top-most decisions or considerations made by the Alpha-Spirit regarding the "*is-ness*" (what things "are") about energy-matter and space-time.

potentiality : the total "sum" (collective amount) of "latent" (dormant—present but not apparent) capable or possible realizations; used to describe a state or condition of what has not yet manifested, but which can be influenced and predicted based on observed patterns and, if referring to beta-existence, Cosmic Law.

POV : see "*point-of-view*" and/or "*POV Processing.*"

premise : a basis or statement of fact from which conclusions are drawn.

presence : the quality of some thing (energy/matter) being "present" in space-time; personal orientation of *Self* as an *Awareness* (*POV*) located in present space-time (environment) and communicating with extant energy-matter.

prevalent : of wide extent; an extensive or largely accepted aspect or current state.

Prime Directive : a "spiritual" implant program that installs purposes and goals into the personal experience of a Universe, esp. any *Beta-Existence* (whether a 'Games Universe' or a 'Prison Universe'); intellectually treated as the "Universal Imperative" in some schools of moral philosophy; comparable to "Universal Law" or "Cosmic Ordering."

"process-out" or **"flatten a wave"** : to reduce *emotional encoding* of an *imprint* to zero; to dissolve a *wave-form* or *thought-formed* "solid" such as a "*belief*"; to completely run a *process* to its end, thereby *flattening* any previously "*collapsed-waves*" or *fragmentation* that is obstructing the *clear channel* of *Self-Awareness*; also referred to as "processing-out"; to discharge all previously held emotionally encoded imprinting or erroneous programming and beliefs that otherwise fix the free flow (wave) to a particular pattern, solid or concrete "*is*" form.

processing, systematic : the inner-workings or "through-put" result of systems; in *NexGen Systemology*, a methodology of applied spiritual technology used toward personal Self-Actualization; methods of selective directed attention, communicated language and associative imagery that targets an increase in personal control of the human condition.

processing command line (PCL) or **command line** : a directed input; a specific command using highly selective language for *Systemology Processing*; a predetermined directive statement (cause) intended to focus concentrated attention (effect).

proportional : having a direct relationship or mutual

interaction with.

protest : a response-communication objecting an enforcement or a rejection of a prior communication; an effort to cancel, rewrite or destroy the existence or "is-ness" (what something "is") of a previous creation or communication; unwillingness to be the Point-of-View of effect (or receipt-point) for a communication.

psychometric evaluation : the relative measurement of personal ability, mental (psychological/thought) faculties, and effective processing of information and external stimulus data; a scale used in "applied psychology" to evaluate and predict human behavior.

—R—

rationality / reasoning (game theory) : the extent to which a player seeks to play (make decisions, &tc.) in order to maximize the gains (or else survival) achievable within any given game conditions; the ability and willingness of an individual to reach toward conditions that promote the highest level of survival and existence and make the best choices and moves to see the desired goal manifest.

reactive control center (RCC) : the secondary (reactive) communication system of the "*Mind*"; a relay point of *Awareness* along the Identity's *ZU-line*, which is responsible for engaging basic motors, biochemical processes and any *programmed automated responses* of a living *beta* organism; the reactive Mind-Center of a living organism relaying communications of *Awareness* between causal experience of *Physical Systems* and the "*Master Control Center*"; it presumably stores all emotional encoded imprints as fragmentation of "chakra" frequencies of *ZU* (within the range of the "*psychological/emotive systems*" of a being), which it may *react* to as Reality at any time; in *NexGen Systemology*, this is plotted at (2.0) on the continuity model of the *ZU-line*.

reality : see "*agreement.*"

realization : the clear perception of an understanding; a consideration or understanding on what is "actual"; to make "real" or give "reality" to so as to grant a property of "beingness" or "being as it is"; the state or instance of coming to an *Awareness*; in *NexGen Systemology*, "gnosis" or true knowledge achieved during *systematic processing*; achievement of a new (or "higher") cognition, true knowledge or perception of Self; a consideration of reality or assignment of meaning.

relative : an apparent point, state or condition treated as distinct from others.

religion : a concise spiritual *paradigm*, set of beliefs and practices regarding "Divinity," "Infinite Beingness"—or else, "God"—as representative symbol of the *Eighth Sphere of Existence* for *Beta-Existence* (or else "Infinity").

repetitively : to repeat "over and over" again; or else "repetition."

responsibility : the *ability* to *respond*; the extent of mobilizing *power* and *understanding* an individual maintains as *Awareness* to enact *change*; the proactive ability to *Self-direct* and make decisions independent of an outside authority.

resurface : to return to (or bring up to) the "surface" of that which has previously been submerged; in *NexGen Systemology*—relating specifically to processes where a *Seeker* recalls blocked energy stored covertly as emotional "*imprints*" (by the RCC) so that it may be effectively defragmented from the "*ZU-line*" (by the MCC).

rhetoric : the art, study or skilled craft of using language eloquently (words, writing, speech preparation); expert communication using "words"; effectively using language for persuasive communication.

Route-0 : a specific methodology from *SOP-2C* denoting "*Creativeness Processing*," as described in the text

"*Imaginomicon*" (*Liber-3D*).

Route-0E : a specific methodology (expanding on *Route-0* from *Liber-3D*) denoting "*Conceptual Processing*" applied to *Ethics Beta-Defragmentation*, as described in the text "*Way of the Wizard*" (*Liber-Three* or *Liber-3E*).

Route-1 : a specific methodology from *SOP-2C* denoting "*Resurfacing Processing*," as described in the text "*Tablets of Destiny*" (*Liber-One*) as "RR-SP" (and reissued in "*The Systemology Handbook*").

Route-2 : a specific methodology from *SOP-2C* denoting "*Analytical-Recall Processing*," as described in the text "*Crystal Clear*" (*Liber-2B*) as "AR-SP" (and reissued in "*The Systemology Handbook*").

Route-3 : a specific methodology from *SOP-2C* denoting "*Communication-Circuit Processing*," as described in the text "*Metahuman Destinations*" (*Liber-Two*); also the basis for *SOP-2C* routine.

Route-3E : a specific methodology (expanding on *Route-3* from *SOP-2C*) denoting "*Ethics Processing*," as described in the text "*The Way of the Wizard*" (*Liber-Three* or *Liber-3E*); also related to "Standard Procedure R-3E."

—S—

Seeker : an individual on the *Pathway to Self-Honesty*; a practitioner of *Mardukite Systemology* or *NexGen Systemology Processing* that is working toward *Spiritual Ascension*.

Self-actualization : bringing the full potential of the Human spirit into Reality; expressing full capabilities and creativeness of the *Alpha-Spirit*.

Self-determinism : the freedom to act, clear of external control or influence; the personal control of Will to direct intention.

Self-honesty : the basic or original *alpha* state of *being* and *knowing*; clear and present total *Awareness* of-and-as *Self*, in its most basic and true proactive expression of it-self as *Spirit* or *I-AM*—free of artificial attachments, perceptive filters and other emotionally-reactive or men-tally-conditioned programming imposed on the human condition by the systematized physical world; the ability to experience existence without judgment.

semantics : the *meaning* carried in *language* as the *truth* of a "thing" represented, *A-for-A*; the *effect* of language on *thought* activity in the Mind and physical behavior; language as *symbols* used to represent a concept, "thing" or "solid."

semantic-set : the implied meaning behind any groupings of words or symbols used to define a specific paradigm.

sensation : an external stimulus received by internal sense organs (receptors/sensors); sense impressions.

slate : a hard thin flat surface material used for writing on; a chalk-board, which is a large version of the original wood-framed writing slate, named for the rock-type it was made from.

SOP-2C : *Standard Operating Procedure #2C or System-ology Operating Procedure #2C*; a standardized procedural formula introduced in materials for "*Metahu-man Destinations*" (*Liber-Two*); a regimen or outline for standard delivery of systematic processing used by *Sys-temology Pilots* and *Mardukite Ministers*; a procedure outline of systematic processing, which includes applica-tions of "*Route-1,*" "*Route-2,*" "*Route-3*" and "*Route-0*" as taught for *Grade-IV Professional Piloting*.

space : a viewpoint or *Point-of-View* (POV) extended from any point out toward a dimension or dimensions; the consideration of a point or spot as an *anchor* or *corner* in addition to others, which collectively define parameters of a dimensional plane; the field of energy/matter mass cre-ated as a result of communication and control in action and measured as time (wave-length), such as "distance" between points (or peaks on a wave).

spectrum : a broad range or array as a continuous series or sequence; defined parts along a singular continuum; in physics, a gradient arrangement of visible colored bands diffracted in order of their respective wavelengths, such as when passing *White Light* through a *prism*.

Spheres of Existence (dynamic systems) : a series of *eight* concentric circles, rings or spheres (each larger than the former) that is overlaid onto the Standard Model of Beta-Existence to demonstrate the dynamic systems of existence extending out from the POV of Self (often as a "body") at the *First Sphere*; these are given in the basic eightfold systems as: *Self, Home/Family, Groups, Humanity, Life on Earth*, the *Physical Universe*, the *Spiritual Universe* and *Infinity-Divinity.*

spiritual timeline : a continuous stream (*continuum*) of moment-to-moment *Mental Images* (or a record of experiences) that defines the "past" of a spiritual being (or *Alpha-Spirit*) and which includes impressions (*imprints, &tc.*) form all life-incarnations and significant spiritual events the being has encountered; in NexGen Systemology, also "*backtrack.*"

standard-issue : equally dispensed to all without consideration.

standard model : a fundamental *structure* or symbolic construct used to evaluate a complete *set* in *continuity* relative to itself and variable to all other *dynamic systems* as graphed or calculated by *logic*.

Standard Model, The (systemology) : in *NexGen Systemology*—our existential and cosmological *standard model* or cabbalistic model; a "*monistic continuity model*" demonstrating *total system* interconnectivity "above" and "below" observation of any apparent *parameters*; the original presentation of the *ZU-line*, represented as a singular vertical (*y*-axis) waveform in space across dimensional levels or Universes (*Spheres of Existence*) without charting any specific movement across a dimensional time-graph *x*-axis; The Standard Model of

Systemology represents the basic workable synthesis of common denominators in models explored throughout Grade-I and Grade-II material.

succumb : to give way, or give in to, a relatively stronger superior force.

Sumerian : ancient civilization of *Sumer*, founded in Mesopotamia c. 5000 B.C.

symbol : a concentrated mass with associated meaning or significance.

sympathy : a sensation, feeling or emotion—of anger, fear, sorrow and/or pity—that is a *personal reaction* to the misfortune and failure of another being.

syntax : from the Greek, "to arrange together"; the semantic meaning that words convey when combined together; the manner in which words are arranged together to provide an understandable meaning, such as following the structure for a sentence.

system : from the Greek, "to set together"; to set or arrange things or data together so as to form an orderly understanding of a "whole"; also a *'method'* or *'methodology'* as an orderly standard of use or application of such data arranged together.

systematization : to arrange into systems; to systematize or make systematic.

Systemology : see "*NexGen Systemology.*"

Systemology Procedure 1-8-0 : advanced spiritual technology within our Systemology, which applies a methodology of systematic practice for experiencing: (1) Self-Awareness, (8) Nothingness and (0) Beingness, introduced for "Crystal Clear" but expanded on for "*Imaginomicon*"; *'one-eight-zero'* is included in, but not the same as application *'one-eighty'*—or else the *Beta-Defrag-Intensive* called "*SOP-180*" or "*Systemology-180.*"

Systemology-180 : an intensive systematic processing routine employing all *Grade-III*, *Grade-IV* and cross-over

Wizard-Level work to date; the total sum of all effective philosophical and spiritual applications necessary to pro-fessionally *Pilot* a *Seeker* to reach a stable point of *Self-Honesty* and basic *Beta-Defragmentation*, as a prerequis-ite to treating "*Actualized-Ascension Technologies*" (*A.T.*) of upper-level *Wizard Grades*.

systems theory : see *"general systematology"*

—T—

Tablets of Destiny : the first professional publication of Mardukite Systemology, released publicly in October 2019; the first professional text in Grade-III Mardukite Systemology, released as "*Liber-One*" and reissued in the Grade-III Master Edition "*Systemology Handbook*"; con-tains fundamental theory of the "*Standard Model*" and "*Route-1*" systematic processing methodology.

teleological (teleology) : using the end-goal or purpose of something as an explanation of its function (rather than being a function of its cause); example—Aristotle wrote (in his discourse, "*Metaphysics*") that the intrinsic (inher-ent or true nature) *telos* of an 'acorn' is to become a fully formed 'oak tree'; the ends are an underlying purpose, not the cause (also known as "final cause"), or else the fam-ous phrase: "the ends justify the means."

terminal (node) : a point, end or mass on a line; a point or connection for closing an electric circuit, such as a post on a battery terminating at each end of its own systematic function; any end point or 'termination' on a line; a point of connectivity with other points; in systems, any point which may be treated as a contact point of interaction; anything that may be distinguished as an 'is' and is there-fore a 'termination point' of a system or along a flow-line which may interact with other related systems it shares a line with; a point of interaction with other points.

thought-experiment : from the German, *Gedankenex-periment*; logical *considerations* or mental models used to

concisely visualize consequences (cause-effect sequences) within the context of an imaginary or
hypothetical scenario; using faculties of the Mind's Eye to
Imagine things accurately with *considerations* that *have
not* already been consciously experienced in *beta-existence*.

thought-wave or **wave-form** : a proactive *Self-directed
action* or reactive-response *action* of *consciousness*; the
process of *thinking* as demonstrated in *wave-form*; the
activity of *Awareness* within the range of *thought vibra-
tions/frequencies* on the existential *Life-continuum* or *ZU-
line*.

threshold : a doorway, gate or entrance point; the degree
to which something is to produce an effect within a certain state or condition; the point in which a condition
changes from one to the next.

thwarted : to successfully oppose or prevent a purpose
from actualizing.

time : observation of cycles in action; motion of a
particle, energy or wave across space; intervals of action
related to other intervals of action as observed in Awareness; a measurable wave-length or frequency in
comparison to a static state; the consideration of variations in space.

timeline : plotting out history in a linear (line) model to
indicate instances (experiences) or demonstrate changes
in state (space) as measured over time; a singular conception of continuation of observed time as marked by event-
intervals and changes in energy and matter across space.

transhumanism : a social science and applied philosophy
concerning the next evolved state of the "*Human Condition,*"; progress in two potential directions, either
"spiritual" technologies advancing *Self* as an "Alpha-Spirit," or the direction of "external"-"physical" technologies
that modify or eliminate characteristics of the *Body*; a
theme describing contemporary application of material
sciences emphasizing only "physical" and "genetic" parts

of the *Human* experience, such as brain activity, cell-life extension and space travel; *NexGen Systemology* recently began distinguishing its emphasis on "spiritual technology" as "*metahumanism.*"

traumatic encoding : information received when the sensory faculties of an organism are "shocked" into learning it as an "emotionally" encoded *Imprint*; a duplicated facsimile-copy or *Mental Image* of severe misfortune, violent threats, pain and coercion, which is then categorized, stored and reactively retrieved based exclusively on its emotional *facets.*

treat / treatment : an act, manner or method of handling or dealing with someone, something or some type of situation; to apply a specific process, procedure or mode of action toward some person, thing or subject; use of a specific substance, regimen or procedure to make an existing condition less severe; also, a written presentation that handles a subject in a specific manner.

turbulence : a quality or state of distortion or disturbance that creates irregularity of a flow or pattern; the quality or state of aberration on a line (such as ragged edges) or the emotional "turbulent feelings" attached to a particular flow or terminal node; a violent, haphazard or disharmonious commotion (such as in the ebb of gusts and lulls of wind action).

—U—

unconscious : a state when *Awareness* as *Self* is removed totally from the equation of *Life* experience, though it continues to be recorded in lower-level response mechanisms (fixed to a simulacrum or genetic vehicle) for later retrieval. See also *Biological Unconsciousness.*

understanding : a clear 'A-for-A' duplication of a communication as 'knowledge', which may be comprehended and retained with its significance assigned in relation to other 'knowledge' treated as a 'significant understanding';

the "grade" or "level" that a knowledge base is collected and the manner in which the data is organized and evaluated.

Utopian Philosophy : a social philosophy and ethic for (primarily) independent rural (country-dwelling or pagan) living communities that adopt a neo-Utilitarian moral philosophy (as suggested by Systemology) to enhance the "greater happiness" and "Ascension" of all participants.

—V—

validation : reinforcement of agreements or considerations as "real."

via : literally, "by way of"; from the Latin, meaning "way."

vibration : effects of motion or wave-frequency as applied to any system.

viewpoint : see *"point-of-view" (POV).*

—W—

wave-form : see *"sine-wave."*

wave-function collapse : see *"collapsing a wave."*

Western Civilization : modern contemporary culture, ideals, values and technology, particularly of Europe and North America as distinguished by growing urbanization, industrialization, and inspired by a history of rebellion to strong religious and political indoctrination.

will *or* **WILL** (5.0) : in *NexGen Systemology* (from the *Standard Model*), the Alpha-ability at "5.0" of a Spiritual Being (*Alpha Spirit*) at "7.0" to apply *intention* as "Cause" from consideration or Alpha-Thought at "6.0" that is superior to "beta-thoughts" that only manifest as reactive "effects" below "4.0" and *interior* to the *Human*

Condition.

willingness : the state of conscious Self-determined ability and interest (directed attention) to *Be*, *Do* or *Have*; a Self-determined consideration to reach, face up to (*confront*) or manage some "mass" or energy; the extent to which an individual considers themselves able to participate, act or communicate along some line, to put attention or intention on the line, or to produce (create) an effect.

—Z—

ZU : the ancient Sumerian cuneiform sign for the archaic verb—*"to know," "knowingness"* or *"awareness"*; in *Mardukite Zuism and Systemology*, the active energy/matter of the "Spiritual Universe" (AN) experienced as a *Lifeforce* or *consciousness* that imbues living forms extant in the "Physical Universe" (KI); *"Spiritual Life Energy"*; energy demonstrated by the WILL of an actualized *Alpha-Spirit* in the "Spiritual Universe" (AN), which impinges its *Awareness* into the Physical Universe (KI), animating/controlling *Life* for its experience of *beta-existence* along an individual Alpha-Spirit's personal *Identity-continuum*, called a *ZU-line*.

Zu-**Line** : a theoretical construct in *Mardukite Zuism and Systemology* demonstrating *Spiritual Life Energy* (*ZU*) as a personal individual "continuum" of Awareness interacting with all Spheres of Existence on the Standard Model of Systemology; a spectrum of potential variations and interactions of a monistic continuum or singular *Spiritual Life Energy (ZU)* demonstrated on the Standard Model; an energetic channel of potential POV and "locations" of Beingness, demonstrated in early Systemology materials as an individual Alpha-Spirit's personal *Identity-continuum*, potentially connecting *Awareness (ZU)* of *Self* with *"Infinity"* simultaneous with all points considered in existence; a symbolic demonstration of the *"Life-line"* on which *Awareness (ZU)* extends from the direction of the

"Spiritual Universe" (AN) in its true original *alpha state* through an entire possible range of activity resulting in its *beta state* and control of a *genetic-entity* occupying the *Physical Universe (KI).*

Zu-Vision : the true and basic (*Alpha*) Point-of-View (perspective, POV) maintained by *Self* as *Alpha-Spirit* outside boundaries or considerations of the *Human Condition* "Mind-Systems" and *exterior* to beta-existence reality agreements with the Physical Universe; a POV of Self *as* "a unit of Spiritual Awareness" that exists independent of a "body" and entrapment in a *Human Condition*; "spirit vision" in its truest sense.

"Today, I'll be spinning on a Wheel
I'm a slave to a Wheel—and there isn't any stopping.
What mistake could I have made?
I'm a slave serving time for a life that I've forgotten."

"Today, I'm a King on the Wheel,
still a slave to the Wheel,
But this time around, I'm smiling.
Keep me cautious, keep me safe, just in case
there's a chance I can leave this Wheel behind me."

"Who's at the center of the Wheel,
the inventor of the Wheel—or another spinning servant?
I'm the Master of my Wheel, of my very own Wheel,
Universal and recurrent."

~SPLASHDOWN, *"Karma Slave"*

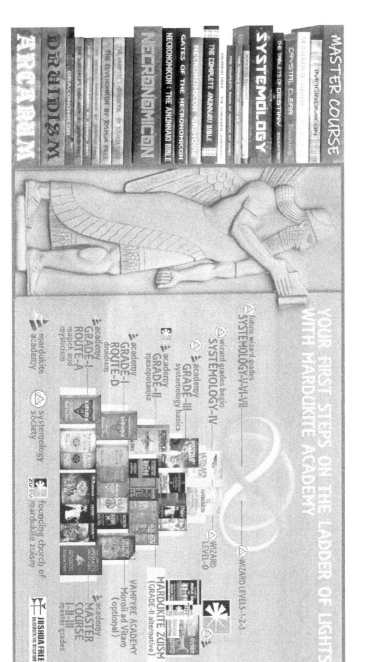

SYSTEMOLOGY
The Pathway to Self-Honesty

CRYSTAL CLEAR

The Self-Actualization Manual & Guide to Total Awareness

by Joshua Free
Foreword by Kyra Kaos

Mardukite Systemology Liber-2B

available in Paperback and Hardcover

Take control of your destiny and chart the first steps toward your own spiritual evolution.
Realize new potentials of the Human Condition with a Self-guiding handbook for Self-Processing toward Self-Actualization in Self-Honesty using actual techniques and training provided for the coveted "Mardukite Self-Defragmentation Course Program" —once only available directly and privately from the underground International Systemology Society.

Discover the amazing power behind the applied spiritual technology used for counseling and advisement in the Mardukite Zuism tradition.

** Revised Second Edition Forthcoming Summer 2022 **

SYSTEMOLOGY
The Pathway to Self-Honesty

A Basic Introduction to
Mardukite Systemology

THE WAY INTO
THE FUTURE

A Handbook for
the New Human

a collection of writings by
Joshua Free
selected by James Thomas

available in
Paperback and Hardcover

Here are the basic answers to what has held Humanity back
from achieving its ultimate goals and unlocking the true
power of the Spirit and highest state of Knowing and Being.

"The Way Into The Future" illuminates the *Pathway*
leading to Planet Earth's true "metahuman" destiny.
With *excerpts from "Tablets of Destiny," "Crystal Clear,"*
"Systemology—Original Thesis" and *"The Power of Zu."*
You can help shine clear light on anyone's pathway!

Carefully selected by Mardukite Publications Officer,
James Thomas, this critical *collection of eighteen*
articles, lecture transcripts and reference chapters by
Joshua Free is sure to be not only a treasured part
of your personal library, but also the perfect
introduction for all friends, family and loved ones.

(*Basic Grade-III Introductory Pocket Anthology*)

SYSTEMOLOGY

The Pathway to Self-Honesty

SYSTEMOLOGY HANDBOOK

*The ultimate operator's manual to the Human Condition
and unlocking the true power of the Spirit.*

** *"Modern Mardukite Zuism"* **
** *"The Tablets of Destiny"* **
** *"Crystal Clear"* **
** *"The Power of ZU"* **
** *"Systemology—Original Thesis"* **
** *Human, More Than Human* **
** *Defragmentation* **
** *Patterns & Cycles* **
** *Transhuman Generations* **

(Complete Grade-III Master Edition Anthology)

MARDUKITE
MASTER COURSE
The Key to Gates of Higher Understanding

Now you can experience the Legendary "Master Course" from anywhere in the Universe, exactly as given in person by Joshua Free to the "Mardukite Academy of Systemology" in September 2020.

800+ pages of materials collected in this volume provide Seekers with full transcripts to all *48 Academy Lectures* of the legendary *"Mardukite Master Course"* combined with all course outlines, supplements and critical handouts from the original *"Instructor's Manual"*—making this the most complete definitive single-source delivery of New Age understanding and spiritual technology.

Referencing 25 years of research, development and publishing, including *"Necronomicon: The Complete Anunnaki Legacy,"* *"The Great Magickal Arcanum," "The Systemology Handbook"* and *"Merlyn's Complete Book of Druidism."*

SYS⸸EMOLOGY
The Gateways to Infinity

**METAHUMAN
DESTINATIONS**

*Piloting the Course
to Homo Novus*

by Joshua Free
Foreword by David Zibert

*Mardukite Systemology
Liber-Two*

*available exclusively
in hardcover*

Drawing from the Arcane Tablets and nearly a year of
additional research, experimentation and workshops
since the introduction of applied spiritual technology
and systematic processing methods, Joshua Free
provides the ground-breaking manual for those seeking
to correct—or "defragment"—the conditions that have
trapped viewpoints of the Spirit into programming and
encoding of the Human Condition.

Experience the revolutionary professional course
in advanced spiritual technology for
Mardukite Systemologists to "Pilot" the way to higher
ideals that can free us from the Human Condition
and return ultimate command and control
of creation to the Spirit.

SYS⌁EMOLOGY
The Gateways to Infinity

IMAGINOMICON
The Gateway to Higher Universes
A Grimoire for the Human Spirit

by Joshua Free

Mardukite Systemology Liber-3D

available exclusively in hardcover

The Way Out. Hidden for 6,000 Years.
But now we've found the Key.
A grimore to summon and invoke, command and control,
the most powerful spirit to ever exist.
Your Self.

Access beyond physical existence.
Fly free across all Gateways.
Go back to where it all began and reclaim that
personal universe which the *Spirit* once called "*Home.*"

Break free from the Matrix;
command the Mind and control the Body
from outside those systems
— because *You* were never "human" —
fully realize what it means to be a *spiritual being*,
then rise up through the Gateways to Higher Universes
and *BE.*

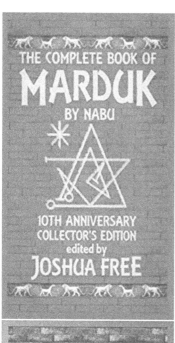

THE COMPLETE BOOK OF MARDUK BY NABU

A Pocket Anunnaki Devotional Companion to Babylonian Rituals

edited by Joshua Free

10th Anniversary Collector's Edition Hardcover Mardukite Liber-W

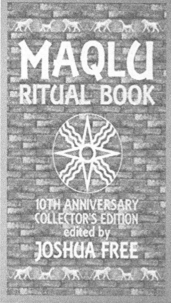

THE MAQLU RITUAL BOOK

A Pocket Companion to Babylonian Exorcisms, Banishing Rites & Protective Spells

edited by Joshua Free

10th Anniversary Collector's Edition Hardcover Mardukite Liber-M

The Original Classic Underground Bestseller Returns!
10th Anniversary Hardcover Collector's Edition.
Explore the original religion on Earth.

SUMERIAN RELIGION
Introducing the Anunnaki Gods
of Mesopotamian Neopaganism

Mardukite Research Volume Liber-50

by Joshua Free

Develop a personal relationship with Anunnaki Gods
—the divine pantheon that launched a thousand
cultures and traditions throughout the world!

Even if you think you already know all about the Sumerian Anunnaki or Star-Gates of Babylon... * Here you will find a beautifully crafted journey that is unlike anything Humans have had the opportunity to experience for thousands of years... * Here you will find a truly remarkable tome demonstrating a fresh new approach to modern Mesopotamian Neopaganism and spirituality... * Here is a Master Key to the ancient mystic arts: true knowledge concerning the powers and entities that these arts are dedicated to... * A working relationship with these powers directly... * And the wisdom to exist "alongside" the gods, so as to ever remain in the "favor" of Cosmic Law.

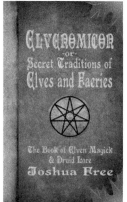

Necronomicon: The Anunnaki Bible : 10th Anniversary Collector's Edition—LIBER-N,L,G,9+W-M+S *(Hardcover)*

Gates of the Necronomicon : The Secret Anunnaki Tradition of Babylon : 10th Anniversary Collector's Edition— LIBER-50,51/52,R+555 *(Hardcover)*

Necronomicon—The Anunnaki Grimoire : A Manual of Practical Babylonian Magick : 10th Anniversary Collector's Edition— LIBER-E,W/Z,M+K *(Hardcover)*

The Complete Anunnaki Bible: A Source Book of Esoteric Archaeology —LIBER-N,L,G,9+W-M+S *(Hardcover and Paperback)*

Anunnaki Bible : The Cuneiform Scriptures—New Standard Zuist Edition : Abridged Pocket Version *(Hardcover & Paperback)*

Sumerian Religion : Introducing the Anunnaki Gods of Mesopotamian Neopaganism : 10th Anniv. Collector's Ed.—LIBER-50 *(Hardcover)*

Babylonian Myth & Magic : Anunnaki Mysticism of Mesopotamian Neopaganism : 10th Anniv. Coll. Ed.—LIBER-51+E *(Hardcover)*

The Complete Book of Marduk by Nabu : A Pocket Anunnaki Devotional Companion to Babylonian Prayers & Rituals : 10th Anniversary Collector's Edition—LIBER-W+Z *(Hardcover)*

The Maqlu Ritual Book : A Pocket Companion to Babylonian Exorcisms, Banishing Rites & Protective Spells : 10th Anniversary Collector's Edition—LIBER-M *(Hardcover)*

Novem Portis: Necronomicon Revelations & Nine Gates of the Kingdom of Shadows : 10th Anniv. Collector's Ed.—LIBER-R+9 *(Hardcover)*

Elvenomicon—or—Secret Traditions of Elves & Faeries : Elven Magick & Druid Lore : 15th Anniv. Collector's Ed.—LIBER-D *(Hardcover)*

Draconomicon : The Book of Ancient Dragon Magick 25th Anniversary Collector's Edition—LIBER-D3 *(Hardcover)*

The Druid's Handbook : Ancient Magick for a New Age 20th Anniversary Collector's Edition—LIBER-D2 *(Hardcover)*

The Sorcerer's Handbook : A Complete Guide to Practical Magick 21st Anniversary Collector's Edition—*(Hardcover)*

The Witch's Handbook : A Complete Grimoire of Witchcraft 21st Anniversary Collector's Edition—*(Hardcover)*

The Vampyre's Handbook : Secret Rites of Modern Vampires 5th Anniversary Collector's Edition—LIBER V1+V2 *(Hardcover)*

JOSHUA FREE

PUBLISHED BY THE **JOSHUA FREE** IMPRINT REPRESENTING

**The Founding Church of Mardukite Zuism
& Mardukite Academy of Systemology**

mardukite.com